Hiking Snohomish County

Ken Wilcox

90 Selected Hikes & Walks
On the Coast, & in the Lowlands, Foothills & North Cascades

Plus Parks, Viewpoints, Water Access & Campgrounds

Northwest Wild Books
Bellingham, Washington

Hiking Snohomish County

ISBN 0-9617879-4-5

Photography by Steve Satushek (*pages* 31, 35, 41, 55, 56, 60, 75, 78, 84, 92, 95,
96, 98, 107, 116, 118, 120, 121, 123, 135, 139, 141, 146, 149, 153, 155, 157,
163, 164, 166 & 170), and the author (*all others*). Maps by the author.

Designed and published by Northwest Wild Books, Bellingham, WA.
Printed on chlorine-free and acid-free recycled paper, 20% post-consumer.
Manufactured in the USA.

Front cover: Glacier Peak and Image Lake, by Steve Satushek.
Back cover: Mountain wildflowers, by Steve Satushek; Boardman Lake old-growth,
North Fork Falls & Spada Lake by the author.

Hiking guides from Northwest Wild Books...
Hiking Whatcom County, 3rd Ed. (1996)
Hiking Snohomish County (1998)
Coming soon...
Hiking the San Juans, Whidbey & Camano Islands
Hiking Skagit County
Hiking King County
*We welcome your comments, corrections, kudos, criticisms, and/or suggestions
regarding current and future editions of these titles. Write us at Northwest Wild
Books, P. O. Box 4003, Bellingham, WA 98227.*

Foreword

Snohomish County, Washington, is a fine place to hike.

I have to admit that I didn't know this during the first few years I lived in the county. On July 4th, 1967, my parents, five siblings, and I crossed the mighty North Cascades in a big truck and a little car to make a new home in the amazingly green and drizzly State of Washington. For this happy camper, Utah was history. We settled in at Alderwood Manor the first few months, as Dad headed out every morning to build tall buildings in Seattle. But Alderwood was just too urban for this bunch, considering the traffic and subdivisions and all. So in a matter of months we were out on the farm—smack between the north and southbound lanes of I-5, near Stanwood. And despite the sound of it, that was when I-5 near Stanwood was about as busy as a dead-end street in Mukilteo.

Out of school and off on my own by the early 1970s, I still failed to appreciate what there was to see and experience in the lowlands and North Cascades of Snohomish County. I owned a dirt bike and got to know logging roads and cow pastures instead. I took a truck-driving job, built a funky log cabin outside Arlington, then complained about all the new development and the loggers taking down so many big trees. The battle for wilderness—an essential ingredient for any civilized society—had begun and I was headlong into it. The fight for wilderness preservation, strangely enough, carried me deeper into the wilderness than I'd ever been before. While I had explored around the edges for a number of years, mostly dayhikes to little lakes and waterfalls, jaunts in the old-growth, and up to the alpine meadows, the majesty of it didn't really strike home, I'm embarrassed to say, until a little trip up Mt. Baker, up in Whatcom County, in the late 1970s. The view was as amazing as the day. I was hooked.

Until then, hiking, I thought, was something you did at the National Park, like in the Olympics or at the Grand Canyon. In 1980, I leaped to the realization that hiking—*walking* really, although that sounds less glamorous—is really what my life was about. In February of that year, my sweetie (at the time) accompanied me to a slide show about a basic mountaineering course being offered by the Everett Mountaineers. We were totally impressed and signed up immediately. And like others who've made the leap, the experience changed our lives profoundly. We learned to "walk" up mountains, with or without a trail. I climbed the ominously subtle Mt. Pilchuck the day Mt. St. Helens blew (we heard it go and hustled to the ridge to watch the mushroom cloud a hundred miles away), then Del Campo and Gothic Peaks. Then the big one, Glacier Peak, and Whitehorse, White Chuck, Dome Peak, and dozens more in subsequent years. I must confess to a prolonged peak-bagging phase that has since evolved into more of a fascination with discovery, beauty, the breathing of fresh air, and the patience to sit and watch the world go by. But climbing, that is, hiking with a rope, ice axe, and things that jangle, in no way reduced the attraction of hiking without all the extra baggage. And today, no one could possibly keep me off the trail or out of the mountains. But these are typical sentiments for the hundreds of thousands of Washingtonians who've taken the time to discover and appreciate wilderness in the Northwest.

While life's unpredictableness soon carried me north to Western Washington University and a career as an environmental and recreation planner in Bellingham, the mountains and trails of Snohomish County have remained a forever-important part of my life. After completing a trail guide to Whatcom County in 1987, the notion of writing a similar book for Snohomish County seemed only natural. I wouldn't have guessed it would take most of ten years to do it. Now that it's done, I just hope it proves to be a useful tool for those who would like to discover what Snohomish County really has to offer.

Wilderness, of which the county has a substantial allotment in our share of the North Cascades, is not, by any means, the only kind of place worth exploring. The coast, urban areas, lowlands, and foothills all have something unique to offer. The walking experiences available are, of course, as varied as the landscape—and the people doing the walking. This book tries to point out some of the more interesting places to walk (or "hike," if you prefer) in many of these natural and human-altered settings. I've tried to include wide geographic coverage, and a range of difficulty levels so that hopefully everyone has something to choose from. Walks along the coast and in town tend to be short and easy, while treks in the Cascades are certainly much more strenuous overall. Yet even in the mountains, some short and easy walks are noted for those who might prefer that to a 15-mile trudge up and down a mountain.

While this book catalogues more than 300 miles of trails—over two-thirds of it in the North Cascades—we can expect even more walking opportunities as time goes on, if the growing numbers of Americans using trails and advocating for more trails is any indication. A number of possible trail projects for this area are noted in the *Introduction*, many of them in the lowland and urban areas of the county. For every existing or planned trail, the hard work of trail advocates, volunteers, city and county park staff, state and federal trail planners, trail-minded politicians, trail crews, and others must be commended. So much of what they do is taken for granted, even among some of the more avid trail users. While there's a lot of good energy available to do more, inadequate funding presents a typical stumbling block. Nevertheless, as competing interests vie for limited tax dollars, trails will still win out on occasion. Perhaps if more people demanded more quality walking opportunities for all the good things they do for families and communities, we'd could really start cruising. Instead, we live in a society where, despite broad public support for trails, a lot of politicians and couch-potato voters think we ought to spend less on trails, parks, and the like, and more on locking up non-violent criminals. I can't prove it but I think that's probably got it backwards.

Trails, it seems, are places to think and feel and communicate with others and with the natural environment, to get clear on priorities, to experience beauty and harmony, and learn to appreciate what's so good about this thing called life. Trails are simple, cheap, attractive, and inviting, if they're designed and built correctly. They're something virtually everyone can enjoy — walking or not. As growth and development in the region seem poised to gobble up every wild corner of the lowlands, as single-occupant automobiles and short-sighted politics rattle across the landscape in unending shock waves, and as more and more families arrive in their big trucks and little cars looking for a new home, trails offer a step back from it all.

And trails, notwithstanding my woeful whining, are just plain fun to walk. I hope this book is most useful in that regard.

Happy trails,

Ken Wilcox, February, 1998

Acknowledgments

I'm lucky to have so many good friends to explore the woods with — and for moral support to get this book done. Special thanks to Steve Satushek for his excellent photographic contributions and early work on the project, to Sara R. and Jim O. for constant encouragement and insight, to Brooke D. and Juliet T. for invaluable editing assistance and support, to Jana W., Clare F., Jim H., Brad R., and especially Kiko A. and Betty P. for their unfailing confidence and generosity, and to Steve W., Bill W., David D., Jim Z., Brandon L., and Liza F. for letting me bore them with my frequent consternations. A special group hug to those who walked with me more than a mile or two: Kiko A., Mel B., Lorraine B., Floyd B., Joan C., Ginger D., Ed H., Jerry H., Steve I., Keith K., Tom K., Brandon L., Peter M., Dennis M., Jim O., Sara R., Ron S., Steve S., Sue S., John W., and — not last and never least — Helene Z., and finally to a couple of very important and still missed canine companions, Bean and Si. Appreciation also goes to Marc Krandel, Dianne Housden, Pat Kenyon and John Tucker with Snohomish Co. Parks & Recreation; Jane Lewis and Daryl Bertholet at Everett Parks & Recreation, Arvilla Ohlde, City of Edmonds, Kathy Johnson formerly with the Lynnwood Parks Dept., Clark Meek, City of Bothell, Dawn Erickson and the helpful staff at the Darrington Ranger Station and Verlot Public Service Center, Tom Davis and Debby at the Skykomish Ranger Station, Kathy White also with the USFS, and Ralph Radford at Wallace Falls State Park. All were quick to offer the information needed to fill in the gaps. I'm especially indebted to Marc K., Dawn E., and Tom D. for sharing their knowledge of trails and for their friendly feedback on pertinent parts of the manuscript.

DISCLAIMER
This guidebook is intended for use by competent hikers who accept the inherent and sometimes unpredictable hazards associated with the activity. Read the introductory material and be sure of your ability to safely hike any of the trails listed before venturing out.
The user assumes all risks!

Contents

Walks & Hikes 👣 = EASIEST / 👣 👣 👣 👣 = MOST DIFFICULT

The Coast

Urban Walks

< Copper Lake from below Vesper Peak

Lowlands & Foothills

North Cascades
🌲 = GOOD SHORT HIKE ALSO AVAILABLE

Trail Location Map

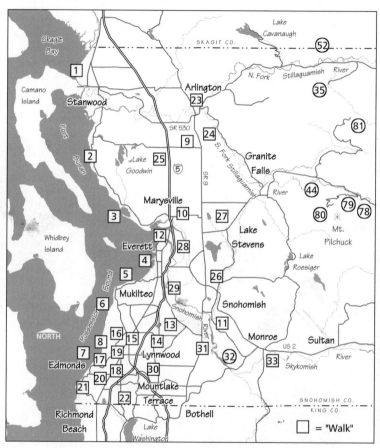

SNOHOMISH

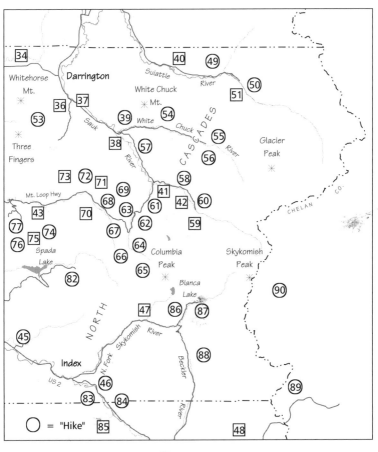

COUNTY

Glacier Basin near Monte Cristo

Introduction

Trails in Snohomish County...

From the wild bluffs and beaches of Port Susan and Possession Sound to the flowery alpine meadows of the Glacier Peak Wilderness, Snohomish County, Washington, is a wonderful place to walk. Hundreds of miles of trails access mountains, glaciers, wildflowers, waterfalls, lakes, rivers, and old-growth forests of the North Cascades, while more than a hundred more miles lead to lowland forests and fields, more lakes, streams, rivers, and wetlands, urban parks and natural areas, historic communities, and saltwater shores.

Hiking Snohomish County offers a wide selection of walks and hikes—doable in an hour or a day—to all of these destinations, from the easiest half-mile stroll on a scenic waterfront, to a marathon grind to a spectacular North Cascades summit. With the major emphasis on dayhiking, well over three hundred miles of walking is described in this guide, along with suggestions for further exploration. Listings are also provided for dozens of public parks, viewpoints, water access areas, and campgrounds throughout the county.

Overall, it's clear that Snohomish County has a lot to offer in the way of walking and hiking trails. However, most of these trails—over 80% of the trail miles in the county—are in the North Cascades, on federal (National Forest) and state (Department of Natural Resources or DNR) lands. The rest is generally spread across a number of city and county parks in the lowlands, most notably Lord Hill and River Meadows County Parks. A few urban-style multiuse trails like the Centennial and Interurban Trails, plus several trailless beach walks, a couple of dike trails, and a few miles within Wallace Falls State Park account for almost all of the balance.

What's in the works...

To someone new to the area or one who doesn't get out on the trail much, it may seem as if all our trail worries are over. Yet despite the sound of it, the overall trail system in Snohomish County is far from complete. Perhaps the most obvious trail deficiencies are the general lack of high-quality hiking trails over vast areas of the lowlands, and the absence of urban trails and greenways in almost all populated areas of the county. Major links between communities are also lacking, with only two exceptions: the Centennial and Interurban Trails. The trail system of the future may never rival the sprawling network we've developed to suit our addiction to the automobile, but certainly much can be done to improve on what we have. In fact, much *is* being done to address these deficiencies.

Thanks to the dedication of many concerned citizens, agency staff, and leaders in the community, there is no shortage of good ideas for future trails in Snohomish County. Among the routes seriously under consideration for near-term development are several major rail-trails, nature trails, park-based trail systems, and a range of trail extensions, links, and spurs throughout the county. To name a few, rail-trail extensions are planned for both the Centennial (all the way to Skagit County) and Interurban Trails within the next several years, as are improvements to the 27-mile Arlington-Darrington (AKA Whitehorse) Trail. Also of interest to hikers are expanding trail opportunities planned along the Snohomish River between Everett and Snohomish (plans emerged in the late 1980s for this route), and at Hubbard Lake and Robe Gorge east of Granite Falls. Trail improvements within existing parks and natural areas county-wide are also in the works, including several within the incorporated cities.

Many other trail projects have been identified for the long-term, as funding, access, and acquisition issues are worked out. These include the 13-mile Maltby and 3.5-mile Kruse Junction rail-trails, both of which would connect with the Centennial; dike trails near Stanwood and along the delta of the Snohomish River; other river trail extensions; trail links between communities and between other major trail systems like the North Creek Trail from the Sammamish River-Burke-Gilman Trail in King County to Silver Lake Park via Thrashers Corner and Mill Creek; Stimsons Crossing to link Kayak Point Park to the Centennial Trail by way of Lake Goodwin; a link from the Centennial Trail at Hartford to Robe Canyon via the Monte Cristo Railroad grade; and a new route from Everett to Marysville via Smith Island. An interpretive riverwalk trail from Lowell to north Everett and the Port Gardner waterfront is part of the grand plan, as is a Green Lake-style loop trail around Silver Lake in south Everett. Barrier-free enhancements are likely in many areas.

Among the shorter trails and connections within communities

that are on the drawing board are linking the Scriber Creek Trail in Lynnwood with Wilcox Park and Meadowdale Beach Park, and the development of new trails along several of the ravines between Everett and Edmonds, such as Powdermill Gulch, Merrill and Ring Creeks, and Pigeon Creeks. New coastal routes could link them all together. A new link from Harborview Park to Darlington Beach is another attractive possibility. Trails along Terrace Creek, Swamp Creek, Wood Creek, and possibly Lake Ballinger are also good candidates for enhancing the regional trail system. Other plans include trails along Narbeck Creek and wetlands, an interpretive trail to Kasch Park bog which drains into Lake Washington, and a trail at Japanese Gulch by way of another abandoned railroad grade. Improving unused street rights-of-way for trail use could further help link schools, parks, and neighborhoods. Also, a "Tidelands Trail" could be developed to facilitate better access to the county's 62 miles of marine waterfront.

In the foothills and Cascades, the emphasis is more on maintaining what exists and bringing some of the poorest trails up to an acceptable standard. The U. S. Forest Service, for example, plans to rebuild several mountain trails in the near future, including the lower wet section of Weden Creek Trail, and the trail to Poodle Dog Pass, both near Monte Cristo. Plans also call for a new loop trail around Heather Lake, and a new bridge over Canyon Creek and the Suiattle River Trail in 1998. This will complement major improvements made by both paid professionals and volunteer trail crews in 1996-97 on the Big Four, White Chuck Bench, and Elliot Creek Trails off the Mountain Loop Highway, as well as Pass Creek and the Lake Serene Trail near Index. Volunteers with the Washington Trails Association, Volunteers for Outdoor Washington (VOW), the Boy Scouts, and several other groups deserve a lot of credit for the thousands of hours of labor donated to these and dozens of other trails in the North Cascades. The Everett Mountaineers, having spent hundreds of volunteer hours restoring and maintaining old fire lookouts (and trails) in the North Cascades, is completing yet another restoration at the Heybrook Ridge Lookout, also near Index. Trails on DNR lands have also benefitted from recent improvements, much of it by volunteers, including Mt Pilchuck, Ashland Lakes, and Cutthroat

Lakes (AKA "Walt Bailey Trail"), in the Mt. Pilchuck area, and Greider Lakes near Spada Lake.

Hopefully, the trail park pass fee system instituted in 1997 will generate enough revenue to make a real difference in looking after trails in the National Forest in coming years. While a number of excellent opportunities exist for new trails on state and federal lands, sensitive ecosystems and the need to protect wilderness values demand a cautious approach to such development. Barrier-free improvements are also needed in some locations. Eventually, trails in the Cascades could be linked with lowland trail systems by way of the Arlington-Darrington rail-trail and other corridors.

A perspective on future trails...

All of this probably sounds ambitious and surely it is. Nevertheless, the public has consistently expressed interest in substantially expanding trail systems for both recreational use and to serve as alternatives to our sprawling, dreary, and expensive car-based transportation system. The demand for trails is clear. In fact, recent planning efforts revealed a shortage of more than one hundred miles of trails in the Everett area alone, based on accepted planning standards. Fortunately, the county's largest city has an abundance of waterfront around the west, north and east sides, plus much less-developed land to the south which offer tremendous opportunities to help address this deficit. Considering the growing number of people who reside in the region and use trails, we can expect the demand for more trails to rise, probably much faster than we can build them.

That raises at least three interesting questions.

First, can we afford to build and maintain an enjoyable and solidly interconnected regional trail system in Snohomish County? Perhaps we can't afford not to. If a decent quality of life is something we want to keep around for awhile, trails must be an integral component in the ongoing development of our communities. And acquiring corridors for future trails will only get more complicated and expensive over time. Secondly, does building more trails (or publishing more guidebooks, for that matter) only attract more trail users to fill them up and thereby diminish the quality of the trail experience? Perhaps, but that seems unlikely for now. People may have to wander a little farther from home or farther from the trailhead on occasion to find solitude as more good people inevitably come to 'our' trails, but the benefits seem to far outweigh the costs. People who walk on trails almost invariably find something valuable in the experience. It might be purely recreational, or personal, or spiritual, or educational, or whatever, but if people value the experience, there's a chance they will also value the place. And what we clearly need more of in the waning years of the second millennium on Planet Earth is more people who value *place*—whether it's an old-growth forest, an unpolluted lake, a quiet marsh, or a spectacular mountain vista. If trails take us to places that mean something to us, maybe we'll be inspired to take care of them.

Finally, can the natural environment withstand us all loving it to death simultaneously? Most likely not. We've seen the damage caused by overuse and abuse in the alpine country where thin soils and a short growing season tend to exaggerate the damage from tents, fires, and the like. We hear plenty about the need to protect water quality around sensitive lakes and streams. Many of us have stopped to pick up other people's garbage along the trail, mystified by the mentality of those who might just as easily trash the planet. We also know how humans can interfere with the needs of wildlife. Wolves and grizzlies desperately need a home, not to mention all the other imperiled species whose last refuge may be the wilderness of the North Cascades.

Certainly we can't all rely on the wilderness as one big happy playground dedicated to the weekend whims of humanity, nor should we presume that less pristine areas are any less sensitive to our numbers or our carelessness. Yet we can enjoy these areas as concerned individuals and learn to explore them in ways that keep them intact and unspoiled. We can learn to coexist with wildlife and the land. We can care about the *place*. We can encourage others to do the same.

About Snohomish County

FROM SEA TO SUMMIT...

Continental glaciers, we know, carved out much of the Puget Sound region over the past 20,000 years or so, then melting ice and huge meltwater rivers dumped thick layers of sediment over much of what we call the lowlands of northwest Washington. As the ice retreated and the climate moderated, vast forests gradually reclaimed the land. Wildlife, salmon, and humans followed. The land, free of this enormous burden of ice, went into rebound as if someone took seven thousand years to step off a 400-foot trampoline. But the sea rose almost as quickly, fed by the melting continents. Eroded bluffs along the marine shore offer an easy view of the sand, clay, and rock that was deposited here.

Before, during, and after the "Ice Age" (some say it hasn't really ended), *alpine* glaciers carved the mountains, as unmelted snow was compressed into ice which, responding to gravity, flowed and still flows like a slow river down the mountain side. Most glaciers are still carving rock from the North Cascades, inch-by-inch, year-by-year. At the same time, the Cascades are still uplifting, perhaps as quickly as they're being chipped away. Streams and rivers carry this stony refuse out of the mountains and onto the floodplains where new deposits are made, reminiscent of and intermingled with the vast glacial deposits that characterize much of the lowlands. Hills and foothills of underlying bedrock, like Lord Hill, stand as remnants of a huge and incomplete wearing down of the landscape.

Scientists can watch these natural processes over decades and lifetimes and then extrapolate from their observations what most likely occurred over spans of time that most mortals can hardly imagine. They help us see the natural landscape as the logical result of something dynamic and at the same time unshakeable, such as entire continents drifting around the globe, pieces of oceanic and continental crust colliding ferociously but in ultra slow-motion nearly invisible to human awareness, volcanoes erupting through the weakened rock where one tectonic plate slides hotly beneath another. In the place we arbitrarily refer to as Snohomish County, volcanic Glacier Peak emerged from this sub-earthen waltz to become what is perhaps the region's most dramatic natural landmark.

First climbed in 1898 by Thomas Gerdine, Sam Strom, and three others, 10,541-foot Glacier Peak was called *DaKobed*, or Great Parent, by the natives. Gerdine and his contemporaries called it Glacier. Over twenty square kilometers of ice mantle its slopes. Perhaps 700,000 years old, the volcano has not erupted in any great measure for about 12,000 years and may be the least active of Washington's five major volcanoes. Its two restless neighbors, on the other hand, Mt. Baker and Mt. Rainier, quite feasibly could erupt within a year, perhaps in a century. While the mountain is buried deep enough in the range to be mostly obscured from view from the western lowlands, it is a dramatic sight from nearby trails and meadows.

The North Cascades—generally all the mountains between Snoqualmie Pass and British Columbia's Fraser River—are at least several million years old. Their amazingly rugged appearance—best appreciated up close and personal—is largely a result of long periods of stream erosion intermixed with periods of glacial advance and retreat. The frequent occurrence of hanging valleys offer evidence of calamitous ice traffic buzzing across preexisting valleys over centuries and millennia. But whatever the geologists say, the photographers assure us that the result is at least as beautiful as it is educational. Hikers and climbers find literally hundreds of scenic peaks to choose from in the North Cascades for their one- or multiday adventures.

In the lowlands and foothills, the shape and feel of the land is more subtle. Dozens of lakes, streams, waterfalls, forests, wetlands, occasional rock outcrops, and mountain vistas become the prized destinations. Here, there are no rules to say all hikes must end somewhere huge and spectacular. Instead, we look for what's beautiful or unique in nature. And the closer we look, the more there seems to be. To our good fortune, Snohomish County has taken great steps to ensure that some unspoiled areas and unique natural features in the lowlands and foothills remain intact for our and future generations to enjoy. These bits of protected land (about six-thousand acres worth), like the higher mountains, are home to a wide diversity of birds, mammals, fish, amphibians, arthropods, unique plants, and other life forms whose future also depends on protecting substantial areas from development, and in some cases, from any human use at all. While wetlands and riparian, or streamside, habitats are turning out to be some of the most valuable places we can protect, we can hope that, some day, viable representative examples of all native ecosystems will be protected.

National Forest lands provide some of this "insurance" for ecosystems, especially designated Wilderness Areas (of the county's 1.3 million acres of land, just under half is National Forest). Yet even Wilderness Areas miss much of the lower forests and streams, while doing a more reasonable job protecting high meadows, rock and ice. Nevertheless, Snohomish County is lucky to have several hundred thousand acres of wildlands set aside within the Glacier Peak, Boulder River, and Henry M. Jackson Wilderness Areas. A small amount of state land is also protected, most notably around Mt. Pilchuck and Spada Lake (about ten percent of the county is managed by the DNR, albeit mostly for timber production).

The human years...

Once inhabited only by wildlife, from salmon and grizzly bear — even bison and woolly mammoth as the ice retreated — to sparrows and butterflies, the land called Snohomish County was eventually occupied by Native Americans. A relatively advanced culture of hunters and gatherers moved into the region, perhaps thousands of years ago to become the expert fishers, hunters, crafts people, traders, and artists who were encountered during Northwest explorations by Captain George Vancouver in 1792, and others before him and since. In the early 1800s, non-native fur traders passed through, but even by the 1840s no one had seriously confronted the Snohomish tribes whose camps and villages lined the region's rivers and saltwater shores. That would soon change, however, as pioneers and fortune-seekers began to make their way into the forested frontier. Conflicts arose with virtually all native tribes in the lowland regions, at times escalating into deadly violence. Military forts were established in many areas of western Washington, but from lessons learned in previous Indian wars of the West, a more concerted attempt at pacification, perhaps, led to the signing of the Point Elliot Treaty at Mukilteo in 1855. Territorial Governor Stevens, his delegation, a number of tribal chiefs, and 2,000 to 4,000 natives assembled for the occasion. In exchange for peace, a few scraps of reservation land, and guaranteed access to hunting and fishing grounds, the natives let go of a vast territory from Seattle to Canada. The treaty, unfortunately, has been violated repeatedly over the years, as much of the Indian land fell into non-native hands, as disastrous attempts were made to forcibly assimilate Native Americans into the white Euro-American culture, and as the salmon catch in particular was unfairly distributed. (The famous Boldt decision in the 1970s helped rectify the latter.)

In 1861, Dennis Brigham homesteaded at the foot of California Street on Port Gardner Bay, and the tiny settlement that would become Everett was born—the same year Snohomish County was split off from Island County. On Port Gardner, originally named by Vancouver, the mud, mills, stumps, and saloons of Everett, Washington, would soon develop into of one of the most important timber towns in the nation—Milltown it was called. The West's infatuation with big timber had spread north from California through the Oregon Country and on to the great wilderness surrounding northwest Washington's inland sea. Big timber was exactly what Snohomish County was made of. While the county's first sawmill was just up the shore at Tulalip Creek, it quickly became clear that Port Gardner, at the mouth of the Snohomish River, was the most strategic place to be. The river was the interior's transportation link to the outside world, as the founders of Lowell, Snohomish, and Monroe could easily see in the latter part of the 1800s. Word spread quickly of Douglas fir and red cedar trees over twelve feet in diameter, and a seemingly inexhaustible ocean of timber from the mountains to the sea. It seemed that easy fortunes awaited the barons, developers, and speculators willing to invest in the region's future. Logging camps and sawmills sprouted up by the dozens in every direction. Communities like Arlington, Darrington, Granite Falls, Hartford, Edmonds, and of course, Everett rapidly took shape around lumber and shingle mills. In 1889, gold ore was discovered at the headwaters of the Sauk River. The Monte Cristo mines brought a railroad and smelter, adding to the inflated promise of wealth for all who might come to Snohomish County.

In the 1880s, completion of the Northern Pacific Railroad to Tacoma had enticed a hundred thousand people to Washington within two years. Hundreds of bankers and investors from New York, Boston, St. Paul, and elsewhere took note of the grand potential to the north, and names like John D. Rockefeller, James J. Hill, Henry Hewitt, Frederick Weyerhaeuser, Wyatt Rucker, Charles Colby, Charles Wetmore, and Colgate Hoyt appeared on the scene. They were the economic movers and shakers, determined to see the place grow and prosper as the "City of Smokestacks," while generating more than a tidy profit for their investments. Empire Builder Jim Hill's 1,800-mile Great Northern Railroad reached Everett, by way of Stevens Pass, in 1893, but it didn't terminate here as these men had dearly hoped. Hill pushed it through to Seattle, and the dream of Henry Hewitt, "father of Everett," that the city would become the New York of the West, was lost. This turn of events, plus a nationwide financial panic the same year sent the city into turmoil. Over the next several years scores of businesses shut down, unemployment surged, wages fell, many lost everything they had, a landlord was shot trying to collect ten dollars rent, thousands of properties went into tax foreclosure, and thousands of people left.

Amazingly, where others saw hopelessness, Jim Hill saw a new opportunity. As the nation rebounded from the worst depression to date, Hill struck a deal with Frederick Weyerhaeuser who bought up nearly a million acres of land from what were the Northern Pacific land grants, for the cozy sum of six dollars an acre, then built the world's largest lumber mill on the Everett waterfront. As the city was revived, mostly through the lumber and shingle industries, Hill could expect, among other things, a vast increase in the use of his railroad to ship wood products and other freight. But industrial capacity rapidly outstripped demand, and markets spiraled out of control. Prices dropped as the supply of lumber increased, then mills would increase production to make up the difference. The industry literally collapsed in 1907. Still, by 1908, more than 270,000 acres of land had been logged off in Snohomish County, and a commission was established to figure out what to do about it. Ultimately, the stumps and slash would be cleared for agriculture and settlement to further the region's economic development.

As workers struggled to survive the winds of boom and bust, many perceived that the greed of industrialists and the politicians they supported were responsible for the poor wages, poor — and at times dangerous — working conditions, mill closures, and unemployment that would plague all the county's lumber towns on and off for decades. Populist sentiments spread among the discontent. Labor unions gained strength. The Industrial Workers of the World, or the Wobblies, became more vigilant, and disgruntled workers flocked to their ranks. Eugene Debs and the Socialists were gaining ground nationwide, and Washington State had become a veritable hotbed of support. The situation escalated into angry demonstrations and arrests, then beatings and shootings, and ultimately the infamous tragedy known as the Everett Massacre on November 5th, 1916. To rally the workers' cause and assert the right of free-speech in Everett, over two-hundred Wobblies boarded a ship in Seattle, steamed north, then were refused a landing by Sheriff McRae and a hundred citizen deputies. A barrage of gunfire broke out, bodies tumbled off the ship and deputies collapsed on the dock. Of the sixty or more wounded, at least thirteen were killed, though no one is sure all the dead were ever accounted for.

In the years following this tumultuous beginning for the City of Smokestacks, conditions slowly improved, and despite the ongoing saga of boom and bust, commerce and industry continued to spread across the county from its social and economic epicenter at Hewitt and Wetmore, in downtown Everett. Logging, lumber, pulp and paper, mining, shipping, bargeworks, agriculture, and all the support services needed to keep them going remained the mainstays of the local economy for much of this century. From a land transportation system that consisted of a few meager routes, like the "road" from Mukilteo to Lowell up Edgewater Creek, and the old Turkey Neck Trail from Lowell to the base of Hewitt Avenue, routes that were often impassable because of muck or high water, a modern, all-weather, albeit not all paved, road system would emerge by the 1940s. In the 1960s, the Boeing boom introduced a big-time aerospace manufacturing element to the county payroll, which, along with spin-off development from Seattle and King County, began to change the face of every community south of Everett. What was rural became suburban, and what was urban ballooned outward into strip development, shopping centers, condominiums, and freeways. Similar growth and development is underway in almost every other community in the county. In the 1990s, the U.S. Navy's Everett Homeport opened, promising an annual infusion of millions of dollars more into the local scene.

An outlook for the future...

In a few short generations, Snohomish County has become a dramatically different place from what Jim Hill, Frederick Weyerhaeuser, or any other astute industrialist possibly could have imagined a century ago. Between 1980 and 1990, the county was the fastest-growing in the state. During that period, the population increased by nearly thirty-eight percent to 465,642, compared to a statewide increase of only eighteen percent (to 4.9 million). Everett grew almost as fast as the county as a whole. From 1990 to 1995, the county grew by another 60,000 people, a five-year increase of thirteen percent, a slower rate than before but substantial nonetheless. At this rate the countywide population could hit 600,000 by the year 2000.

Anyone who's watched this growth take place over the past two decades can scarcely fathom what might transpire over the next two decades. Growth and development shows little sign of slowing down much at all. In theory, the hotly debated Growth Management Act is a potent law that is supposed to help by ensuring orderly and efficient development, while protecting the most critical areas from being destroyed. Yet at the rate new subdivisions and shopping centers have been replacing farms, fields, and forests, one can only wonder how or where it might possibly stop.

In the meantime, it's not just the development or pains of growth, politics, and economics that define what Snohomish County is. It is, more importantly, a *place*. It is a coast, lowland farms and fields, lakes, wetlands, streams, rivers, waterfalls, wooded foothills, and the rock, ice, alpine meadows, and old-growth forests of a magnificent range of mountains called the North Cascades. And, of course it is a community of Northwesterners, some of whom like to hike.

The uncertainty is whether we can keep it that way.

What To Know Before You Go

Climate & season...

Although prospectors and surveyors were blazing trails into the North Cascades a century ago, few roads pierce this stronghold of nature. Development in the eastern half of the county has been limited by precipitous terrain–and a lot of precipitation (mostly snow). Except for a few low elevation trails along the Suiattle, Sauk, Stillaguamish, and Skykomish Rivers, most hiking areas are buried in deep snow six months out of the year. More than 150 inches of water, including as much as fifty feet of snow, falls on Glacier Peak annually. This compares to 35 inches in Everett (mostly rain, of course) and 90 or more inches in the foothills. The east slope of the Cascades receives only about half the rain as the west slope. The warm Pacific High usually dominates the summer weather over much of northwest Washington, while moist marine and dry continental air masses compete to influence the weather during the rest of the year. The lowlands experience a mild (but moist) climate and remain reasonably accessible throughout the seasons. In the light breezes of springtime, lowland jaunts are ideal while the Cascades are still snowed in. Hiking doesn't have to be limited to sunny days, as some might suppose. Beach walks are great any time, but beware of rising and falling tides, especially during stormy periods. The casual hiker, properly clothed and shod, will find that a November sunset stroll along a windy shore can be just as enjoyable as an April day hike to Wallace Falls, or a cool October outing to Lake Valhalla.

In summer, the flowering alpine meadows high in the North Cascades on a warm day are especially inviting and difficult to surpass in their soothing beauty. Mid-July through mid-September and sometimes June and October are the best months for good weather and snow-free trails in the North Cascades. In heavy snow years, the higher trails may not even start to open up until late July. Wildflowers and snowfields may have all but disappeared by September, with fall colors peaking by early October. Snowpack in the mid-elevations (2,000 to 4,000 feet) is a crap-shoot year to year. A lake at 3,000 feet may be just as likely to be snowbound in June one year as it is to be snow-free in April the next. Remember, too, that the higher south-facing slopes can be free of snow a month or more before nearby north-facing slopes, so save the latter for later.

In the mountains, the weather can be fast-changing and unpredictable, so good raingear and layers for warmth are essential. Many days of cold rain and/or gusty winds can be expected anywhere anytime with or without any warning. Thunder storms are not unusual, so avoid ridge tops, taller trees and open water if you think lightning may strike in the vicinity. Snow is possible any day of the year above 5,000 feet. HYPOTHERMIA, therefore, IS A MOST SERIOUS CONCERN, having claimed the lives of more than a few unprepared victims. In the lower elevations, if you're dressed for the weather, hiking season can last all year.

Preparation...

A rewarding trip is usually one with good prep: proper dress, adequate food and water, and a few basic safety items in the knapsack. Unsolicited advice: tell someone where you're going and when you'll return. Know your limits under the conditions around you. Sharpen your senses before and during your walk. Go at a comfortable pace and make it an enjoyable outing for yourself and your companions. Travel in a small group–three to six is ideal. Anticipate problems that might arise and prepare for them. Is the weather unstable? When does it get dark? When does the tide come in? Will there be snow on the trail?

The shortest walks require little more preparation than what's needed to check the mail up the street. Longer hikes require much more foresight, especially in remote areas. Overnight trips are another matter altogether. This guide is not intended to prepare you for overnight backpacking, though many of the hikes listed offer great potential. Consult libraries, sporting goods stores, outdoor clubs and knowledgeable persons about furthering your skills in backcountry wilderness adventure. Numerous books are available that address clothing, equipment, navigation skills, camping, weather, ice axe use, hazards and other elements you may or may not be familiar with. Remember that trail conditions change due to any number of factors, so the trail descriptions in this book are not cast in concrete. Always carry along a bucket of common sense.

Clothing & equipment...

For convenience, a suggested clothing and equipment list is included below. Volumes have been written on the selection and use of gear for a variety of hiking environments. Outdoor shops are excellent sources of information. Dressing comfortably means wearing loose-fitting layers that can be added or removed as necessary. Just being fashionable won't do. Under typical northwest skies, the best combination in the mountains often includes a fast-drying synthetic layer against the skin, a light wool shirt or sweater, wool or synthetic durable pants (avoid cotton), a heavy wool sweater or pile jacket, a wind and water-resistant shell, top and bottom, gloves or mittens, and a wool hat or balaclava. Feet need special attention. A boot that fits is mandatory. Thick socks over thin help absorb friction away from your skin. Wet clothes, especially denim and other cotton fabrics, can lead to a rapid and dangerous loss of body heat. Add layers, gloves, a hat, and a parka in colder weather. Nights in the mountains, even in summer, are usually cold. A wool hat that pulls down over the ears makes a great thermostat. Put it on before you start shivering and remove it before you sweat or overheat. Fashionable sunglasses with UV protection, and sun cream (SPF 15 or better) are appropriate for bright days, cloudy days in the snow, and hot tub parties.

For short day trips, a large waist or fanny pack may be useful to carry food and drink, a nature guide, camera, windbreaker, etc. A backpack or rucksack will be required for mountain trips. Some of the higher trails can still be snow-covered in summer and an ice axe and the ability to use it may be necessary for safety. Contact outdoor shops or clubs to learn proper ice axe technique. In remote areas, care must be taken to avoid getting caught in darkness or bad weather without the essentials in your rucksack. Carrying plenty of water is also very important (caffeinated sodas are a poor substitute). Study the following list and notice what other experienced hikers carry with them. For those who may be "hiking" by wheelchair (let's hear it for accessible trails), modify the list as needed.

Short walks:

Food, water, proper clothing, footwear, camera, binoculars, guidebook, sunglasses, sun cream.

Short hikes:

Same as above, and sturdy, lug-soled boots, small pack, extra clothes (sweater, raingear), pocket knife, whistle, flashlight, batteries, first aid kit. Some now carry a cell phone (less reliable in the mountains).

Longer dayhikes:

Same as above, and extra food and water, more clothes and raingear, map and compass (learn to use them), matches, fire-starter, foam pad, toilet paper, insect repellent, emergency shelter.

BACKCOUNTRY SANITATION...

Cleaning yourself or your food containers and cook pots should always occur well away from water sources. Use common sense if you need to make a nature call. Get well off the trail and a good distance—100 feet or more—from streams or water bodies. Dig a shallow hole into the humus soil layer then cover it up well with soil, rocks, and sticks. If it's safe (damp and raining), burn your toilet paper; otherwise pack it out along with any trash or recyclables. Never discard anything but body waste in a wilderness privy. Leaves or snow work well if you forget the TP. Whenever possible, take care of these little duties before you hit the trail.

CONDITIONING...

The better shape you're in, the more enjoyable the hiking. And the best way to get in shape may be (surprise!) to go for a hike. If you hike often, each trip better prepares you for the next, each becoming more and more effortless as your condition improves. Most trips require only average physical condition. To cover more miles while avoiding burnout, maintain a comfortable pace. Check with your doctor if there's any doubt about your health or ability to make the trip. If you're not in the greatest shape, start with shorter walks and slowly work up to more strenuous hikes. Don't push yourself to the point that you are gasping for air or listening to your pulse pound in your head. This is supposed to be fun. Take plenty of breaks, relax and enjoy the natural surroundings. Think, ponder, contemplate. Discover meaning in your hiking partner's sniffle. . .

SOME RULES & PRECAUTIONS...

In the Cascades, check on park or forest regulations, trail conditions, and other details before arriving at the trailhead. Just because a hike is included in this or any other book doesn't mean it will be totally safe. Conditions can change dramatically in a short period of time. Prepare well, and turn back if trail conditions or the weather are seriously deteriorating, or if you suddenly find you're in over your head. On federal park and forest lands, a few rules need to be noted: keep the party size small, never more than twelve; practice 'no trace' hiking and camping; don't trample or destroy vegetation by camping on it or short-cutting trails; pack out your garbage; control your pet (pets are not allowed in certain areas); avoid building fires outside of designated areas, especially in meadows or dry forest; carry a small backpack stove for cooking; and camp only in developed or approved campsites. Trail park passes (*see page 21*), and free backcountry permits are required at many trailheads.

Some knowledge of first aid is highly recommended and essential when traveling in remote places. Carry plenty of water. Stream or lake water must always be boiled or purified, or you run an increased risk of catching the giardia bug and other serious health maladies. Beware of changing conditions and unseen hazards. Creek crossings can be dangerous during high runoff periods. Notice that streams often fall during the night and rise in the afternoon. In early season especially, avoid all steep open snow slopes, due to avalanche danger. If you're unsure, don't chance it. Sturdy, water-resistant lug-soled boots are recommended for mountain trails and on snow. Stay on the trail and don't lose it. *If you do get lost, calling out, staying put, and marking your location so it's visible from the air may be your best options. Keep dry and exercise if needed to stay warm.*

On logging roads, watch out for large trucks hauling their heavy loads of timber off the mountain and give them the right-of-way. Washouts, rocks, water, and windfall are common on roads from fall through spring so keep a sharp eye out to avoid disaster. Be cautious during hunting season (generally in the fall). Wear bright orange when large mammals are in season, or don't go. If a large mammal like a bear or cougar decides (unlikely as it may be) that *you* might be in season, consider the following. Grizzly bears are extremely rare in the North Cascades. In the unlikely event you see one, savor it for a moment then back away slowly. Some say it's unwise to look them in the eye, and far worse to run. Running from black bears or cougars also may only encourage them to engage their predator instincts and come after you. Stand your ground if an attack seems likely (some say play dead if it's a grizzly). A charge may be a bluff, so there's always hope. Occasionally, a problem bear can spoil your day by going after you or your food because careless others have taught them to associate humans with food. Be wise. Cook away from your tent, and always hang your food, garbage, toothpaste, etc. high when camping overnight. Fortunately, problem bears are uncommon in the Cascades, thanks to bear-proof garbage cans and bear-wise campers.

With cougars, use firm language and make yourself look big. If attacked fight back aggressively. Climbing a tree is probably moot since both black bears and cougars climb much better than we do. The best defense against these animals is probably not to approach them in the first place. Stay clear of their young and don't get between a mother and her offspring. If you stumble on a partly eaten carcass, it's best to move on. Be heard and seen when hiking in the woods or backcountry, although the risk of a dangerous encounter is so low in the North Cascades, bells and the like are normally dispensed with as more of a nuisance than they're worth. Avoid hiking alone, especially if you're a smaller person without much of a pack. Keep kids and pets close by. Report unusual wildlife sightings or encounters, or any grizzly or gray wolf sighting to an area wildlife official or ranger. Wolves, by the way, are very rare in the Cascades and will generally go out of their way to avoid you. The vicious attacks often portrayed in the movies are far from the reality of gray wolf encounters, even in Alaska.

If the worst happens (it rarely, rarely does) and you are confronted by a wacko, thieving, troublemaking *human* on the trail, try to stay cool. Cooperate if it will avoid something violent happening to you or your party. Attract someone's attention, if necessary, and scream, run, or fight back as good old common sense dictates. Give up your valuables if that's what it takes to protect your life. To reduce the risk, don't travel alone. Trust your instincts when you encounter someone who makes you uneasy. Avoid them or leave. Remember details if this is something that should be reported to the police. Report any criminal activity to the proper authorities, and/or call 911 if there's an emergency. Fortunately, violent crime seldom occurs on the trail (I have neither experienced a violent offense on the trail nor have I ever known anyone, in twenty years of hiking, who has). Common sense would suggest that walking alone at night on a deserted, unlit city street or trail would be one of the riskier scenarios. Hiking with a group during daylight hours, of course, would normally be a better choice.

Criminal activity, fires, accidents, lost hikers, and the like should be reported to local emergency officials, or just call 911. Search and rescue activities are coordinated through the County Sheriff. *Call the Sheriff or 911 if you need help with an injured party, or to report an overdue hiker.* Forest fires can be reported to 911 or to DNR at (800) 562-6010, or to the local Ranger District. For non-emergency related inquiries, contact the local park agency, or for questions involving National Forest lands try the toll-free information line in Mountlake Terrace at (800) 627-0062.

If big and threatening wild animals—whether two-legged or four legged—haven't frightened you out of the woods altogether, consider, then, the most hideous and terrifying wilderness creatures of them all: bugs. Actually, bugs aren't bad at all, rather it's their bites and stings that can spoil an otherwise perfect outing in the hills. For more sensitive folks (you probably know who you are), stings can be downright dangerous and may require immediate care (check with your doctor ahead of time if you think you might be susceptible to a reaction). However, for most of us, bug bites are just part of the package. The worst tend to be yellow jackets. They nest in rotten stumps and logs or holes in the ground, and once disturbed, they are amazingly quick to sting. Sooner or later, just about everyone who hikes regularly will encounter them, although if you stay on the trail when you're below timberline, the odds of stepping on a nest are almost nil. Mosquitos and no-see-ums are also a pain, but usually only in the early morning and early evening, although there are exceptions. To ward them off, find a high breezy place to relax, use a little jungle juice (citronella seems less intense than deet, but might have to be applied more often), cover yourself with clothing or mosquito netting, light up a cigar (the smoke deters them; don't inhale, of course), or try moving a few hundred yards (away from moist areas). Deer flies and black flies (black flies tilt steeply to bite) can be worse than mosquitos and can be intense even in the heat of the day. Similar techniques may allow you to escape their wrath. Horse flies are the big ones that zip around as if on a string. They can bite hard, but fortunately, there aren't usually a lot of them buzzing around you at the same time. In good weather from May through July, expect a lot of bugs in the mountains, and plan accordingly. Numbers tend to drop off later in summer and in cool or wet weather.

One other pesky life form we're supposed to worry about now is the *hantavirus*, a rare but deadly malady carried mostly by a few deer mice. When someone comes into contact with an infected rodent, say, by cleaning, disturbing, or sleeping near one's nest, it's possible to inhale tiny airborne particles of mouse urine, saliva or feces which could then cause the occurrence of *hantavirus pulmonary syndrome*. Just over a dozen cases have been confirmed statewide in recent years, including one in Snohomish County in 1996. About half the incidents are fatal. Fever, chills, muscle aches, and other flu-like symptoms develop within one to four weeks of contact, then rapidly turn into severe respiratory distress. Deer mice, the principal carriers, are about six to seven inches long to the tip of the tail and have a cute white belly and feet. Prevention is the key. Avoid the mice and their nests, as well as crude cabins, shelters, or other enclosed areas that may be infested or which are not well ventilated. Consider sleeping in a tent rather than on bare ground. Keep food and utensils sealed and protected from rodents. While the odds of contracting the illness are remote in Washington, reducing the risk to a minimum isn't a bad idea.

All in all, there are far more friendly and benign critters in the wild to marvel at than there are creatures to be feared in Snohomish County. So, be wise — not paranoid — and enjoy the wilderness.

Finally, take time to learn about the natural environment before and while you're in the middle of it. Bring your natural history guide to the wildflowers rather than the other way around. Exercise respect for other walkers, wildlife, and the environment. At home, take time on occasion to speak up for trails and wilderness. Before you and I arrived on the scene, others were doing that for us.

Trail park passes...

Trail park passes are now required in the National Forest. For information, or to purchase a pass contact the Darrington Ranger Station (360) 436-1155, the National Forest office in Mountlake Terrace (425) 775-9702 or 1-800-627-0062, or the Verlot Public Service Center (360) 691-7791. Passes are also available at many businesses near the National Forest that cater to trail users.

Beginning in July, 1997, the US Forest Service instituted a trailhead parking permit system to raise money for much-needed trail and trailhead maintenance on federal lands. Permits are required year-round for nearly all trailheads on National Forest land in the county. A day pass is $3 and an annual pass $25, subject to change, of course. Discounts are available for trail volunteers, seniors, and the less able-bodied among us. A pass purchased for the Mt. Baker-Snoqualmie National Forest (that's our Forest in Snohomish County), is good at surrounding Forests as well, including the Olympic and Wenatchee, and three others in Oregon. Eighty percent of the money raised goes to trail and trailhead maintenance. The program is called "experimental," but could remain in effect for the foreseeable future. In 1997, an "annual" pass was only good for the calendar year, *not* twelve months. Hopefully, that will change.

Are these fees fair? There is some good debate about what we, as taxpayers, ought to expect from our government in the way of basic public services, and what ought to be paid for through user fees. These lands belong to us all. As co-owners, we all have equal access and an equal responsibility to ensure that future generations have the same opportunity to enjoy them. If some people choose not to enjoy their public lands, should the rest of us pick up the cost? Instead of cutting maintenance budgets to make ends meet, shouldn't Congress and the President be insisting that all public facilities be well taken care of first? At the same time, most folks probably don't mind shucking out a few dollars for a nominal fee, that is, unless you're strapped financially. But if the money raised goes directly to support the trails, that's good too.

Obviously, there are merits to both sides of the argument, and the best solution may be a combination of user fees and budget appropriations. The trail park pass program is worth a try, as long as it doesn't become an excuse for axe-happy politicians to duck their responsibility to properly fund public facilities. If the money gets siphoned off for non-trail expenses, public support for the program will surely plummet. For now, however, the outlook is good. The Forest Service has done a good job involving people in the debate, listening to and incorporating ideas, and developing a pass program that seems mostly reasonable. Let's hope it stays that way.

PRIVATE PROPERTY...

Veteran hikers in the county may notice that some lowland trails are not included in this book. This is not because the author missed them necessarily, but rather that many of them traverse private lands whose owners might not wish to advertise their use by the general public. Liability for injures, vandalism and fires are common concerns (although landowners are well protected from liability by state law). A few careless people appear to be responsible for most of the public access problems being experienced. Local residents, outdoor shops and land managers are possible sources to consult in locating these semi-secret places.

A lot of good hiking country is under private timber company ownership where access is sometimes a little easier. You can generally avoid trouble with these folks by obeying all signs, closed gates, fences, seasonal fire closures, or other indications that your presence is not welcome. Obtain permission where necessary. Descriptions in this guide should not be construed as permission to violate private property rights. Always assume that camping and campfires are not permitted outside of designated sites.

As for your own private property–your personal valuables–don't leave them in your car at trailheads. Way too many brainless thieves have a habit of showing up at the oddest hours to break a window and make off with your goods. Report thefts to the authorities.

BEACH ACCESS...

It is often assumed that any old beach is open to the public. That is generally true in Oregon, Hawaii, and other coastal states, but it's not so cut and dried in Washington. Regrettably, the State of Washington sold off its best tidelands around our inland sea to private interests over much of this century. Not only was it an absurd thing to do, it left us with major difficulties in finding good access to more than a fraction of the county's scenic shores. The practice was banned around 1970, but the damage was done. However, there is still a legal argument — and the author agrees — that the public never gave up its right (i.e. the public trust) to use tidelands to access public waters, whether for commerce or recreation or whatever, even though the mud and the crud may belong to an adjacent landowner. The county's 1994 Comprehensive Parks and Recreation Plan puts it this way: "the tidelands may still be used for public access including trails — provided no other activities are included in the process that would infringe on the private property owner's other uses of the land." All that said, private property still deserves some respect.

Private or otherwise, the vast majority of tideland owners are not snobs and couldn't care less whether you and I go for a harmless stroll along a remote beach. However, they are not inclined to advertise these places to the general public due, in part, to the problems caused by a few individuals who abuse the privilege. Obnoxious behavior, litter and vandalism are primary concerns, especially where waterfront homes are located close to the shore. Fortunately, remote areas are more interesting to visit, and responsible hikers will encounter few problems with anxious landowners. On all beaches (public and private), use common sense: don't take or leave anything, don't start fires, be quiet, avoid large groups, respect wildlife and the marine environment, smile, be courteous to residents, stay off the stairs and pathways leading up to their yards, and watch out for trains if there's a need to cross the tracks.

Beach walks are good almost year-round, except during stormy periods, and in November and December when lower-low tides occur after dark. The suggested coastal walks (Walks #1 - 8) include those with public beach or access, and areas that have been used regularly by the public in the past. While it would take a title company and a survey crew to know for sure which areas are private, there are substantial public tidelands present. It is the user's responsibility to obtain prior authorization if necessary. Plan your visit during lower tide levels (check the tide tables), and be aware of rising tides which can surprise, strand, and/or drown you if you're not careful. **Walk these and all other areas at your own risk!**

How To Use This Book

When, where & how far?

To make best use of this guidebook, first read the *Introduction* and *What to Know Before You Go*, then decide on a walk or a hike. Check the *Trail Location Map* on pages x-xi for possibilities, read the trail descriptions, then check other maps in the back of the book (*p. 188 & 204*) for possible side trips to parks, viewpoints, water access, or campgrounds in the vicinity. Trails have been divided up into "walks" and "hikes," as noted on the *Trail Location Map*, to reflect the level of difficulty one might expect to find. *Walks* generally require less than an hour or two round trip, are usually 0.5 to 3.0 miles long, and are not particularly steep or difficult. *Hikes* are more strenuous but vary greatly in length, steepness, and overall difficulty. Of course, what may seem to one person to be an easy stroll may be a real workout for the next. Refer also to the 🚶 symbols in the table of contents (*p. vii-ix*). Round-trip distance to one or more destinations, approximate time needed, elevation gain, best months to visit (this varies year to year, of course), and directions from I-5 or the nearest town or highway, including milepost (MP) notations, are provided for each listing. The estimated times are loosely gauged for walking speeds of one to two miles per hour. Three miles per hour is brisk, and four is almost a trot and difficult to maintain over much distance. Additional time is added where elevation gain is more significant. Read the trail description to see what the times and distances given refer to.

Trips are divided into four geographical areas: the coast, urban areas, the lowlands and foothills, and the North Cascades. Some hikes don't fit clearly in one category or another, like the woodsy Buck Island walk next to downtown Monroe, or the White Chuck Bench Trail which is clearly in the North Cascades but at a low enough elevation to keep it accessible most of the year. For consistency, trails that generally stay below 2,000 feet elevation for their entire length are listed under lowlands and foothills. While these areas can be snowed-in part of the year, they can also be snow-free in the dead of winter if the weather's been mild. A special emphasis has been given to walks and hikes which are not adequately de-

On the go (on the ground) near Columbia Peak

scribed in other guidebooks, especially between the coast and foot-hills. A number of other potential trips are mentioned at the end of the numbered trail listings. These are not described in detail for a variety of reasons: limited space, lack of information, well covered by other guides, private property issues, etc. A determined adventurer will soon cultivate the detective skills needed to locate these and other worthwhile trails.

A listing of public parks briefly describe the location and facilities available, and may include short walks not listed elsewhere in the guide. Viewpoints and water access are accessible by car, bike, or a short walk and are self-explanatory. A list of public campgrounds is provided for those who might want to combine one or more dayhikes with a comfortable evening in the woods. All maps in this book are intended for general reference only, not for navigation. Far better full-sized topographical maps to all areas are available at many outdoor shops. USGS and Green Trails™ maps are excellent choices and may be indispensable for most hikes in the North Cascades.

For More Information...

Hiking Snohomish County is the only guide with broad coverage for the entire county, from the saltwater shore to the crest of the Cascades. However, several other guidebooks cover trails and overnight backpacking opportunities in the North Cascades, most notably Spring and Manning's *100 Hikes in the Glacier Peak Region* (The Mountaineers, 1996), and Darvill's *Hiking the North Cascades* (Sierra Club, 1982). Sterling's *Best Short Hikes in Washington's North Cascades & San Juan Islands* (The Mountaineers, 1994), and brief trail guides published by the Forest Service and the Northwest Interpretive Association are other useful sources. For lowlands, foothills, and the rest of the county, try *Walks & Hikes in the Foothills & Lowlands Around Puget Sound* (Manning, Manning/The Mountaineers, 1995), *Walks & Hikes on the Beaches Around Puget Sound* (Manning, Manning/The Mountaineers, 1995), and the *Footsore* and *Afoot & Afloat* series also published by The Mountaineers (varied publication dates). For beach access, try the Washington Public Shore Guide: Marine Waters (Scott, University of Washington Press, 1986). USGS and Green Trails™ topographic maps also deserve mention here as requisite tools for the mountains. Some of the older guidebooks may be out of print, while others are available at book stores and hiking shops in the region. In the cyber world, the Washington Trails Association maintains an excellent Web site (http://www.wta.org./wta/) loaded with information, including literally thousands of trail reports filed by users and management agencies, details on volunteer opportunities, and other trail resources and information.

Several local outdoor clubs and environmental groups sponsor guided hikes throughout the year, usually free of charge for members. These are listed at the end of the book, along with emergency contacts and various land management agencies. Libraries, outdoor shops, and resource agency staff are other excellent sources of "how-to" and "where-to" hiking information. Fred Beckey's *Cascade Alpine Guide: Stevens Pass to Rainy Pass* (The Mountaineers again, 1996) offers excellent local history and geology notes, as well as North Cascades climbing information for the experienced mountaineer. A couple of other good sources for local history include Harvey Manning's *Walking the Beach to Bellingham* (Madrona, 1986), and

Norman Clark's classic, *Mill Town* (University of Washington Press, 1970). See also *Pacific Northwest: Essays in Honor of James W. Scott* (Western Washington University, 1993) for several interesting essays, including Kathryn Utter's "What Shall Be Done When the Timber is Gone?" For natural history, a whole range of titles are available. Personal favorites include Matthews' *Cascade-Olympic Natural History* (Raven Editions, 1988), and Pojar and MacKinnon's *Plants of the Pacific Northwest Coast* (Lone Pine, 1994). Inquire at libraries and bookstores for the latest editions of these and other worthwhile titles.

Get involved in trails...

If you enjoy using trails, consider giving something back to the community on occasion, say, by calling or writing your representatives in Olympia or the other Washington to encourage them to support trails programs, or donating time or money to a local trail education or maintenance program. Snohomish County Parks and Recreation offers many opportunities to do volunteer work on trails, or to even patrol them on foot, by bike, or on horseback. Call them at (425) 339-1208 for information about volunteer opportunities, up-

coming projects, or how to connect with other trails organizations. To learn more about volunteering for trail work in the foothills and North Cascades, contact the Washington Trails Association or Volunteers for Outdoor Washington (addresses and phone numbers are in the back of the book). You may be surprised at how enjoyable this kind of work can be—and it's a fine way to get plugged into the local trail scene, pick up some hard-to-find trail information, discover new places, maybe meet a new hiking buddy. . .

Ashland Lakes Trail

Coastal Areas

Big Ditch Slough in winter

< Mukilteo Lighthouse

Beach north of Edmonds >

1. Big Ditch Slough

Distance: 0.5 - 2.5 miles roundtrip   Time: Allow 1 - 2 hours

Elevation gain: None   Season: Year-round

Bring the binoculars and bird guide for this easy scenic saunter along the southeast shore of Skagit Bay within the Skagit Wildlife Recreation Area. The latter encompasses 12,800 acres of sloughs, islands, and tidelands spread across the broad delta of the Skagit River, from Stanwood nearly to La Conner. The dike along Big Ditch Slough, despite the name, offers a fine coast walk, with good views and good odds of seeing many species of birds and other wildlife, particularly in winter and spring. Harbor seals, otter, beaver, mink, and deer are all possible. There's a catch, though: a fishing or conservation license is required to use the area (*see p. 205*).

To reach the dike and trail, head west on SR 532 from I-5 and turn right on Pioneer Highway (SR 530) at Stanwood. Drive past pleasant farms and views of Skagit Bay and the lands that embrace it, namely Camano, Whidbey, Fir, and Fidalgo Islands. In 2.7 miles, turn left at the bottom of a hill onto Old Pacific Highway. Cross the tracks, but continue straight on a gravel road signed "Big Ditch Access" that leads to the bay and parking area. Closed after dark. (An overgrown dike just east of the parking area might be cleared some day for a possible link to Stanwood.) Walk over a small bridge crossing the slough and go left 0.2 mile for a look south and west across mucky flats to Camano Island. Whidbey's Strawberry Point lies beyond and right. Some wandering is feasible at lower tides, but so is getting stranded—best to stay close to the dike.

The main walk leads north from the slough bridge and tends to be higher and drier. Rich, marshy wetlands abut the dike to the west, alive with birds and critters. Watch for eagles, hawks, red-winged blackbirds, great blue herons, ducks, and a variety of shorebirds and upland fliers. Beached logs, rootwads still attached, lie across the flats like fluked whales. After a mile of good walking and, weather permitting, nice views of Mt. Baker and the Twin Sisters Range, the dike passes a little colony of beach cabins built on piling, with wooden walkways that have a "don't trespass" look to them. Just beyond, the trail begins to fade, although the dike continues another long mile to Milltown and another access point for more dike walking in Skagit County.

To reach the latter by car, head north on Pioneer Highway 2.4 miles north of the Big Ditch access road and turn left at Milltown Rd. The road climbs over the railroad tracks and bends north to a gate and limited shoulder parking. The dike south to Big Ditch is back where the road crossed the tracks (no parking here). A newly rebuilt dike runs north from the gate and parallels Tom Moore Slough and the South Fork Skagit River to Conway (behind the Conway Ballfield off the west end of Main St.). In less than a mile from the gate, go left at a junction and cross Fisher Slough on a wooden bridge to more wandering on old roads and dike. A right at the junction leads to an unmarked crossing of the tracks (caution). It is feasible to cross Fisher Slough on a floodgate walkway with railing on the west side of the highway bridge. The obvious dike continues north another long mile to Conway.

2. Kayak Point

Distance: 0.5 - 5.0+ miles roundtrip   Time: 1 - 3+ hours
Elevation gain: 0 - 100 feet   Season: Year-round

For some easy beach wandering, nice views across Port Susan to Camano Island, and a chance at seeing an orca whale, try Kayak Point County Park south of Stanwood. There's even a small stand of old-growth forest on the bluff with some giant trees. From I-5, take the SR 531exit at Smokey Point and go west 2.3 miles to a stop sign, turn right and continue another 6.2 miles to Marine Dr. (where SR 531 goes left to Lake Goodwin, don't turn; continue straight on Lakewood Rd.). Turn left on Marine Dr. and find the park entrance on the right in 2.2 miles (jog right then left at stop signs).

Pass the self-service fee station ($3.00/day in 1997) and continue down to the beach. Either head for the pier, hit the beach, or check out the short staircase trails on the bluff. For the latter, look for a path at the foot of the bluff due east of the fishing pier. The first of

Camano Island from Kayak Point beach

several large Doug-fir trees (seven feet across) is a few paces up on the left, followed by a big grand fir. Head right at the next two junctions (more big Doug-firs), then stay left to return to the parking area less than 200 yards from the start. There are a few other paths in the park, though not nearly as interesting.

Tides, of course, dictate when and where you can walk, although even at higher tides one can stroll above the drift logs on gravel, grass, or path. The park has 0.6 mile of good walkable waterfront, half of it below the high bluff. Picnic shelters crowd the shore north of the pier. At lower tides, say, below five feet or so, it's possible to walk much farther north and south. However, high eroding bluffs shed trees and debris, producing obstacles that are potentially dangerous if you get caught during a rising tide. From the south edge of the park, a 100-foot high bluff quickly gives way to McKee's Beach (homes near the water), then more bluff beyond, rising to 300 feet and higher. To the north, more homes line Kayak Cove, followed again by high bluffs, then the substantially inhabited shores of Warm Beach, two miles north. There are no public access points at any convenient distance north or south, so plan to retrace your steps.

3. Tulalip Bay

Distance: 1.0 mile loop

Elevation gain: Negligible

Time: 1 hour

Season: Year-round

Before Captain George Vancouver stopped at Tulalip Bay on June 4th, 1792, native people had already fished and crabbed and lived here for countless generations. When the ship's anchor dropped, Mr. Whidbey went ashore, intrigued by the large native village that existed here. The natives welcomed their visitors with hospitality and a parade of canoes. Vancouver, in return, staked his claim for the British Crown. Said he, "I had long since designed to take formal possession of all the countries we had lately been employed in exploring, in the name of, and for his Brittanic Majesty, his heirs and successors. . ." Today, an interpretive sign above the bay wisely acknowledges how tenuous such claims were. "Undoubtedly," it reads, "Capt. Vancouver failed to realize that these lands had been the Northwest coast natives' homelands for thousands of years and were not available as a birthday gift for the King."

To share some of the history of this area with the public, the Tulalip Tribes and Washington Department of Natural Resources have developed an interpretive walk along the bay called *A Walk with the Ancestors*. Improvements are minimal, but the history is fascinating. The walk begins at the Tulalip Bay Marina west of Marysville. From I-5 Exit 199 head west on Marine Dr. about 4.8 miles and turn left on 64th St. NW, then right on Totem Beach Rd. in 0.4 mile. Continue 0.7 mile to the historic St. Anne's Church (1904) on the right; turn left into the Tulalip Bay Marina and grab one of the first parking slots on the left. A big sign with a map of the walk offers a little history of the area. Check out the boats, then walk north past the marina and along a narrow paved road above the beach. To the left, the Mission Beach peninsula wraps around half the bay, and Hermosa Point guards the north. Pass a road on the right (an optional return route later) and keep going straight until reaching a guardrail and another road, about 0.4 mile from the start. Walk left across Tulalip Creek to an interpretive sign on the left next to what remains of William Shelton's Story Pole. Keep walking left to a

Tulalip Bay Marina, Camano Island in the distance

grassy area with another sign and a view of the bay over wild rose and blackberry bushes.

Return to the dam and two large interpretive signs and benches across the road. One elaborates on Vancouver's landing two centuries ago. The other tells us that the first sawmill in Snohomish County was built on Tulalip Creek. Walk along the main road 0.2 mile to two more signs, one on the origin of two silos (assimilation of native culture by turning fishers into farmers), and the other a language lesson, including the words for counting one to ten in Snohomish. Then either turn right on 36th Ave. NW to reach the road leading out of the marina, or take the next right to find the historic St. Anne's Catholic Church in 0.4 mile. Cross here to return to the starting point.

4. Jetty Island

Distance: 0.5 - 4.5 miles rountrip   Time: 1 - 4 hours

Elevation gain: None   Season: Summer-plus

At about two miles long and hardly anything wide, Everett's Jetty Island is barely three dimensional. The north part was once a heap of spoils from the dredging that makes the city's waterfront (Port Gardner) navigable, while the south part is a more conventional jetty made of big rocks piled in a long line that helps break up the waves and swell rolling in from Possession Sound. From this not so glamorous beginning Jetty Island has become a little haven of nature jointly managed by the Port of Everett and the city park department. Views, wildlife, an interpretive trail, and some nice walkable beach make the island attractive to footsters.

The best — or at least easiest — time to visit is in summer when the Everett Park Department runs a free foot ferry to and from the island about every half-hour (from the 4th of July through Labor Day, 10:00-5:30 Wed-Sat, 11:00-5:30 Sun, no boat Mon-Tue). The ride is a freebie and takes a grueling five minutes each way. The boat can fill up quick on a nice day so expect to wait a little, or go on a cloudy day when more folks are home grumbling about the weather. Catch the boat at the big public boat launch at Marine Park off Marine View Dr. and the west end of 10th St.

On the island, park staff offer guided nature walks daily, or you can explore a half-mile interpretive trail on your own. Two miles of beach on the west shore and northern part of the island offer several hours of wandering, but don't trample the vegetation, of course. It's feasible to find your own way to the island at other times — experienced kayakers have an obvious advantage here — but no camping is allowed. Always give wildlife a wide berth, and by all means, leave only footprints.

5. Pigeon Creek to Point Elliot

Distance: 0.5 - 3.0 miles one-way   Time: 1 - 3 hours

Elevation gain: Negligible   Season: Year-round

For a pleasant stroll on a good beach southwest of Everett, head for Howarth Park just off Mukilteo Blvd. While it's feasible to wander three miles to Mukilteo at lower tides, the best walking is in the first mile where the beach is generally much wider, sandier, and plenty scenic. From I-5 take Exit 192 and follow 41st St. west a few blocks, cross Evergreen Way, pass Forest Park, and in another 1.5 mile find Howarth Park on the right at Seahurst Ave. Pass the first parking area and park at a viewpoint, then head toward the bluff to find the high footbridge over the railroad tracks. The westerly of two Pigeon Creeks flows across the beach just right of the footbridge.

It's important to time a walk with the tide. At higher tides, many areas are impassable, if not downright dangerous. The first mile or so of beach is usually accessible at a moderate tide level of, say, six feet or less. Closer to Mukilteo, unique circumstances present a potential hazard not to be taken lightly, even at this tide level. *Be*

Footbridge at Howarth Park, from Pigeon Creek

cautious below the rock wall that supports the railroad tracks, since if the tide comes in while you're there, you could be trapped. The only escape may be a difficult vertical rock climb. Barnacles growing six feet above the beach offer a stark clue as to how high the water rises each day. Time your walk with an outgoing tide. The narrow parts toward Mukilteo are most walkable at tide elevations of four feet or less. For those who can deal with the tide issue, the walk offers a much better chance at solitude than the stretch closer to Pigeon Creeks. Maybe stash a bike at one end, or catch a bus for the return.

From the bridge, descend to the beach and head left for the best walking; right leads toward downtown Everett along a narrow and less appealing shore. The drone of the city's industrial waterfront carries easily across the bay, but so does the musical barking of a sea lion colony that often hangs out at Jetty Island and near the Navy Homeport in fall and winter. It's about a mile to the far end of the wider beach to the west. Either turn around there, or if the tide's out, continue as far as conditions allow. For the longer trek toward Mukilteo, several streams must be crossed (Glenwood, Merrill, Ring, Narbeck, Powdermill, and Edgewater Creeks) which can be some-what inconvenient when there's much runoff. But these streams are also significant deposition zones that produce small deltas and bet-ter beach to walk on. The upper part of the beach usually offers easier going on packed sand or gravel, although some areas are bouldery and/or slimed with algae. A steep, wild, eroding bluff rises behind the tracks, hiding most homes from view. Drift logs, weathered stumps, scattered boulders, old piling, islands, Mt. Baker, and a curious seal or two add to the scenery. At lower tides in fall and winter, watch for eagles, ducks, herons, and other shorebirds.

The walk to Mukilteo ends at an informal access area off the end of a dirt road east of the ferry. To find it from Howarth Park, follow Mukilteo Blvd. 3.3 miles to Mukilteo Speedway. Turn right (not the ferry line), and right again on Front St. across from the ferry termi-nal. Jog right then left at railroad tracks and continue 0.4 mile to another sharp right; instead, go straight on the bumpy gravel road to a small parking area at the end of a long concrete wall that shields a former Defense Department fuel tank farm (closed and under clean-up). This access area is closed at night (8:00 pm to 6:00 am).

6. Point Elliot to Picnic Point

Distance: 1.0 - 5.0 miles one-way   Time: 1 - 5 hours
Elevation gain: Negligible   Season: Year-round

From Mukilteo State Park, there's a good walkable beach leading south below railroad tracks and an almost continuous wall of bluffs all the way to Picnic Pt., five miles afar. The problem, however, is that it can only be done at lower tides, say, three feet or less. The railroad crowds the shore the entire distance, largely built on fill and revetment atop the upper beach and tidelands. There's nothing terribly odd about that, considering that nearly half the county's shoreline has more or less been turned over to the railroad. But it does seem rather unfortunate that so many miles of relatively wild shore are so difficult to access and enjoy. There is no convenient way to access the beach on foot other than at Points Elliot or Picnic, so unless you can time a walk with a lower, outgoing tide, stick to the higher and drier stretches near these two end points. The walk is described from north to south—flip it around if there's a strong wind bounding up Possession Sound.

Morning on the beach at Pt. Elliot

Find Mukilteo State Park near the Whidbey Island ferry terminal, left off the end of Mukilteo Speedway. (One could spot a car first at Picnic Pt., or stash a bike at Mukilteo, then drive to Picnic Pt. for a start there and a bus-bike combo for the return; *see Walk #7 for directions*.) The famous beach at Pt. Elliot (*see Park #22*) may be walkable at more moderate tides for a half-mile or more. If not, one is soon forced up onto the railroad tracks which is not something to be recommended here, mainly because there is little room to get out of the way of speeding trains, but also because you might be trespassing. Like with the beach east of Mukilteo, getting caught by rising water below the intermittently steep rock wall that supports the tracks is a hazard to be avoided. Assuming there's still a beach to walk, round a point and continue as far as time and conditions allow. Watch and listen for harbor seals or Stellar sea lions (fall and winter) browsing and blowing along the shore, and perhaps a bald eagle and great blue heron. Thousands of ducks and grebes may feed offshore in winter. Whidbey Island is just a few gull flaps to the west, and Possession Sound fills the view north and south.

After 1.5 miles or so, there's an obstacle to negotiate (a possible turn-around point) in the form of a dozen beach cabins perched between the tracks and a big concrete seawall. There's no car access to this idyllic neighborhood. The way continues like before, although some places can only be walked at the lower tides of three feet or less. A few homes appear along the bluff, and a small sewer plant is passed, as well as a couple of small streams emerging from gulches. At about four miles, another obstacle appears, this time a rotting hulk of something that may have been seaworthy fifty years ago, next to an unfriendly looking homestead waterward of the tracks. The beach here is nice, but littered with dozens of "private beach" and "no trespassing" signs which might be moot if you stay below the high-water mark. At least we can hope so (*see page 22 for details*). Proceed at your own risk, however. Beyond, a few more homes have gravitated toward a small lake perched behind a causeway supporting the tracks, and finally, at its other end, comes the wide beach at Picnic Point.

7. Picnic Point to Brackett's Landing

Distance: 1 - 6 miles one-way   Time: 1 - 6 hours
Elevation gain: Negligible   Season: Year-round

Walks along the Emonds waterfront and at Picnic Pt. are among the nicer beach strolls to choose from in the county. If the tide is right (best under three feet or so) the entire six-mile stretch from one to the other is about as wild a walk as you'll find in southwest Snohomish County. High bluffs keep most of the voracious residential development above and out of sight, though there are gaps where homes have drifted close to the beach. The railroad still dominates the upper beach as before, and frequent trains squeal past, but somehow, they're more tolerable than a busy highway. The trek is described north to south, but reverse it if there's a brisk southerly kicking up chop.

To reach Picnic Point Park, take Highway 99 to just south of SR 525 and head west on Shelby Rd. which becomes Picnic Point Rd. in a few blocks. Stay right at a Y and find the park 1.4 mile farther at

A view north from Edmonds

the mouth of a small canyon. Scamper across the big footbridge and out to the beach. North (right) leads to Mukilteo (*see Walk #6*). Head south for Edmonds.

Immediately cross the outwash from a small creek, then in a bit over a mile, pass a wharf at Norma Beach, followed by Meadowdale Beach Park in 1.5 miles. This beach makes a good turn-around for a shorter walk, or maybe stash a car or bike at the upper end of the Lunds Gulch Trail for the return to Picnic Point (*see Walk #8 for details*). Now enter Browns Bay, as Whidbey Island slips into the distance off your right shoulder and the view opens up to bigger water, the Kitsap Peninsula, and Olympic Mountains beyond. Contour around the bay a half-mile to 162nd St., the only good public access point between Edmonds and Meadowdale Beach (very limited parking, however). It's a good 3.5 miles from here to Edmonds.

To continue, skip past the old Haines fishing wharf (big blue and white buildings), leaving Browns Bay behind in another mile. A few small streams are easily crossed, and occasionally the flats grow wide and inviting when the tide is out. This center portion of the walk is great for relative solitude, especially weekdays, or in the off-season, or on less-than-perfect summer weekends. The final stretch to Edmonds seems to arrive too soon, so plan a break accordingly to savor the smells, the sounds, and the beauty of Washington's inland sea. But don't shrug off the time thing altogether, so as to avoid getting forced up on rocks or over the railroad tracks which makes for an unpleasant scurry back home.

The beach walk more or less ends a Brackett's Landing, an Edmonds city park next to the ferry terminal. The park is located at the base of Main Street, just across the tracks. It's a popular place, so if the lot is full, try Sunset Ave. close by, north of Main. This makes a good option for a shorter beach walk as well, maybe combined with a stroll along the city's pedestrian-friendly waterfront, or a gavotte uptown to Edmonds' historic core at 5th Ave.

8. Meadowdale Beach

Distance: 2.4 - 3.5 miles roundtrip   Time: Allow 2 - 3 hours
Elevation gain: 450 feet   Season: Year-round

To get to Meadowdale Beach Park's namesake beach, plan on a 1.2-mile walk each way, via the steep, quiet trail through Lunds Gulch. There's a significant loss in elevation involved on the way in (425 feet) so allow plenty of time for the climb back out to the parking area. The trail is wide, perhaps too wide in places, and is buzzed frequently by fast boys on bikes. That alone suggests the need for an alternative narrow track for hikers that more or less parallels the main trail at an appropriate distance. A few sets of stairs here and there would help keep the bikes off. For barrier-free access to the beach, there is handicap-only access via the service road off the north end of 75th Pl. (reached from Meadowdale Rd.). The rest of us may only approach the beach area from the trailhead (*see also Walk #7*).

From 52nd Ave. W. north of Lynnwood, turn west on 160th St. SW (park sign), then right on 56th Ave. and left on 156th St. The park and trailhead are a few blocks ahead (gate may be locked after sunset). The trail rounds a grassy area and enters young Douglas fir forest, with bigger trees beyond. The path steepens at stairs and a big switchback, and by the first half-mile most of the elevation loss to the beach is history. Pass several large cedar stumps, then walk easier path among hardwoods closer to the creek to a junction at 0.8 mile. Either fork leads to a low tunnel under the railroad tracks and the sandy beach beyond. The Olympics are prominent across Possession Sound. Edmonds is to the south. For strolling north or south, plan for a tide of five feet or less. The rules posted at the beach are typical of public parks everywhere. A sign reads (almost verbatim): "No-no-no-no-no-no-must be-do not-must be-no." Pretty basic stuff. Apparently, some people still need to be told.

Meadowdale Beach Park

City ducks

9. Arlington Airport

Distance: 5.0 mile loop   Time: Allow 2 - 3 hours

Elevation gain: None   Season: Year-round

Joggers and bikers may find the five-mile loop trail around the Arlington Airport appealing, but hikers might rather be in the woods somewhere else. Nevertheless, the trail is easy, uncrowded, and a good place to gander at small airplanes, including ultralights and other creative craft, as well as Cessnas and Pipers. Expect busy roads and much development along the south and east margins of the airport. Avoid these by walking the more tolerable north and west sides, then retrace your steps rather than making a full loop. Look for trail signs and limited parking near the corner of 172nd St. NE and 43rd Ave. NE, and by the airport entrance on 59th Ave. about a half-mile north of 172nd. Tread is a mix of grass, gravel, roads, and paved path. A number of ballfields exist in the area, and a future link with the Centennial Trail to the east is likely. (The loop trail could be improved immensely if there was some way to move the south section away from the road. Some strategic landscaping, a meandering alignment, and better surfacing would help too.)

10. Jennings Nature Park

Distance: 0.5 - 1.0 miles roundtrip   Time: Allow 1 hour

Elevation gain: Negligible   Season: Year-round

Saunter through an urban park with paved and unpaved paths, big rolling lawns, woods, and extensive wetlands at Jennings Nature Park in Marysville. This is a good family destination with a lot of room for kids to burn off excess Btus. Head east on 4th St. to 47th Ave. Turn left then right in a few blocks into the park. Or, keep going east on 4th (SR 538) another 0.5 mile to a small parking area on the left (a nice kids' play area here). This side may be less crowded, probably the better start. Wander the obvious paved path. Cut left across lawn to a picnic table perched on a hump for a good view of the wetlands along Allen Creek (bring binoculars in spring for bird-ogling). Where the paved trail ends, head west (left) past a ball diamond and over the hill to a short loop trail around the duck pond. Return the way you came. Figure close to a mile round-trip.

11. Snohomish Historic District

Distance: 0.5 - 2.0 miles roundtrip   Time: Allow 1 - 2 hours
Elevation gain: Minimal   Season: Year-round

Downtown Snohomish, settled on the north bank of the Snohomish River in 1859, is easily one of the more attractive historic districts in the state. Fascinating architecture and excellent maintenance of the area's many historic buildings offer a reasonable image of what western Washington's early boomtowns might have looked like, albeit dressed up in fresh paint and an abundance of potted flowers to please the tourists. There are literally dozens of shops in town selling good food, good beer, souvenirs, used books, antiques and more antiques. Thanks to the Snohomish Historical Society and their fine guide to old buildings, an enjoyable and informative walk awaits anyone curious enough to wander.

Park near First St. and head for the historic information sign and map near First and Ave. B, with a list of sights. The walk up and down First is mandatory, but burn some calories before getting

Historic downtown Snohomish

sidetracked by all the good eats. Some of the more interesting historic sites on First St. include (west to east) the Northern Hotel (1890) which survived the big fire of 1911, Pioneer Market (1890), the only three-story building in town, the Marks Building (1888) where the town's first flush toilet was installed, old Snohomish City Hall (1927), First National Bank (1907), Princess Theatre (1900), Oxford Saloon (1890), Eagles Hall (1904), and the Alcazar Opera House (1892).

From First St. walk a half-block up Ave. B to find the nicely preserved Blackman House (1878), built by an eminent logging family, and home of the first mayor, now a museum with original wallpaper, and a piano that sailed around South America. Ask for a "walking tour" brochure. Up another block on the right is the Methodist Church (1885) and the county's first church bell. Continue up to Fourth St. to the Stevens House (1887) built for the man Stevens Pass was named for. Catty-corner is the Snyder House (1888) with 22 rooms, five fireplaces, and a ballroom on the third floor. All these homes, except Blackman, are privately occupied, so no intruding. Turn east one block then right on Ave. A past other turn-of-the-century homes, including the "Gingerbread" House (1887) south of Third St., then little cottages known as Soap Suds Row (1889) where loggers and mill workers dropped off their laundry. Turn left on Second St., pass the St. Johns Episcopal Church (1893) originally built for $250, then turn right on Union to find many interesting shops across from a City Hall that was designed after Philadelphia's Independence Hall (1938). Head south another block to the site of Snohomish founder E. C. Ferguson's prefab house (1859), the town's first home. Then look for a new riverfront trail just beyond and walk downstream to steps leading back up to First St. at Ave. A.

Other points of interest include a State Senator's home (1889) at Union and Third, the gigantic Iverson House (1908) near Third and Ave. D, covering more than 8,000 square feet, Snohomish Hardware (1906) on Ave. C near First St. (has a water-powered elevator), the Odd Fellows Lodge (1886) at Second and Ave. C, and Pioneer Village Museum at Second and Pine with an 1875 log cabin, homes from 1889 and 1892, and a 1910 general store and blacksmith shop. A totem pole stands at Kla Ha Ya Park near First and Ave. C, just east of the American Legion Building (1887).

12. Port Gardner

Distance: 5.3 - 6.5 miles roundtrip   Time: Allow 2- 5 hours

Elevation gain: 200 feet   Season: Year-round

The possibilities for urban walks in Everett are many, but the following suggested loop offers a variety of natural, scenic, and
cultural features that should make it far more interesting than a
pointless jaunt down Evergreen Way. The description begins at Legion Memorial Park at 2nd St. and Alverson Blvd. (parking on the
west side), but start anywhere on the loop and bump the directions
accordingly.

Check out the view of the waterfront then wander northish along
Alverson Boulevard to Marine View Dr. Turn left and walk the paved
path and sidewalk down the viaduct to sea level, then soon pick up
the path through North View and South View Parks at the water's
edge (a bit over a mile to here). Maulsby Swamp is across the road
to the northeast. Keep walking south a short distance to 10th St. and
turn right for a half-mile side trip (roundtrip) to Marine Park. Return to Marine View Dr. and walk to 14th for the Firefighters Museum (a long block to the right), and on to the Everett Marina at 18th
St. Walkways and promenade lead past boat slips and around a
collection of shops and restaurants and even a hotel should you
decide to make this an overnighter.

Back at Marine View Dr., continue south up a viaduct with a
good view of the Navy Homeport, built for a seven ship battle group,

including a nuclear-
powered aircraft car-
rier, four destroyers,
and two frigates. The
project created thou-
sands of jobs and will
supposedly contribute
hundreds of millions
of dollars to the

*Everett waterfront from
Grand Ave. Park*

regional economy. Head up the ramp and take the bridge at 25th St. to Grand Ave. (without the side trips it's about two miles from North View Park to 25th and Grand). Turn left and walk to Grand Avenue Park at 17th St., then look down on the route you walked below. Continue north on Grand and Alverson to the start, 2.3 miles north of 25th St. The route also works well on a bicycle.

13. Silver Lake

Distance: 0.5 - 3.0 mile loop
Elevation gain: Negligible

Time: Allow 1 - 2 hours
Season: Year-round

Someday, if many citizens and park planners have their way, a Greenlake-style urban trail system for cyclists and walkers (and non-walkers, for that matter) could encircle Silver Lake in south Everett. But considering how much development already crowds the shoreline, and the high cost of acquiring lake frontage, it may take awhile before such an undertaking could be seriously undertook. Nevertheless, it's a worthy proposition that shouldn't be shrugged off as too costly or ambitious or impossible. Perhaps to get a head-start on things, a pedestrian way has been marked on much of the road shoulder along 19th Ave. SE and Silver Lake Rd., so hardcore pedestrians can circumnavigate the lake, despite the distractions and hazards of big-city traffic. The entire 2.5-mile walk can be done briskly in an hour or leisurely in two. Start at Thornton A. Sullivan Park on the west side (off Silver Lake Rd. a few blocks west of 19th Ave. SE) and essentially follow your nose to the most logical paths and roads.

If the lake loop is too much, try a much shorter nature trail in the woods across Silver Lake Rd. from the parking area at T. A. Sullivan Park. A trail sign and white posts mark the beginning (accolades to the Kiwanis Club and Boy Scouts for assistance). Several short loops are possible with minor ups and downs. Or stay right at junctions on good trail to complete a longer 0.5-mile loop that returns you to the starting point. The forest is lovely, but screaming traffic on I-5 next door obviously impacts the experience.

14. North Creek Woods (McCollum Park)

Distance: 0.5 - 1.5 miles RT

Time: 1 - 2 hours

Elevation gain: None

Season: Year-round

For a short walk in the woods on easy trail, try the little circuit at McCollum Park south of 128th St. SE, just east of I-5. North Creek—a salmon spawning stream—splits the park and a portion of the forest. While there is some traffic noise drifting into the trees, the creek's soothing gurgle helps neutralize it. Adopt-A-Stream Foundation and volunteers have worked to enhance the creek and trails for both salmon and people (respectively speaking), also built an interpretive/education center, and have made interpretive improvements along the creek.

Park south of the swimming pool and head for the footbridge over North Creek. Go left through pretty forest to begin one of several possible loops. Just off the trail are some excellent forested picnic sites (with grills) in the shade of modest-sized Douglas fir trees. Walk past a spur on the left leading to another footbridge and reach a fork just beyond, about 300 yards from the start. The longer loop begins and ends here. Imagine a path around the perimeter of the forest with several other paths cutting through the middle, and you will have a sense of where you're headed. If you head right (a counter-clockwise start) then generally keep right at major junctions to complete the loop. Or go left to do the opposite. The outer loop is a pleasant half-mile stroll through Douglas fir, red cedar, and western hemlock forest, with some red alder and a few old stumps, plus an understory of vine maple, salmonberry, red huckleberry, Indian plum, wild rose, sword fern, and salal. The terrain is gentle, and much of the trail system may be wheelchair accessible, with some bumps, for the more advanced folks on wheels.

15. Interurban Trail

Distance: 1.0 - 10.0+ miles roundtrip   Time: Allow 1 - 5+ hours

Elevation gain: Negligible   Season: Year-round

The recently developed Interurban Trail along I-5 between Lynn-wood and Everett is a major accomplishment, although some parts may not be quite exciting enough to be of much recreational interest to hikers. Some sections of the trail are noisy, disjointed, hard to follow, aesthetically dull, maybe even ecologically defunct, though there are exceptions. But before getting too critical, it's important to recognize that the trail is a major urban facility that was designed to provide a significant nonmotorized transportation alternative—not some cozy garden path for the footloose. It's also still under development. So, despite its less appealing qualities as a walking trail, it is improving. We should be grateful that Lynnwood, Everett, Snohomish County, and the local PUD #1 came together to allow it to be built in the first place. Incidentally, the newly paved trail follows what was a rail corridor for the electric Interurban Trolley that ran from Ballard to Bellingham in the early 1900s.

Interurban Trail near 112th St.

For the Interurban to become a more attractive urban greenway for hikers, new links and sidepaths are needed, pocket parks and traffic bypasses should be constructed, along with freeway noise barriers and interpretive facilities. Most importantly, native trees, shrubs, ferns, and wildflowers should be restored throughout the corridor. Some of this is already happening, like the new bicycle/pedestrian overpasses about to be constructed over 44th Ave. W near I-5, and across I-5 near 36th Ave. W which will add tremendously to the trail's appeal. Until they're completed, it may be better to explore these sections by bike, though even on wheels freeway noise and impossible traffic at major intersections are just plain unnerving. Watch for future trail extensions north and south, including a new section between SR 526 and Madison St. in Everett in 1998.

The Interurban Trail is worth a walk, if for no other reason than to inspire good ideas about how to make it better. Forward those ideas to local park officials. To walk the trail try the sections between South Lynnwood Park and Scriber Creek Trail (*see Walk #20*), and between 128th St. SE and Everett Mall where busy crossroads are more easily avoided. For the latter, park at Thornton A. Sullivan Park on Silver Lake, then walk 112th St. SE across I-5 (west) to the obvious trail entrance. There is a trail underpass here which allows one to head north or south without having to cross the street above. Trail access and parking are also feasible at Everett Mall (good access behind the cinema off W Mall Dr.), at the 164th St. Park-and-Ride, at McCollum Park (off 128th St. SE), and at Alderwood Mall. Another stretch perhaps worth exploring (noisy) is east of I-5 between 164th St. and the drive-in theater south of 128th St.

16. Meadowdale Playfield

Distance: 0.5 - 1.0 mile loop   Time: Allow 1 hour

Elevation gain: None   Season: Year-round

Another simple opportunity to get out of the house and loosen up the body can be found on the trails around Meadowdale Playfield in Lynnwood. About a mile of mostly paved paths, mostly barrier-free, exists at this multi-agency urban park and sports complex. From SR 99, head west on 168th St. SW, staying right at Olympic View Dr. Turn right again onto 66th Ave. W and enter the park just ahead. The walk needs no real description other than to say paved paths generally meander around and between the ballfields, trees, and play areas. Go when it's busy and catch a little sports action by some talented, energetic youngsters. Of course, any route will do, but don't forget the duck pond on the north side next to a picnic area. Thoughtful rock sculpture adds a bedazzling touch. An unpaved path parallels Meadowdale Rd. north of the park, becoming sidewalk farther down the hill. If you don't mind the road walk and the climb back up, it feasible to wander this walkway all the way down to the waterfront. At a junction with 75th Pl., not quite a mile from the duck pond, cross to pick up another paved path that leads 200 yards to railroad tracks, a road crossing, and when it's safe to cross, the beach just south of Meadowdale Beach Park (*see Walk #8*). Allow another hour or two and a couple miles roundtrip for this option.

17. Southwest County Park

Distance: 0.5 mile loop or 2.0 miles RT   Time: Allow 1 hour
Elevation gain: Negligible   Season: Year-round

Urban wanderers may be surprised to find a limited though reasonably good trail system slicing through pretty forest in what is otherwise a large, undeveloped county park near Edmonds. Several loops ranging from good to poor condition exist here, including at least a mile of well maintained trail, and other sections that are not so good. The steeper "paths" which are, perhaps, misplaced or, more likely, bootlegged in should be avoided due to the erosion and damage to vegetation they cause (not to mention the slips and falls). The area makes a reasonable destination for a lazy or crummy day, and will certainly get better as trails are improved and extended. From Puget Dr. in Edmonds head north on Olympic View Dr. about two miles to a shoulder parking area on the right immediately before 180th St. SW. Park near the park sign and walk into the woods on the obvious wide path. Stay right in fifty feet to follow a pleasant half-mile loop in Douglas fir forest. Narrower side-paths offer additional exploring. Or, from the park sign, cross the road and walk left a few yards to another half-mile path running parallel to Olympic View Dr. back to the western park boundary. Side trails here tend to be steep and are best avoided so as not to contribute to the damage others have caused. Otherwise, grades are gentle and easy to walk.

18. Lynndale Park

Distance: 0.5 - 1.0 miles loop   Time: Allow 1 hour
Elevation gain: Negligible - 100 feet   Season: Year-round

One of Lynnwood's finer parks, Lynndale has a wide range of facilities for everyone, including more than a mile of paths, mostly in a cozy forested setting. About half the trail distance is paved and barrier-free, although the loop described below is mostly unpaved. There are several ways to access the park. The main entrance is off the south side of Olympic View Dr., about 0.3 mile east of 76th Ave. W. Park up the hill near the big log shelter.

Either wander through the park aimlessly, or for a hilly, but easy half-mile loop on good trail, head left on the paved path between the parking area and the log shelter. Cross the access road near the exit from the parking lot to pick up a gravel path. This leads down 50 yards to a junction. Turn right, climb a little and follow this path along a narrow wooded ridge, then down steeply a few paces and soon to a four-way junction in a small valley. Head left up the stairs or go straight and take the next left (right goes over a rise and leads toward the park entrance). Stay on the main traveled path through Douglas fir and sword fern to a fork under the power lines. Turn left to reach another junction where one more left heads back to the start. Instead, go right. This leads to a paved path. A left here returns to the log shelter. Trails around the shelter and several spurs leading to more developed areas of the park are barrier-free.

19. Sierra Park

Distance: Less than 0.2 mile   Time: Allow 1 hour

Elevation gain: None   Season: Year-round

The short paved path at Sierra Park in Edmonds gets a mention for two reasons. First, there's a small and informal arboretum that's taken hold here containing a modest variety of native and non-native trees and shrubs. Second, the path was developed specifically for the blind. Low railing, benches, pavement edges, large rocks, and vegetation produce a three-dimensional environment that can be explored quickly and easily by just about anyone. Fragrant, flowering plants (spring and summer) add a fourth dimension to the experience. Find the park north of 196th St. SW on the west side of 80th Ave. W, but south of 190th St. SW. Parking is off 190th. Pick up the path at either end of the parking lot. The walk makes a short loop (less than a quarter-mile) through forest and flowers but requires no real description. Interpretive signposts are unique and written only in Braille. Big pines grow here, and the diversity of shrubs and flowers is enough to suggest bringing along a plant guide. Benches and picnicking are also available.

20. Scriber Creek & Scriber Lake

Distance: 2.3 RT or 0.7 mile loop   Time: Allow 1 - 3 hours

Elevation gain: None   Season: Year-round

Hidden behind the urban hubbub of noisy cars and rumbling trucks zipping along 196th St. SW in the heart of Lynnwood is a little gem of a lake named for a family who settled here in the 1890s. Like the natives before them, the Schreibers and other settlers found the area rich in game, with good fishing to boot. Later, a resort was developed at the west end, and the lake's name would be phonetically adjusted to Scriber Lake. The area became a park in 1981. A pleasant 0.7-mile loop surrounds the lake and is linked to the Interurban Trail by a 0.8-mile path that generally follows Scriber Creek.

To do just the loop, take 196th St. SW east of SR 99, turn south onto Scriber Lake Rd., then left on 198th St. Park near the restrooms and take the path on the right for a counter-clockwise loop around the lake. Trail surface varies from sawdust and shavings to pavement and boardwalk (some barrier-free). The woods and scrub provide important habitat for wildlife. Bird boxes have been installed to give cavity nesters a better shot at raising a family here. In a quarter-mile, a spur on the left leads to a discreet viewing area with a bench and interpretive sign. Just beyond, go left and across a footbridge to continue the loop, or straight to another junction (a left here crosses a second bridge and leads to 196th St.; right heads uphill to a grassy picnic spot; go straight to continue on the Scriber Creek Trail). On the lake loop, several more "duckblinds" are passed before reaching a floating walkway with artsy benches—a fine spot to watch for ducks, beaver, or muskrat. The loop ends shortly beyond (head right to reach the 196th St. crosswalk and Wilcox Park).

Scriber Creek Trail leads from the lake to 200th St. SW. Walk left (east) a block and cross 200th St. and 50th Ave. W at the light to pick up the trail at Scriber Creek Park (more parking). Follow either paved or unpaved path (they rejoin shortly) and continue a few blocks to a junction with the Interurban Trail at a Park-and-Ride lot next to I-5. A right here takes you another 1.5 miles or so on the Interurban to its end at South Lynnwood Park near 211th St. and 63rd Ave. W.

Scriber Lake

21. Edmonds Woods Walks

Distance: 0.5 - 2.0 miles RT   Time: Allow 1 - 3 hours

Elevation gain: Negligible   Season: Year-round

There are three mostly wooded parks in south-central Edmonds that are all within a few blocks of each other, and each offers a little woods walk. Do one or do them all in few hours or less. (See the park listings for Maplewood, Yost Memorial, and Pine Ridge Parks for directions.) Maplewood Park is probably the least interesting of the three to walk, although it is a lovely spot for a quiet family picnic. From the northwest side of the lawn-covered hill, find the path across the drive. The trail leads past beauteous groundcover and several large trees as it drops down to a footbridge over a seasonal creek, fading not far beyond. Down and back is about a quarter-mile.

Yost Memorial Park offers a mile of paths looping through woods (mostly red alder), in and out of the ravine containing Shell Creek. Numbered interpretive stops are posted for those looking for an

Big-leaf maple

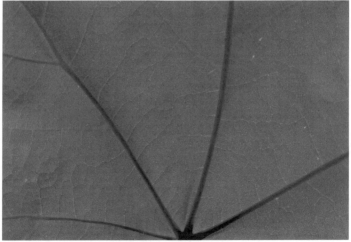

education—good for kids (check with the park folks for details and/ or a brochure). Walk down the service road (handicap parking access) a short distance to a good trail on the left. Follow this into the ravine to a junction. Straight leads to Main St. near 12th Ave. N and to a minor viewpoint of an old retention dam for a water system downstream. But go right, cross the creek, and follow this awhile, partly on boardwalk, until you reach a four-way intersection. Left goes back to Main St. with a link to the first spur trail to Main St., and straight up the hill loops back in that same direction. Go right then right again to reach a gravel road which leads back toward the pool and the original starting point. The full loop plus a little wandering on spur trails tallies up to about a mile.

At Pine Ridge Park you can wander an easy, flat trail through Douglas fir-western hemlock forest to Goodhope Pond and adjacent wetlands with a bench to sit and wait for birds and other wildlife to materialize. From the parking area off 83rd Ave. W, walk the wide trail about 250 yards to a small fenced "duck pond" and a short distance beyond to the larger pond and wetlands. The two paths beyond this point only connect to adjoining neighborhoods. To do a loop, walk back around the north side of the fenced pond (narrow path next to the fence) and find another good path leading up to a junction. Right goes to a partially obscured overlook of the Goodhope Pond (with another bench); left leads back to the start. Figure a light half-mile walk for the loop.

22. Terrace Creek

Distance: 1.2 miles RT

Time: Allow 1 - 2 hours

Elevation gain: 100 feet

Season: Year-round

Terrace Creek Park in Mountlake Terrace is a 52-acre forested oasis in the midst of a city. The park is not intensively developed and contains one major trail corridor, offering a mostly quiet walk in the woods, about a mile each way. A small parking area and trailhead exists on the west side of 48th Ave. W. near 233rd St. SW. Follow the paved path left around a play and picnic site and large lawn area that makes up part of a unique disc-thrower's "golf course." Unless you brought your bag of competition "discs," skip the "tee-off" and head around a ballfield to where the main path enters the woods.

The hike continues on unpaved but good trail and old road bed another 0.5 mile, passing a small clearing near a service road, followed by a gradual climb up the valley to the trail's end at 221st St. SW. Several narrow paths and boot tracks intersect the main trail at various points and most lead to the numbered "holes" of the "golf course." If nobody's playing, you could potentially extend the walk a mile or more by exploring these "side paths." But beware, routefinding can be "clumsy" if you don't know "the course." A few benches along the main trail allow time to rest and listen for "birdies" (okay, couldn't resist).

North Fork Stilly from near the South Fork confluence

23. Stillaguamish Forks

Distance: 0.5 - 1.0 mile roundtrip   Time: Allow 1-2 hours
Elevation gain: None   Season: Year-round

On 44 riverfront acres in Arlington, Twin Rivers Park is better known for its ballfields, but there are also a few paths here along the South Fork of the Stillaguamish River which lead to a summer beach and extensive gravel bars at the confluence with the North Fork Stilly. Late summer through early spring are better times to visit, since the park can be crazy busy with sun and sports fans in summer. If you go in summer, go early to beat the crowds, which happens to be a better time for wildlife viewing anyway. If it's raining hard (or just did), you may want to avoid some areas. Several paths are so silty and the silt is so fine that you may find yourself walking on a trail surface that has about the same consistency as sauteed slug slime — as in really slick. When the river is up, the flood channel blocks access to the big gravel bar. Of course the river can move around too and trails can simply wash away (best to stand back from any eroding edges). Much of the area is subject to seasonal flooding.

Find the park on the west side of SR 530 just north of the South Fork Stilly bridge as you head out of Arlington. Drive to the west end and park near the apparent trailhead. The park extends from SR 530 to the confluence with the North Fork about a half-mile downstream and paths will take you there most of the year. Various small loops cut through forest between the river and the ballfields and you can easily reach the river bank at several locations. Unless the river is running high, you should be able to cross a dry flood channel and keep heading downriver to the big gravel bar close by. The North Fork rides in from the right. Both forks are usually deep and swift, even later in summer. The old railroad bridge, soon to be a new segment of the Centennial Trail, spans the river just downstream.

24. River Meadows

Distance: 1.0 - 6.0 miles roundtrip   Time: Allow 1 - 3 hours
Elevation gain: 0 - 100 feet   Season: Year-round

With perhaps the best lowland river walk in the county, River Meadows Park near Arlington is well worth a visit anytime, but expect crowds on sunny summer weekends. The 200-acre park is largely undeveloped but nicely maintained, and quiet. Silt and sand trails follow a long bend in the river and connect with mowed paths among grass and wildflowers, creating a six-mile network of easy walking trails. Many bird species, deer, and other wildlife are often seen. A guide to animal tracks could be useful here. Historic features and interpretive displays also exist and tent camping is available. The park opens early but closes at dusk.

From Arlington follow SR 530 a half-mile north of the South Fork Stilly bridge and turn right onto Jordan Road. Stay right in a mile and continue three more miles to the park entrance on the right. Drive down to the flats and park near the river. There is no real need for directions since aimless wandering works quite well here. But if a hint would be helpful, try walking the wooded path down-

South Fork Stilly at River Meadows Park

river. Several spur trails access river bars and beaches (some sandy), plus views of a high eroding bluff across the river. The Stilly can be deep and swift so young'ns should be eyed closely. The forest includes cedar, fir, hemlock, birch, alder, cottonwood, and many native Northwest shrubs, herbs, and ferns. At some point duck out of the woods and walk the edge of Cove Meadow to Homestead Terrace (orchard, flowers, view). Cross the access road at the base of a hill, walk along Funnel Meadow past an oddly-trunked hemlock tree to a pleasant cedar grove with a giant bigleaf maple with pudgy serpentine limbs. More wandering almost any direction is feasible. Toss in a checkered cloth and lunch, and find a spot to sit and enjoy.

25. Twin Lakes Park

Distance: 0.9 mile roundtrip   Time: Allow 1 hour
Elevation gain: None   Season: Year-round

If you can stand the freeway noise (earplugs anyone?), Gissberg Twin Lakes County Park north of Marysville isn't such a bad place for an easy stroll around two artificial lakes. The lakes resulted from the removal of fill material for the development of I-5 in the early 1970s, and while they don't seem too appealing through the wing window at 70 mph, the walk around them is actually kind of scenic.

From I-5 (Smokey Point exit) head west on SR 531 a short distance and take a left on 27th Ave. NE. The park is on the right in 0.7 mile, essentially abutting I-5. The walk around the lakes on a grassy path needs no description. Each lake is roughly 400 yards long by 150 yards wide, and they are joined by a narrow channel near the west end which prevents one from walking around just one lake—unless you're up for a short swim or waist-deep wade (more or less). The full loop is just under a mile long. The 'peninsula' between the lakes has a rough path leading through cedar and birch trees to the channel. Watch for ducks, geese, other birds, and small mammals. Even a river otter isn't unheard of here. Swimming is an at-your-own-risk proposition. To avoid the heavy decibels, try early Sunday mornings when the big grey ribbon is usually a little quieter.

26. Centennial Trail (Lake Stevens-Snohomish)

Distance: 0.5 - 7.8 miles one way   Time: Allow 1 - 5 hours

Elevation gain: None   Season: Year-round

The old railroad grade which has become the county's preeminent lowland trail, the Centennial Trail, was originally developed as the Seattle, Lakeshore & Eastern Railway in 1889. The line extended north from Snohomish, eventually to Arlington. The railroad was sold to Northern Pacific in 1892, then later to Burlington Northern Railroad in 1970 who shut down the line north of Hartford in 1972, then the rest back to Snohomish by 1987, nearly a century after it was built. The county bought the land in 1990 for a trail, hence the name "Centennial Trail." Washington State, founded in 1889, celebrated its centennial in 1989. While the existing trail from Snohomish to Lake Stevens is just under eight miles long, the grand plan calls for a 45-mile trail from King to Skagit County, including a ten-mile section between Lake Stevens and Arlington slated for construction in 1998 (*see Walk #27*).

Since 1990, the old grade between Snohomish and Lake Stevens has been developed to the "superhighway" standard for trails — wide, paved, landscaped, and embellished with traffic signs, interpretive signs, bollards, gates, benches, bridges, and the like, plus two major trailheads. An equestrian path parallels much of the route. While an expensive trail of this standard seems like a natural in an urban environment where bicycle transportation is a primary goal, the facility does feel somewhat overdone for a rural area. At the same time, this is a major trail corridor that's intended to serve a lot of needs for a lot of people, and not just the nature walker who might prefer a narrow winding path over a fat straight ribbon of blacktop. With that in mind, it is a remarkable facility, largely made possible by the hard work of the Snohomish-Arlington Trail Coalition, the late Mike Parman (the county's dedicated trail planner to whom the Centennial itself is dedicated), and many citizens and civic leaders who worked hard to make the trail a reality.

Access the Centennial at any of several points. In Snohomish, find the current southern terminus at Maple and Pine St. (street parking), or drive north 1.6 miles to a large trailhead parking area on the right. The trail heads north from here about 3.5 miles past farms and rural homesteads to another big trailhead at Machias Station. By car, turn west off S. Machias Rd. onto Division St. then go left on Virginia St. to find the trailhead. This makes a better start for hikers since the trail is back from the road and not so noisy for the next mile. Mt. Pilchuck, Three Fingers, and White Horse Mt. are visible to the northeast (right to left). About 2.5 miles from Machias, the trail crosses 16th St. near a ballfield with more trail parking. In late 1997 the paved trail ended at 20th St., 0.3 mile beyond (no parking). An unimproved section continued north a short distance, then fizzled, although this should become passable later in 1998. The SR 92 underpass was already built. The trail is managed as a park and closes after dark. Wander as little or as much as the day takes you, and expect friendly crowds of walkers, joggers, bikers, and bladers on all but the crummiest weekends.

27. Centennial Trail (Lake Stevens-Arlington)

Distance: 0.5 - 10.0 miles one way　　Time: Allow 1 - 6 hours
Elevation gain: Negligible　　Season: Year-round

In late 1997, north of Lake Stevens, the Centennial Trail was an unimproved, but mostly passable, abandoned rail corridor (*see Walk #26 for trail history, etc.*). However, county park staff was predicting the completion of a new ten-mile stretch from Lake Stevens to a point just short of Arlington by 1998, which means the present trail description will soon be out of date. Nevertheless, the new trail will still follow the route of the existing railroad grade, so directions will hardly change. A new trailhead is planned south of Edgecomb off 67th Ave. NE north of 152nd St. NE, which will make a great starting point for a walk south.

Until this good work transpires, consider parking on the shoulder of 84th St. NE, 0.5 mile east of SR 9, and walk north or south as far as conditions allow. The unofficial trail is in generally good shape, but expect pockets of mud or standing water in the wet season. From here it's about four miles south to the SR 92 underpass, and about 4.5 miles north to the planned trailhead at 67th Ave. Poor sight distance at 108th St. NE requires care crossing (a new underpass is planned here to improve safety). Perhaps the best thing about this stretch of the Centennial is the relative scarcity of adjacent roads, which means less traffic noise than the stretch south of Lake Stevens.

Within a few years, the trail will likely be extended into Arlington, across the Stillaguamish River, and beyond to the Skagit County line and a more northerly trailhead at an historic farm recently acquired by the county. Portions of this grade were passable in 1997, although most was either seriously overgrown or closed to the public, awaiting improvements to address drainage, trailhead parking, street and water crossings, bridge decks, and other safety issues.

Skagit County hopes to continue the trail north to SR 20 at Sedro Woolley, although major portions of that right-of-way are still privately owned.

A soggy Centennial Trail north of Lake Stevens, before the upgrade

28. Smith & Spencer Islands (Langus Park)

Distance: 0.5 - 9.0 miles roundtrip   Time: Allow 1 - 5 hours
Elevation gain: None   Season: Year-round

A fine riverwalk on paved trail close to Everett is found at Langus Riverfront Park on Smith Island next to the Snohomish River. The paved trail leads to a 3.5-mile trail system on Spencer Island, offering strolls of varying length, views of Mt. Baker and Mt. Rainier, and excellent birding in the winter and spring. Bicycles and dogs are prohibited on Spencer Island to help minimize disturbances to wildlife. Reach the park from SR 529 in north Everett. Exit north of the Snohomish River bridge and follow signs from Ross Ave. to Smith Island Rd. (stay right at a fork instead of crossing I-5). The park is just ahead on the right.

For a shorter walk, wander the shore from the north end of the park to the big I-5 bridge and back, about one mile total. Or, walk south along the river, passing under I-5, to a confluence with Union and Steamboat Sloughs, a mile or more from the start (depends on

Spencer Island wetlands

where you parked). Benches here and elsewhere suggest a relaxing pace and time to sit and watch whatever goes by. A few workboats ply the river and great blue herons reconnoiter the slough's muddy banks. Continue around the bend to the left and up Union Slough another 0.6 mile to a road junction and access to Spencer Island. The paved trail ends at 'keep out' signs about a half-mile north of here. The trails are barrier-free to here, and nearly so on Spencer Island.

By the time you cross the bridge to Spencer Island, freeway and city noise have diminished considerably. So, look for interpretive signs and a trail map near the bridge. Two loops, referred to as the South Trail (1.5-mile loop) and North Trail (2.5-mile loop), present several options. Maybe head south on boardwalk just left of a dike, passing a cattail marsh overlook and another trail junction in 0.1 mile. Right (South Trail) leads back along the east side of Union Slough, then along Steamboat Slough. Left cuts across the island past freshwater wetlands on the left, and saltwater marsh and intertidal areas on the right — a good place to set up the spotting scope. Not long ago, dikes were breached on the right, allowing natural estuarine conditions to be reestablished, which not only explains all the dead trees, but contrasts nicely with the freshwater system on the left. Watch for distinct waterfowl and shorebirds — nearly 200 species have been observed making use of these valuable habitats. At the next junction, 0.3 mile from the last, head right for the shorter South Trail loop, or left up Steamboat Slough for the North Trail loop (beware of hunters in duck season).

Swans on the lake, an uncommon view

29. Lowell Riverfront Trail

Distance: 1.0 - 3.5 miles roundtrip   Time: Allow 1-2 hours

Elevation gain: None   Season: Year-round

A pleasant stroll along the Snohomish River on an easy paved trail near Lowell is one of the newer additions to the lowland riverfront trail system developing in the Everett area. The walk is barrier-free in a natural setting and well suited to all ages and abilities. It's a good place for wildlife viewing as well. To find it, cross I-5 on 41st St. (east) and follow the signs to Lowell. Pass Lowell Park, curve left and in a few blocks turn left at a stop sign. The park is just beyond the railroad tracks.

Walk either direction on the obvious paved path. Going upriver (east), the path ends in a quarter-mile at a boat launch (eventually a trail may continue upriver from here all the way to Snohomish). Or, go downriver for the longer, more interesting walk along the grassy riverbank, past wetlands, woods, and fields. At a big bend, the Mt. Baker volcano near Bellingham is prominent to the north, while several big peaks of the North Cascades scratch the sky to the east. An historic homestead stands quiet on the opposite shore of the river.

The paved path fizzles at a railroad crossing in about 1.3 miles, a good turn-around point—trains slither through here fast and frequently. Eventually, the trail will be extended north to Smith Ave. To head back, one can follow dirt paths east of the tracks to loop back to the parking area. Or, just follow the path back along the river for a better chance at seeing more wildlife. Then imagine how high this river must rise to flood almost the entire valley—something it's done many times this century.

30. Bailey Farm Wetlands (North Creek Park)

Distance: 0.5 - 1.5 miles roundtrip   Time: 1 - 2 hours
Elevation gain: Negligible   Season: Year-round

An impressive boardwalk trail through extensive wetlands and peat bog south of Mill Creek is the highlight of North Creek Park, a new facility developed by the county in 1995-96 on what used to be a dairy farm. The Bailey Farm was originally homesteaded in 1891, and now, a century later, the public can enjoy the area's natural beauty and diversity. The boardwalk trail is barrier-free although a small hill must be negotiated at the start. The boardwalk design is clever: it floats when the water rises. Find the park on the north side of 183rd St. SE a half-mile west of SR 527.

The path, gravel at first, leads past an overlook then down a gentle grade for 100 yards to the start of the boardwalk. In 0.1 mile go left at a junction for a closer look at the peat bog and lots of forget-me-nots in summer. Sedges, rushes, cattails, and hardhack (spirea) also seem to love this place. From the junction continue 0.2 mile to another junction. Left goes 0.1 mile to a beaver pond. Straight continues another 0.2 mile to the end of the boardwalk and another 0.1 mile of gravel path connecting with 9th Ave. SE (there's no parking at this end of the trail system). Plans call for additional boardwalk construction in the not-so-distant future.

A persistent birder will likely see dozens of species in winter and spring and perhaps a few more in summer and fall. Depending on the season you may be able to see bald eagles, red-tail hawks, harriers, kingfishers, marsh wrens, and a variety of ducks includ-

ing mallards and canvasbacks. Fauna species you might get a glimpse of include muskrat, deer, rodents, frogs, and pond turtles. To give them a little peace, bikes can be walked but not ridden on the boardwalk.

31. Thomas Eddy

Distance: 1.4 - 2.0 miles roundtrip   Time: Allow 1 - 2 hours
Elevation gain: Negligible   Season: Year-round

Rivers ought to be simple, right? Water flowing between two banks. There might be a flood once in awhile, but hey, that's just a flood. And a river's just a river. Or is it? In the way so many of us think, it may be that a river is *not* a river at all. At Thomas Eddy, south of Snohomish, it's easy to understand why a river might be more correctly thought of as an entire landscape. Not a static one where the water is over here and the banks and bars are over there, but a dynamic place without any boundaries, where almost everything in sight is linked together in some way, and where things are always, always changing. Here on the Snohomish River, a broad floodplain of braided channels, islands, and gravel bars offers a perfect natural "laboratory" in which to ponder an imperfect definition of this word, "river." But if the pondering is too much to bother with, the wandering around part is at least as entertaining.

The Snohomish River at Thomas Eddy

To find the trail to the river, head for the new Bob Heirman Wildlife Park at Thomas Eddy (named for a local long-time resident and wildlife park advocate). From SR 9 about 2.4 miles south of Snohomish, turn east at the Broadway light, then go left in 0.8 mile on Connelly Rd. The park is on the left in another 0.8 mile; closes at dusk. There are a few picnic tables on the bluff with a partially obstructed view of the river in the distance and a small lake up close. Lord Hill rises to the southeast. An old road, now a trail, leads down through meadows and pasture about 0.3 mile to the river bank. Wander downstream (good views) another 0.3 mile to a junction and stay right. The path continues 0.1 mile to the edge of the river bed (this was the case in late 1997, but the "river" could change that). A half-mile or more of wandering may be feasible depending on water level and other conditions. Be sure to memorize the trail's location for the return. At low water in October 1997, it was possible to walk down a very wide dry channel (with sun-dried salmon carcasses) about 0.2 mile, then right (clockwise) around a low island between this and the main channel. This adds an easy half-mile loop to the walk. The County plans to build a small dock soon to make it easier for boaters to tie up and enjoy the place.

Maybe check out the lake on the way back (bring the bird book and binoculars). At the bottom of the hill about 150 yards from the start, one can wander left along one of two paths about 100 yards to the lakeshore. Approach cautiously to avoid scaring off the ducks. Barrier-free improvements to the lake are planned (it might be nice to see the two paths joined near the lake and a simple duckblind installed at some point, creating a short loop for wildlife viewing without a lot of disturbance). Note that dogs are not allowed in this park.

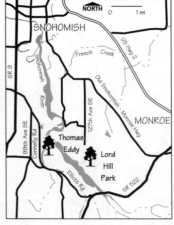

32. Lord Hill

Distance: 3.5 - 10.0 miles + roundtrip   Time: Allow 2 - 6 hours +
Elevation gain: 300 - 1,000 feet +   Season: Year-round

Named for an original 1870s settler on the hill, Lord Hill has a long history of farming and logging — with virtually all the old-growth eliminated by the 1930s. Of the 4,000 acres that make up this conspicuous volcanic ridge south of Snohomish, the county has acquired just over 1,300 acres of emergent forest, lakes, ponds, and wetlands which provide both habitat for wildlife and a good recreation spot for not-so-wild humans (mountain bikes and horses are also frequently sighted). Nearly ten miles of trails have been opened up, mostly on old logging roads and along a natural gas pipeline corridor. While the forest is still a bit scraggly from excessive timber harvest, it's growing fast and will surely reclaim its former majesty, twig by twig, decade by decade.

In the meantime, Lord Hill offers a quiet walk in the woods, a rest by a marshy lake, an occasional view through the trees, and even a 500-foot descent to the river. Steep terrain to the southwest offers great view potential, and volunteers have been working hard to improve those views as well as fix up the trails. Many loops are feasible. To reach the trailhead from Snohomish, follow 2nd St. east to Lincoln and turn right. This shortly becomes the Old Snohomish-Monroe Highway. About 2.5 miles from 2nd St. turn right on 127th Ave. SE and drive another 1.6 miles to the park and trailhead on the

left (*map, p. 70*). Check out the trail map to plan a hike that suits the group (map-brochures should be available here), or try one of the hilly loops described below.

The main trail descends more than it as-

A view from Lord Hill

cends the first 0.4 mile to a junction. Head left another 0.4 mile to Beaver Lake (bigger than it looks). Go right up the Pipeline Trail about 0.3 mile to a four-way intersection. Left adds the Temple Pond Loop (a mile-plus) to your itinerary; right bypasses it. Spurs off the Temple Pond Loop lead to two smaller ponds, while the main loop passes Temple Pond and rejoins the pipeline 0.2 mile south of the four-way. Head right to the four-way, then go left 0.1 mile to reach the Central Loop. Here, a right goes 0.6 mile back to the first junction (before Beaver Lake), passing the Devil's Butte Lookout trail on the left in 0.2 mile (for the latter, walk the old road about 0.5 mile to a junction and stay left, keep walking straight another 0.2 mile to a clearing with a partial view through fast-growing vegetation; a narrower path leads straight and right to a good view of the river toward Everett; another drops left to more partial views — and more confusing trail junctions). For another loop and a hike to the river, head left at the Central Loop junction noted above. Walk 0.7 mile, then right to descend 350 feet to the river in about 0.8 mile. A left leads not quite as far as Temple Pond.

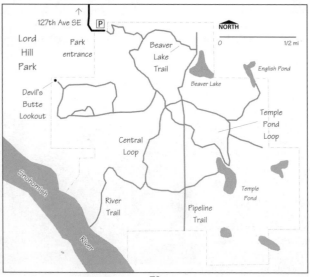

33. Buck Island

Distance: 0.5 - 1.5 miles roundtrip   Time: Allow 1-2 hours
Elevation gain: None   Season: Year-round

On the lower Skykomish River in Monroe, Buck Island offers an easy stroll through a surprisingly beautiliferous forest of bigleaf maple and cottonwood. Walk it anytime, although a cool, clear day, fall through spring, would be especially nice. Several short loops are possible. The trail may eventually connect with the Centennial Trail and an abandoned railroad bridge over the river. The island is also known as Al Borlin Park, a big city park hidden behind an industrial area. Directions are circuitous: From SR 2, turn south onto Main St., cross the tracks, then go left on Woods St., left on Fremont, left on Ann, and right on Simon Road. Drive into the park and park near the gated trailhead on the right (trail map here).

Follow excellent wide trail (Al Borlin Nature Trail) into the woods. At the first junction go right to a view of a very tame Woods Creek with an interpretive sign, or go straight to continue. Big cot-

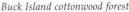

Buck Island cottonwood forest

tonwood trees, some four feet across, are mixed with bigleaf and vine maple, red alder, tall salmonberry, red elderberry, red huckleberry, snowberry, and some ever-invasive blackberries, together filling up the understory. A few other trees and shrubs, plus a variety of ferns and flowers enrich the scene. At the next junction, a quarter-mile from the start, a right takes you around the larger loop and left links with the return trail nearby. Stay right and soon reach a large grassy area; go right to cross Woods Creek on a bridge built on gabions—intended to survive the next flood. This also leads to Lewis Street Park. Or go left to continue the loop. Several spur trails head for views of the Skykomish River. Watch for a large contorted bigleaf maple tree with ferns growing all the way up the trunk and out the branches. At a major junction stay right (left leads a few yards to the path you probably just walked). The trail ends at an unpaved road; go left 200 yards to reach the parking area, or turn right to explore more of the river bank upstream.

Woods Creek is a salmon spawning stream slowly recovering from severe impacts of decades of logging in the Woods Creek watershed. During Monroe's lumbering heyday, parts of the creek were channelized to facilitate the movement of logs and shake bolts downstream to the mills in town. Lake Roesiger, incidentally, is 15 miles upstream.

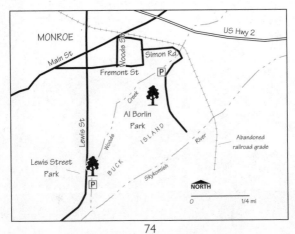

34. Fortson Mill Ponds & N. Fork Stilly

Distance: 0.5 - 1.0 mile + roundtrip   Time: Allow 1 - 2 hours +
Elevation gain: None   Season: Year-round

Snohomish County has had good success acquiring old railroad grades for trails, and the former Darrington Branch line from Arlington is about to become an important east-west corridor for recreation and non-motorized transportation. Originally developed in the late 1800s, the old railroad grade was abandoned in the early 1990s. Twenty-seven miles worth was acquired from Burlington Northern through rail-banking by Snohomish County Parks in 1993. While nature is busy reclaiming much of the old grade with alder, blackberries and the like, portions of the route are still accessible. However signs have been posted by the County closing much of the corridor to public use until it can be properly developed and maintained. Park staff guestimates it may be several years before funding is available to improve and open what could be called the "Whitehorse Trail." For now, the emphasis is on protecting the grade

North Fork Stilly below Darrington

from washing away in the next flood.

In the meantime, look for the grade as you drive SR 530 to Darrington, or stop at the old Fortson Mill Ponds to see one stretch of it while you explore old mill structures, building skeletons, the site of a local railroad station, other miscellaneous mill stuff, and most interestingly, two mill ponds — now fish and wildlife ponds — all put to use by a once-flourishing sawmill. Old roads and the railroad grade make it easy to explore.

To find it, drive SR 530 about six miles west of Darrington and turn north on Fortson Mill Road. Park at the end of the pavement in 0.2 mile. Try walking the right-most gravel road to the first pond (second is straight ahead), then follow roads and trail counter-clockwise around the first pond which is now a juvenile-only fishing area. A small wooden footbridge crosses the pond's inlet stream and a short railroad bridge crosses the dammed outlet. The other larger pond to the east may offer better wildlife viewing, but approach cautiously so as not to scare off the ducks. The North Fork Stillaguamish River is close by and several narrow paths provide access for fishers. The layered summit ridge of Mt. Higgins is visible downriver. A great blue heron may squawk at you from overhead, and a killdeer might call to lure you away from its nest. A short distance to the east is a good view of Whitehorse Mountain from the old railroad grade. With rubber boots and a hot cup of tea, this makes a good winter or spring breather after breakfast. Eventually, the trail will be accessible from Backman Park as well, just south of Darrington.

35. Boulder River

Distance: 2.4 - 8.0 miles roundtrip
Elevation gain: 100 - 600 feet

Time: Allow 2 - 6 hours
Season: Almost year-round

This popular, low-elevation, old-growth forest and river walk offers a sumptuous immersion into the North Cascades' Boulder River Wilderness. And that's gratifying when you consider how much of the year the higher elevation forests are buried in snow. Never exceeding 1,600 feet elevation, the Boulder River trail is sometimes snow-free even in the middle of winter, although ice could make the going interesting in places. If you like waterfalls, do this trip during mild rainy weather in the spring or fall. That's when the river roars and the falls are spectacular to watch. Nevertheless, the falls do fall year-round, and the walk through old-growth forest is a good plan anytime.

From SR 530 about 8 miles west of Darrington, turn south onto

USFS Rd. #2010 (may be unsigned) immediately next to the MP 41 marker. Drive 3.7 miles to the trailhead at the end of the road (900 feet). The first half-mile is wide and flat (an old road bed) and traverses a long moss and fern-covered rock wall with a modest drop-off. A brief rise leads to the Boulder River Wilderness boundary at 0.9 mile. In another 0.3 mile, a thin streamer of a falls from an unnamed tributary is a tease for the much bigger one just beyond. Unless you catch it at low water, this second high falls, often called Boulder Falls, spreads out across the coarse rock face like a thick and lacy apron, noisy and beautiful to watch. The exact height is uncertain but it's surely well over 100 feet. Just upstream the river takes a nice drop next to a cabin-sized boulder.

The trail climbs somewhat over the next quarter-mile, passing giant trees six feet or more in diameter, then finally descends to a not-as-tall-but-lovely-anyway waterfall about a mile upriver from the last. After four miles, the way ends at a ford crossing of the river (1,400 feet) where an old trail (not maintained) once continued up steep forest to Tupso Pass and the summit lookout on Three Fingers Mountain (*see Hike #81*). Obviously, the ford should only be considered by experienced hikers at low water.

Noisy water enters the Boulder River

36. Frog Lake

Distance: 0.5 - 2.0 miles roundtrip
Elevation gain: 400 feet

Time: Allow 1 - 2 hours
Season: Almost year-round

An old trail, hardly used, and nice enough in the beginning to lure you upwards, then leaving you wishing for more... Save Frog Lake for an off-season stretcher, say fall through early spring when the bugs and brush are down, and traffic on the adjacent logging road (also goes to the lake) has diminished or, better yet, disappeared. Forget it when there's snow in downtown Darrington.

From Darrington, head south and east on the Mt. Loop Highway about three miles to the National Forest boundary and less than a half-mile farther to the trailhead and parking area just beyond the Clear Creek Campground, but before crossing the bridge over Clear Creek (600 feet; *map, p. 80*). Take a gander at the Sauk River parading down-valley to Darrington, then head up moderately steep trail through lovely, mature Douglas fir forest. The path quickly rises above Clear Creek and the little gorge that contains it. In a quarter-mile there's a good view off a precipice into the deep, vertical-walled canyon (hang onto the little guys) — a fine destination for a mini-trek and perhaps the most interesting part of the hike.

To reach the lake, continue up through mixed forest, crossing little bridges and a curious footlog, while pretending the logging road nearby isn't real. A narrow old road is soon reached; turn left and find Frog Lake about forty hops away, a mile from the start (1,000 feet). Rising steeply to the southwest is the back side of Jumbo Mt., prominent also from Darrington and a close neighbor of the amazing and dramatic Whitehorse Mountain. (For a good summer hike with excellent views of the latter, head for Squire Creek Pass (*see Hike #53*) by way of the logging road you didn't take to Frog Lake.)

Frog Lake Trail

37. Old Sauk

Distance: 1.0 - 6.0 miles roundtrip   Time: Allow 1 - 3 hours
Elevation gain: Negligible   Season: Almost year-round

There are at least two good reasons to put this river walk on your to-do list: this part of the Sauk is a scenic, low-elevation, mountain river flanked with patches of old-growth forest, accessible almost any week of the year; and, it's a great place to watch for eagles and spawning salmon in the fall and winter. The trail parallels the river for three miles with parking at either end (maybe stash a bike upstream for the easy ride back to the car). Most of the old-growth is along the downstream (northern) half. To start there, drive the Mountain Loop Highway a couple of miles out of Darrington to MP 1 and find the signed trailhead on the left (600 feet); or continue to a paved shoulder parking area at the upstream trailhead near MP 3.5. The trail was repaired by volunteers in 1996.

Follow the obvious path on the right into an impressive Douglas fir forest with many trees three to five feet in diameter. After the first quarter-mile the path runs close to the river bank and short

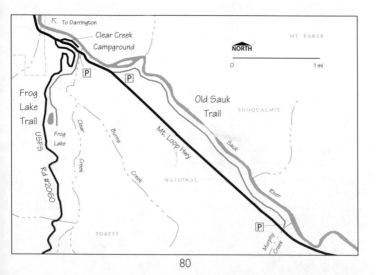

spurs offer views up and down. Salmon and steelhead migrate upstream in late summer and fall, then spawn into the winter. Except for a few minor ups and downs the trail is generally smooth and flat, and depending on flows and the location of meandering channels, it may be possible to access gravel bars at several spots. Portions of the area were logged in the 1930s so there are several distinct plant communities and a wide diversity of native species to be seen throughout the corridor. Most apparent are: Doug-fir, western hemlock, red cedar, red alder, bigleaf maple, black cottonwood, vine maple, salmonberry, thimbleberry, red elderberry, red huckleberry, Oregon grape, salal, devil's club, foamflower, Indian pipe, bunchberry, youth-on-age, bleeding heart, and trillium, plus sword, deer, oak, lady, and maidenhair ferns.

After a mile or so, cross a small stream on a footbridge with cottonwood and bigleaf maple forest beyond. The trail pulls away from the river bank for a half-mile, then returns to mature forest close to the rushing water. At a bit over two miles another bridge crosses

the Constant Creek groundwater channel that was enhanced in 1991 for wild coho and chum salmon. There is a salmon life-cycle interpretive sign here. This could be the best spot to watch for spawning salmon (fall and winter). The way reenters second-growth forest for the balance of the walk, passing a tiny sandy beach before bending up Murphy Creek to another salmon life-cycle sign and the south trailhead.

Old Sauk Trail in early morning

38. Beaver Lake

Distance: 1.0 - 3.0 miles one way
Elevation gain: 200 feet

Time: Allow 1 - 2 hours
Season: Almost year-round

Following the route of an old logging railroad grade southeast of Darrington, the way to Beaver Lake and beyond offers an excellent river walk and off-season wildlife excursion on mostly flat trail. Fall and early spring walks are best for color and views, and for avoiding the worst of the bugs. Access the path at its west or east end and either walk it both ways, stash a bike, or trade car keys for the return. Note: there's a 200-foot descent from the east trailhead.

Follow the Mt. Loop Highway from Darrington into the National Forest and find the west trailhead on the right at MP 6.2, opposite the USFS Rd. #22 junction (1,000 feet; *map, p. 83*). Walk down slightly then follow the good path along the Sauk River, noisy and tumbling at first, smoother and quieter beyond. A big view of Mt. Pugh fills the horizon upriver before reaching the small marshy lake near the walk's mid-point, 1.5 miles from the start. Watch for ducks, beaver, deer, upland birds, and other wildlife, then cross a neck of still water on an old trestle. To the northeast White Chuck Mountain's jagged summit appears through the hardwood forest canopy.

Big, old-growth cedars are scattered beyond the lake. Where the trail and river channel run up close to the hillside, pass a slide area (may be tricky or impassable, a possible turn-around point) and more good views. If safe, continue on trail beneath the remains of an old railroad trestle, then follow around a bend to the northeast between two gigantic cedars. A steep 200-foot climb leads the final quarter-mile to the east trailhead (at MP 8.6).

Old logging trestle at Beaver Lake

39. White Chuck Bench

Distance: 6.7 miles one-way   Time: Allow 4 - 5 hours

Elevation gain: 800 feet   Season: April - November

From a bluff above the confluence of the White Chuck and Sauk Rivers southeast of Darrington, an old trail runs 6.7 miles up the White Chuck through second-growth forest, flood plain, and old-growth forest north of the river. Low elevation means the trail, partly on an old logging railroad grade, is accessible most of the year—even in winter if it's mild. But expect some muddy spots most times and wet (occasionally tricky) stream crossings during periods of higher runoff. Big cedar trees and river and mountain views make the trip worthwhile even on a marginal day. The White Chuck River Rd. follows the opposite side of the river and ends at the White Chuck River Trailhead (not to be confused with White Chuck Bench). The trail can be walked from either end. Maybe spot a car or trade keys with a hiking buddy midway, or stash a bike at the upstream end, then drive back to the lower trailhead for the walk and an easy ride back to the car. For a walk in and back, the trailhead upriver makes a more interesting start.

To reach the downstream trailhead from Darrington, turn left off Mountain Loop Highway at MP 6.2 onto USFS Rd. #22, pass the river boat launch in 0.2 mile and take the next right. The new trailhead is 0.3 mile up the hill on the right just around a bend (1,100

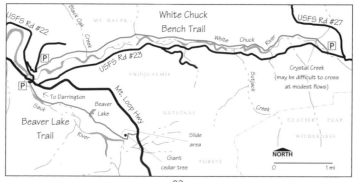

feet). There are good views of Sloan and Bedal Peaks, Mt. Pugh, and White Chuck Mt. near the trailhead from atop a high eroded bluff (the edge is unstable so stay back). For the upriver trailhead, leave Mountain Loop Highway at MP 6.3 and head east on the White Chuck River Rd. (USFS Rd. #23) 5.5 miles to the parking area on the left, just after a bridge over the river (1,600 feet). The hike requires little description from either direction. Volunteers did a lot of work here in 1997.

The best old-growth is along upper two miles. The middle third is mostly in floodplain fairly close to the river. It can be a little hard to follow at a couple of spots but is mostly good trail. Cross Black Oak Creek on a footlog, 1.2 miles from the west end. Toward the west there are also good views of Mt. Pugh, White Chuck Mt., and the river below. Crystal Creek is crossed a half-mile from the east end and is the trickier crossing, difficult or impossible at moderate to high water levels — the old footlog here has collapsed. When the creeks and rivers are up, it might make sense to start from the east to be sure Crystal Creek is crossable, rather than walking six miles upriver only to find it isn't. At low to moderate flows, footlogs over the other creeks generally remain passable. Near Crystal Creek is an impressive view of Mt. Pugh. A little farther west, watch carefully for a glimpse of Glacier Peak upriver through the trees.

Along the White Chuck Bench Trail

40. Buck Creek

Distance: 0.5 - 1.6 miles roundtrip   Time: Allow 1 - 2 hours

Elevation gain: 0 - 200 feet   Season: April - November

For a pleasant short hike along a rushing whitewater creek, try the old trail up Buck Creek, a northern tributary of the Suiattle River (not the Buck Creek on the east side that drains into the Chiwawa River). The unmaintained trail leaves Buck Creek Campground at MP 15 on the Suiattle River Road (USFS Rd. #26). Reach the latter from SR 530 seven miles north of Darrington. The hidden trailhead is at the high point of an upper loop road on the west bank of Buck Creek (1,200 feet). If it's busy and you're not paying for a campsite, you may have to park back down the road.

The trail quickly enters the Glacier Peak Wilderness and for the first quarter-mile stays close to the tumultuous creek, passing steep bouldery drops and only minimal flatwater. Several large boulders suitable for sunning line the edge of the stream. Until the flows drop later in summer, the creek is too swift and deep for swimming, and many jammed logs and debris create nasty hazards at several locations. On the path, expect some rough spots and possibly a few down logs and slide areas.

The trail climbs slightly through a beautiful Douglas fir forest, passing a number of giant trees over six feet in diameter. Western hemlock and red cedar add to the canopy above vine maple, huckleberry, salal, Oregon grape, devil's club, gooseberry, salmonberry, boxwood, many ferns (sword, deer, oak, lady, and maidenhair), bleeding heart, miner's lettuce, foamflower, false Solomon's seal, and trillium, among others. At a large slide area one may be able to descend fairly easily to the creek and a sunny lunch spot. Just beyond, the trail climbs several short switchbacks to avoid another slide then continues higher above the creek. Two little streams with delicate waterfalls are crossed before the trail fades at a steep gully about 0.8 mile from the start (1,400 feet).

"Chicken of the woods"

41. North Fork Sauk Falls

Distance: 0.5 mile roundtrip
Elevation gain: 150 feet

Time: Allow 1 hour
Season: April - November

The short hike to North Fork Sauk Falls is a perfect companion to a longer outing elsewhere in the North Fork Sauk River basin, such as the North Fork Sauk River Trail, an old-growth forest hike that starts a few miles upriver (*see Hike #59*). The river can be torrential in spring creating an exceptionally powerful waterfall that literally explodes into swirling mist and a raging pool below (see the photo on the back cover, taken just two weeks after the one below). Yet even at lower water levels, the falls are still beautiful to watch, as is the bending river that rolls through a gorge downstream.

Find it by driving the Mountain Loop Highway southeast of Darrington to MP 13.2; turn east onto USFS Rd. #49 and head up the North Fork Sauk River 1.1 mile to the tiny trailhead and parking

area on the right (1,600 feet; *map, p. 115*). The way down through alder-maple forest is obvious, and the thunder builds as you settle into the canyon. Beware that there is a sheer cliff at the edge of the viewpoint and a narrow exposed ledge that might look tempting to some. Avoid it, though, to increase the odds of making it back up the trail in one piece. The view is excellent so there's no need to risk limbs, lives, or trampled vegetation for some other imperfect camera angle.

North Fork Falls in spring

42. Harold Engles Memorial Cedars

Distance: 0.5 mile roundtrip

Elevation gain: Negligible

Time: Allow 1 hour

Season: April - November

In April, 1981, a friend and I were lucky enough to run into Harold Engles near the summit of Whitehorse Mt. on an early season climb from Darrington (not recommended by this guide). I had read about the man and knew he was legendary, an early Forest Service Ranger with decades of service and one who had been the first to ascend some of the region's more impressive peaks. He and his contemporaries built many of the original trails and fire lookouts out of Darrington in a time when protecting the woods from wildfire and timber poachers were among a ranger's principle duties. I'll always remember Harold, pushing his eightieth birthday, tearing his shirt off in the high cold air and rolling in the snow at the edge of a glacier 6,000 feet above his home in Darrington. "Invigorating," he said with a glint. Since then, I've practiced the habit myself on occasion at his inspiration. Harold was an extraordinary man of the mountains and a dedicated steward of wilderness. It is only proper that a memorial grove of big cedar trees he set aside for all of us years ago is now dedicated to his memory.

To reach the grove from Darrington, head south and east on the Mountain Loop Highway to the North Fork Sauk Rd. at MP 13.2; turn left and drive another 3.4 miles to a small turnout and information sign summarizing Engles' life in the Forest Service (1,900 feet; *map, p. 115*). A short path leads to a gigantic cedar tree—nearly fourteen feet across. Wander left to view the river and more big trees, or right to find a nice stand of cedars with so many limbs they create the feeling of a cedar chamber, a refuge from the rain. Watch for wood violet, trillium, bleeding heart, lady fern, vine maple, elderberry, red alder, and cottonwood.

43. Youth-On-Age

Distance: 0.4 mile loop
Elevation gain: None

Time: Allow 1 hour
Season: Almost year-round

For an easy walk through an ancient forest of giant Douglas fir, Sitka spruce, and western hemlock trees, the Youth-On-Age interpretive trail is particularly good for families, young kids, seniors, and those of us who might be a little less mobile than the rest. The trail is paved and practically level. The area is named for an unusual plant (youth-on-age) that grows little leaves on the backs of mature leaves. As the older leaves wither and die, the new leaves send roots into the soil and a new plant takes hold.

Find this trail on the south side of the Mountain Loop Highway at MP 18.7 east of Granite Falls (1,300 feet). Cross the footbridge and stroll beneath a tangle of vine maple with several large Sitka spruce trees close by. Spruce needles are sharp and the bark is thinner and smoother than some of the other large trees. This species is the largest spruce in the world, and the principal timber tree in Alaska. Spruce more than eight feet in diameter grow in the Olympic Rainforest and on Vancouver Island, but are far less common in the Cascades. Walk through salmonberry and pass another spruce with a huge base, a bird-pecked snag, and a patch of red alder trees poking through more vine maple. Then near the river, see up close a giant Douglas fir tree with deeply furrowed bark and flat, stiff needles — bottlebrush-like, but not sharp. This tree and others nearby are more than 500 years old and 200 feet tall.

The bank of the South Fork Stillaguamish River seems to move each year and the path has been known to erode and be swept away. Chances are that a good trail remains and you can continue the walk after enjoying the view up and down the river. More big Douglas fir trees, birch, bigleaf maple, a variety of ferns (sword, lady, and deer), spiny devil's club, and another spruce whose mossy branches seem to glow in morning or late afternoon sunlight. The loop ends near the starting point after less than a half-mile of walking.

44. Old Robe

Distance: 3.5 miles roundtrip
Elevation gain: 200 feet

Time: Allow 2 - 3 hours
Season: Almost year-round

A lovely stretch of river, tumbling whitewater, and two old tunnels built for the Monte Cristo Railroad in the 1890s are highlights of this newly improved trail east of Granite Falls. At less than 1,000 feet above sea level, the area is generally accessible all year, but beware of ice in cold, wintery weather. The trail is managed by Snohomish County Parks and was a favorite for esteemed trail guru and friend, Mike Parman who, most regrettably, left this life just as the trail was being dedicated. Plans call for extending the trail several miles downstream to link with a new trailhead and Hubbard Lake south of the river, where some trail improvements could happen as soon as 1998. The Stillaguamish Citizens Alliance and River Network were major players in the county's acquisition of 956 acres here, including the lake, wetlands, forest, and the river gorge. The Alliance also helped develop the trail system.

Wetlands above the Monte Cristo Railroad at Old Robe

To reach the trailhead at what is now being called "Robe Canyon Historical Park" drive east from Granite Falls on the Mountain Loop Highway and park on the shoulder at MP 7.1 near the red brick trail sign across from Green Mt. Rd. The area can be busy on nice summer weekends. A good path snakes quick through a thicket and into a clearcut where a steep hillside offers a great view of the river and wetlands below. The trail switchbacks down to pick up one old railroad grade that leads to another, reaching the river in less than a mile near the site of the old Robe Station. Continue downstream past the mostly invisible townsite of Robe on the right. Frequent flooding sent the town to high ground near the highway in 1907. Hop over two small streams and suddenly enter the gorge of the Stillaguamish River's South Fork.

A century ago, the steep canyon and moody river from here to a point several miles downstream turned out to be more than the construction engineers had bargained for. Periodic floods ripped the old railroad grade to pieces at many locations, and after several rebuilds the railroad was abandoned in the 1930s. Several tunnels have collapsed, abutments and fills have washed away, so that today only Tunnel 5 and Tunnel 6 are accessible. Both lie just ahead.

Pass an active slide area (if not passable the hike ends here) and find Tunnel 6 in a quarter-mile. Imagine rolling and clacking along the grey-white bedrock, nose against the glass, looking straight down at the swirling whitewater just before the lights go out in this tall, curved and nervy tunnel, 1.6 miles from the car. Through the tunnel and into the light and sound of the river, then an alley of sword fern and maple-cedar rainforest. Then comes little Tunnel 5 a quarter-mile more, and suddenly the end of the trail at a worse slide area, unless and until this stretch gets reconstructed (should you be tempted, Tunnels 4 and 3 are impassable).

45. Wallace Falls

Distance: 4.0 - 8.0 miles roundtrip
Elevation gain: 800 - 1,400 feet

Time: Allow 2 - 5 hours
Season: Almost year-round

Probably the most famous waterfall in Snohomish County, Wallace Falls north of Gold Bar also happens to be one of the better hikes in the foothills, especially late fall through spring when runoff is usually higher than the rest of the year, and the crowd factor has diminished. The place can be totally jammed on sunny weekends late spring through summer. The 265-foot falls of the Wallace River are indeed spectacular, and visible from several vantage points—including SR 2 west of Gold Bar. The best view, though is two miles up the trail, or three miles if you opt for a gentler old logging railroad grade that winds away from the river. The area was acquired as a State Park in 1977.

To reach the trailhead, head east on U.S. Hwy. 2 about thirty miles east of Everett to the town of Gold Bar and take a left at the big park sign. The park entrance (300 feet) is two miles ahead—expect to pay a day-use fee. The obvious wide trail heads under transmission lines and splits: right is the steeper Woody Trail closer to the river; left is the longer, easier, but less interesting railroad

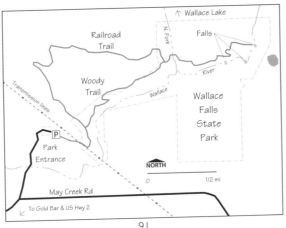

grade. The two routes rejoin 1.5 and 2.5 miles ahead, just before a bridge over the North Fork Wallace River (700 feet). There's a view of the falls 0.3 mile from here on steeper trail (scenic pools and rock), but keep going another 0.2 mile for the up-close-and-doggone-awesome view. The trail continues up steep switchbacks to more views from above, and finally an upper falls viewpoint 1.5 miles from the North Fork bridge. Just beyond, another trail heads up through woods to old logging roads leading northwesterly to Wallace Lake, three miles from the upper falls (watch for signs—there's a risk of getting lost on old grades that have led some folks dazed and confused all the way to Startup). Incidentally, the falls, river, and a lake up the North Fork were named for a Skykomish Indian woman.

Wallace Falls

92

46. Heybrook Lookout

Distance: 2.2 miles roundtrip
Elevation gain: 900 feet

Time: Allow 2 - 3 hours
Season: March-December

When the mountains are snowed in but the lower foothills aren't, Heybrook Ridge beckons. The hike is moderately steep but short, and close enough to sea level to miss most of the winter snowpack that's normally dumped on the Cascades November to March. In mild years the trail might be accessible in the middle of winter. The ridge's strategic location between precipitous walls of Mt. Index, Mt. Persis, and Mt. Baring—none more than five miles away—means great views. A clearing just below the top looks across to the first two plus Bridal Veil Falls. For the bigger picture, the top of the old fire lookout is the place. Unfortunately, the building deteriorated, was demolished, and the remaining tower was still closed in late 1997. However, thanks to the Everett Mountaineers, a five-year project to rebuild and reopen the lookout began in 1997.

The trailhead's at the west end of a big parking area on the north side of U. S. Hwy 2 east of Index at MP 37.6 (800 feet; *map, p. 160*). A straight-forward, steep woods walk on generally good trail under maturing Doug-fir leads one long mile to the old fire lookout, 900 feet above (1,700 feet). Despite some serious clearcutting in the 1920s the forest has retaken most of the ridge. Just as the tower comes into view, a cleared swath offers the best view for now. Highway traffic noise is a little less obnoxious and you can hear the river. Bridal Veil Falls streams below the hanging valley of Lake Serene to the southwest. Mt. Index is above it, Mt. Persis to the right. From the lookout, Mt. Baring will be visible way left, and Puget Sound is thirty miles west, left of Index Town Wall. Ignore the old logging road on top; it only leads to some unsightly transmission lines and clearcuts.

Mt. Baring from the lookout

47. Troublesome Creek

Distance: 0.6 mile loop
Elevation gain: 100 feet

Time: Allow 1 hour
Season: April - November

For a great little family woods walk next to a pretty creek in the mountains, try the nature trail at Troublesome Creek Campground northeast of Index. Even if you're not camping at Troublesome the trail is worth a visit, perhaps combined with other short walks farther upriver (*see Walk #87*). However, beware of dangerous fast water here much of the year (a fatal, off-trail accident occurred in 1997). From US Hwy 2 at MP 35.7, turn north onto the North Fork Rd. (signed for Index) and drive just over 11 miles to the first of two entrances to the campground (1,800 feet). Either park on the shoulder near the bridge over Troublesome Creek or drive into the campground and stay left to find the trailhead close by.

Walk left along the creek and pass under a bridge, and continue upstream in forest past benches to the obvious footbridge ahead. From the bridge there is a great view of Troublesome Creek crashing through a narrow slot of granite like it can't wait to impale the river a few hundred yards downstream. Once across the bridge go

straight on the main trail to continue the loop back to the campground. The trail climbs gently to another junction. Stay right (straight leads muddily back to the road directly across from the second entrance to the campground). The path drops back down to the creek. Stay left here and walk back under the road bridge reaching another footbridge over the creek farther downstream. Cross to return to your starting point. The Forest Service plans to improve this trail in 1998.

Troublesome Creek

48. Deception Falls

Distance: 0.6 mile roundtrip
Elevation gain: Negligible

Time: Allow 1 hour
Season: April - November

Across the line in King County, west of Stevens Pass, is a cluster of beautiful waterfalls all within minutes of the highway. A half-mile loop trail accesses two falls on the Tye River, and a barrier-free path goes to a third on Deception Creek. Park on the north side of US Hwy 2 near MP 57, eight miles east of Skykomish. Interpretive signs and a map at the trailhead speak to the remarkable railroad history of the Stevens Pass area. Nearby, in the winter of 1893, the last spike was driven for James J. Hill's 1,816-mile transcontinental Great Northern Railway between Puget Sound and St. Paul. The original grade literally switchbacked up the pass until 1900 when the old Cascade Tunnel was opened. In 1929 twelve miles of grade was abandoned with completion of a nearly eight-mile-long tunnel. (The old grade is now the Iron Goat Trail; *see p. 187.*)

For the close-up view of Deception Falls, walk east on the obvious path to a catwalk under the highway. (South of the highway, a serious mountain trail continues up Deception Creek and enters the Alpine Lakes Wilderness Area.) Head back toward the restrooms for a quick tour of the nature loop. A beauteous Douglas-fir forest and an excitable river make the loop enjoyable anytime it isn't buried in snow (November - March are the iffy months). In the woods, look for the long needles of one of the our less common conifers, western white pine. The first falls viewpoint is five minutes from the car, and a second right-angle waterfall is just beyond. Here, the bedrock's stout resistance to erosion creates a puzzling sight, dramatic when the river is high. The trail continues through a grove of large cedar trees and returns to the parking lot.

Falls on the Tye River

Glacier Peak from the northeast

49. Green Mountain

Distance: 5.0 - 8.0 miles roundtrip

Elevation gain: 1,700 - 3,000 feet

Time: Allow 4 - 7 hours

Season: July - mid-October

Those who keep coming back to Green Mt. in mid-summer return for good reason: views and wildflowers. Most years, from mid-July to early August, the forever-stretching meadows of Green Mt. are saturated with the rich color and sweet smell of mountain paradise. And if you wait for the flowers to fade, blueberries appear, which means this place stays plenty busy all summer, weekends especially. The mountain and the old fire lookout on top are conspicuous from the Milk Creek Trail bridge over the Suiattle River (*see Hike #51*). To reach the trailhead, take the Suiattle River Rd. (USFS Rd. #26) from SR 530, about seven miles north of the Darrington Ranger Station, and follow it 19 miles to USFS Rd. #2680 (signed for Green Mt.). Turn left and drive six more miles to the parking area (3,500 feet).

The trail is steep at first and passes through mature, moss-draped forest before entering big meadows only a mile from the start. This

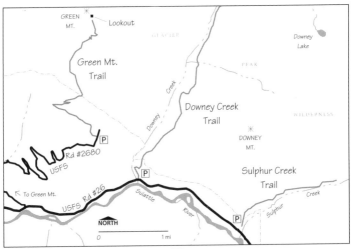

is a good place to pull out the wildflower guide in mid-summer. In another 1.5 miles the trail passes two little lakes (5,200 feet) with campsites and a privy just below. Beyond, the meadows become more fragile and camping is not recommended. Revegetation efforts are underway to restore areas damaged by improper trail use and camping. Snow fields can linger well into summer and may or may not cover the trail depending on seasonal conditions.

If the trail is passable, continue another steep zigging mile to the old Green Mt. fire lookout at the 6,500-foot crest. The building, locked up and in need of repair, is one of only a handful in the Cascades that still functions on occasion as a true fire lookout (the Forest Service was studying what to do with the building in late 1997). The panorama is impressive: Sloan Peak, Mt. Pugh and White Chuck Mt. to the southwest, Mt. Chaval and Snowking Mt. to the north-northwest, Mt. Buckindy not far to the northeast, Dome Peak to the east, and the oft-hidden volcanic monarch of Snohomish County, Glacier Peak, thoroughly conspicuous to the south-southeast. The Suiattle River is a vertical mile below.

Summer mist, Green Mt. meadows

50. Sulphur Mountain

Distance: 11.0 - 14.0 miles roundtrip   Time: Allow 7 - 12 hours

Elevation gain: 4,500 - 5,500 feet   Season: July - October

The 5.5-mile hike (one-way) to Sulphur Mt. is long, hard, and steep, though fortunately, there's a big scenic payoff at the end: the icy north flank of Glacier Peak, plus other seldom seen summits of the North Cascades. UNNfortunately, you have to walk almost to the end of the trail before you see much of anything. So, if a hard hike in the woods on a sometimes lonely trail is appealing, keep reading. Keep in mind that after the first quarter mile there is essentially no water on the route (carry at least two quarts per person on a warm summer day). Camping on the narrow ridge is impractical, although sites in the woods and near Sulphur Mt. Lake are feasible.

The trail begins a short distance up the Suiattle River Trail from near the end of the Suiattle River Rd. From SR 530 seven miles north of Darrington, turn east on the Suiattle River Rd. (USFS Rd. #26) and drive this 22.7 miles to the parking area near its end, just beyond Sulphur Creek Campground (1,600 feet). Walk the river trail 100 yards to a junction and head left for Sulphur Mt. The Glacier Peak Wilderness boundary is just ahead. The tread is in good condition all the way up and maintains a steep grade almost the entire distance. The only stream is crossed in the first quarter mile (after a short descent). After four long miles and a gain of about 3,500 feet,

the trail slips beneath a rock slide (camping is feasible just beyond). Meadow is reached in another mile, then an easier half-mile climb leads to the scenic ridge crest and two flowery high-points with spectacular views of surrounding peaks. The second ridge bump makes a good turn-around point (6,100 feet). Western anemone, valerian, lupine, and other wildflowers add some flair to the scene.

Glacier Peak lures to the south. Tenpeak Mt. is behind and left, Fire Mt. and Lime Ridge are to the right. White Chuck Mt. is visible to the west, partly obscuring Three Fingers. Whitehorse Mt. and the Suiattle River valley are to the right. Green Mt. and Mt. Baker lie to the northwest, with snowy Snowking Mt. and Mt. Buckindy to the right. The Picket Range is visible far in the distance. To the northeast are Sulphur Mt. Lake, and toward the horizon, Spire Point, Dome Peak, and Sinister Peak. Rambling Sulphur Mt. fills the skyline from east to southeast. More experienced hikers with some legs left could continue on less-traveled path southward, losing 200 feet in woods, before climbing to other high points and a 6,735-foot summit on the rocky crest in a mile or so. To reach the lake, among woods, rock, and meadow, return to the point where the main trail first hit the ridge crest, then turn left instead of right. It's about 800 feet and nearly a mile down to the lake (camping and water here).

Glacier Peak and western anemonies from Sulphur Mt.

51. Suiattle River

Distance: 2.0 - 13.2 miles roundtrip   Time: Allow 1 - 8 hours
Elevation gain: 100 - 900 feet   Season: May - November

The trail up the Suiattle River is a popular route for backpackers and equestrians with four days or more to explore wild mountains in the heart of the Glacier Peak Wilderness. But even if you only have a day or even an hour to burn, the walk up the river makes a pleasant outing that can be kept as short or long as you like. The entire trail upriver extends half-way around Glacier Peak and dead ends after twenty miles and a gain of only 2,500 feet. A half-dozen trail junctions offer access to the high country, but to really enjoy these options you'll need at least three days. For a one-day, early or late-season walk, consider hiking all or part of the 6.5 easy miles to Canyon Creek. Only got an hour? The two-mile roundtrip to the river bridge, described below, is a good alternate.

Find the trailhead (1,600 feet) at the end of the 23-mile Suiattle River Road (USFS Rd. #26) which leaves SR 530 just east of the Sauk River bridge at MP 56.6 (*map, p. 99*). Walk the wide path along what used to be a road through beautiful old-growth Douglas fir. Some trees exceed eight feet in diameter. At a junction in 0.8 mile, stay left to continue upriver on the main trail, or head right on the Milk Creek Trail another 0.2 mile to a bridge crossing the river. Look downstream to spot the green mountain, appropriately named "Green Mt." In good light the old fire lookout on top is easy to see. Milk Creek Trail continues through more old-growth forest with big trees another 6.5 miles to a junction with the Pacific Crest trail.

From the fork before the Suiattle River bridge, the main trail up the river quickly leaves the old road grade and gently rises and falls with the terrain, staying close to the river most of the way. Several streams are crossed and small clearings offer occasional glimpses of the surrounding high country. Canyon Creek is reached in 6.5 miles from the start (2,300 feet). This is a reasonable turn-around point for a longer day-hike. (The bridge over Canyon Creek was scheduled for reconstruction in 1998. The trail may be closed at this point from spring til early summer; check with the USFS to be sure.)

52. Mt. Higgins Lookout & Myrtle Lake

Distance: 2.0 - 8.5 miles roundtrip   Time: Allow 1 - 6 hours
Elevation gain: 600 - 3,500 feet   Season: June - October

One of the most westerly summits of the North Cascades is Mt. Higgins, a distinctly layered, mile-high summit visible to the north of SR 530 between Arlington and Darrington. While the true summit is best left to experienced mountaineers, the slightly lower west summit can be reached by a fairly good trail and offers an equally dramatic view of the North Fork Stillaguamish River valley and ragged skyline of the North Cascades.

From MP 37.9 on SR 530, about 5 miles east of Oso, turn north on a gravel road (DNR Road #5500, might be unsigned) and cross the North Fork Stilly in about a half-mile. Continue on the main road, ignoring the less traveled spurs, for about two miles and find the trail just past a wide open area on the right suitable for parking

(1,400 feet). The path climbs moderately through a regenerating forest and suddenly breaks out into a clearcut in the first mile. Views are excellent; Whitehorse Mt. dominates the scene to the southeast. This is a good turn-around for an off-season trek. Or, climb more steeply through some tight switchbacks among rocky outcrops, passing a little memory carved into the rock by Sam Strom, one of

A spring view from the site of the old Mt. Higgins lookout

Darrington's more illustrious gun-totin' pioneers.

Leave the steep clearcut on DNR land and enter a picturesque old-growth forest at the National Forest boundary. The grade moderates and continues up through woods another two miles, crossing Dicks Creek before topping out at a junction in gentle subalpine meadows (3,700 feet). A left takes you down slightly to little Myrtle Lake, a half-mile away. Go right to skirt lovely wetlands and to climb the last steep mile in woods and rocks to Higgins' west summit at 4,849 feet (can be snowy early summer). An old fire lookout existed here from 1926 until heavy snow flattened it in the mid-1960s. The panorama (clockwise): Glacier Peak in the distance, Darrington and the North Fork Stilly, Whitehorse Mt., Three Fingers, Boulder River, Mt. Rainier, Puget Sound, the Olympics, Mt. Baker, and the middle and east peaks of Mt. Higgins. The hike is attractive early in the season when the lower meadows melt out (May or June), but skip the summit, if necessary, to avoid exposure to avalanche danger.

53. Squire Creek Pass

Distance: 4.0 - 8.0 miles roundtrip   Time: Allow 4 - 7 hours
Elevation gain: 1,000 - 2,800 feet   Season: June - October

For an exceptional hike in the Boulder River Wilderness, on some good trail and much crummy, replete with classic North Cascades scenery—which helps make up for the longish drive to the trailhead—consider a little adventure on the trail to Squire Creek Pass south of Darrington. The trail reaches big talus slopes with wide open views about two miles in, a great destination for a shorter day hike. However, by this point most of the hard work is over, so a complete trudge to the pass is the better idea.

From the corner of Fullerton Ave. and Darrington St. in Darrington (several blocks south of SR 530 and west of Mountain Loop Highway) head west on the Squire Creek Rd. Leave the pavement behind and stay on the main traveled road for about five miles, passing a view of Whitehorse Mt. just over a small bridge where the peak profiles like a spire. Watch the road shoulder; portions have sloughed away. (In July 1997, the road was very rough the last half-mile and it may be necessary to park short of the road end.) When the immense 2,000-foot high granite face of Squire Creek Wall comes into view, you're near the trailhead (1900 feet)..

The trail follows abandoned road bed through an old clearcut for the first half-mile then crosses a small creek and enters old-growth forest near the wilderness boundary. The grade is easy to moderate for the first mile, passes some big cedars, then steepens

Squire Creek Wall from near the trailhead

and ascends switchbacks for about 500 feet of elevation gain. Cross a steep boulder wash with views of waterfalls and the mammoth wall of mountains across the valley. Three Fingers is toward the left end. Just after the trail seriously flattens out, enter a large rockslide area with giant flakes of scattered granite and unobstructed views. Smooth high walls on both sides of the valley dominate the scene. This is a good early-season turn-around (in June, the trail is likely to be under snow near the pass).

The path climbs through talus to the base of another wall just up valley. A stand of dead trees is passed before ascending more forest and finally easing off in subalpine meadows thick with huckleberry bushes. The trail crosses bright granite slabs and then more granite at the gentle pass marked by mountain hemlocks and views to the east. Glacier Peak's snowy cone is visible between the trees. Mt. Pugh is closer and just left of it. White Chuck Mt. is to the east-northeast. The entire subrange of Whitehorse, Bullon, Three Fingers, and Big Bear Mt. is seriously impressing, especially in morning light. Once the snow has retreated one can wander south a half-mile through open meadows and granite, perhaps some snow, up to an excellent ridge crest view.

To explore the old and unmaintained Eightmile Trail (a less scenic approach to the pass from the east), continue straight across slabs from the point the trail reached the pass and follow a mostly good trail, narrow with some cairns and blazes, and sometimes hidden under huckleberry bushes, angling down slightly through an extensive subalpine area. Several small tarns, some clear with rocky bottoms, and over a half dozen small streams sliding down more granite slabs, are passed. By arranging a ride at the Eightmile Trailhead one could keep descending, taking extreme care not to lose the trail. After a half-mile, the way drops more steeply into forest and becomes wider and muddier. Cross a boulder-filled gully in a clearing then drop down a few switchbacks (partial view of the pass here). The route drops below a high rock wall and leads through heavier brush and vine maple to the base of Three O'Clock Rock, a local rock climbing area. White Chuck Mt. is visible to the northeast. Where the trail meets the base of the wall, look for it hiding in brush to the left, then down and right and finally back to more woods and more switchbacks. Pass a big cedar tree next to the wilderness boundary and leave the old-growth forest behind. The trail leads to an old logging grade and descends this the final half-mile through a thicket of young trees to the trailhead, 2.5 miles from the pass. To reach this trailhead by car, drive the Mountain Loop Highway about two miles from Darrington to just past the National Forest boundary, then turn right on Clear Creek Rd. (USFS Rd. #2060) across from the Clear Creek Campground. This road may be rough in places. Stay right at a fork in 5.6 miles. The signed trail is on the right 0.6 mile beyond.

54. Meadow Lake & Meadow Mountain

Distance: 15.0 - 19.0 miles roundtrip   Time: Allow 8 - 13 hours
Elevation gain: 1,600 - 2,500 feet   Season: July - October

Meadow Mt. has long been a favorite for the locals, not only because the meadows and views are great, but because access used to be a breeze. But when lovely alpine meadows are matched against wandering crowds of smiling bipeds, the meadows inevitably lose. To reduce the impact, the USFS closed the logging road leading to the main trailhead on the west end of the mountain, thus requiring a five-mile road walk to reach the trail followed by a 1.3-mile hike to the first good meadow. For most of us then, Meadow Mt. is now an overnight hike. But if you're leggy and ambitious you can still make a long day of it to the meadows and to Meadow Lake 2.5 miles from the road end (a 15-mile round trip).

There is also a good trail leading up the east end of Meadow Mt. by way of the White Chuck Trail and Fire Mt. (*see Hike #55*). While this approach avoids the long road walk, figure about the same

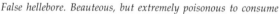

False hellebore. Beauteous, but extremely poisonous to consume

amount of effort for a similar scenic payoff. Riding or walking a mountain bike up the road for a quick ride down gives diminishes the drudgery of the western approach described here. Drive the Mountain Loop Highway south of Darrington (MP 6.3), turn east on the White Chuck Rd., then go left in 5.9 miles on USFS Rd. #27. Follow this 2.5 miles to the trailhead where a berm blocks an old logging road on the right. Park here and walk USFS Rd. #2710 five miles to its end at the former trailhead (3,900 feet). Mt. Pugh towers across the valley to the southwest.

The trail climbs 1,200 feet in under two miles, passing a meadow, and reaching a junction. Go left 0.7 mile to Meadow Lake, a 300-foot descent north and west from the crest. The pretty lake is nestled in a pocket of meadow, trees, and cliffs. Keep right to wander the meadowy ridge of Meadow Mt. with many ups and downs and excellent views of Glacier Peak and other high summits of the North Cascades. From the junction it's about six miles to Fire Mt., followed by a 4.5-mile descent to the White Chuck Trail 1.5 miles from White Chuck Rd. Spot a car here or arrange a lift for the return.

Arctic lupine

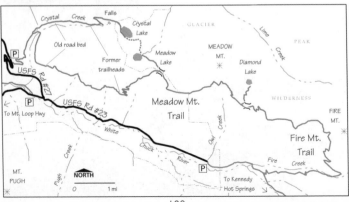

55. Fire Mountain

Distance: 12.0 - 16.0 miles roundtrip   Time: Allow 7 - 12 hours
Elevation gain: 3,200 - 3,900 feet   Season: July - October

The trail to Fire Mt. is also the eastern access for a 19-mile hike over Meadow Mt. (*see Hike #54*), most of which traverses scenic high country northwest of Glacier Peak. Stronger hikers could plant a car at one end and walk the entire distance in a long day, but the area is really too beautiful to rush through, so save the longer haul for an overnight trip. To boot, there's a five-mile road walk at the west end which makes the east end a bit more attractive for a day-hike. The latter includes several miles of easy walking, with some nicely spaced flat stretches to break up the grunty parts. Officially, the trail begins about 1.5 miles up the White Chuck Trail from the end of the White Chuck Rd. (*see Hike #56 for directions; map, p. 108*).

Leave the parking lot (2,300 feet) on flat trail and pass the trail register and Glacier Peak Wilderness boundary in 0.7 mile. Continue another easy 0.8 mile to a junction, 200 yards past the footbridge over Fire Creek, and head left on the Meadow Mt. Trail (right goes to Kennedy Hot Springs).

Glacier Peak from Fire Mt. Trail

After a half-mile of easy walking, some minor muddy spots, and a half-dozen switchbacks, rise to an unusually large and forested bench. Here begins another mile of easy wandering in nice woods (minor mud here too), followed by a half-mile of steepish and a half-mile of flattish trail adjacent to Fire Creek. The route crosses the creek on a hewn footlog (may be slippery) four miles from the parking lot (3,700 feet).

The next mile is steeper with several switchbacks and peek-a-boo views through openings left from an old burn. At a left hairpin (4,600 feet), Glacier Peak makes a stunning appearance. In fact, the best views of the mountain are found along the next 0.2 mile of trail, but you either have to stop to enjoy it or hike backwards — not something this here guidebook author is likely to recommend. Lighting for photos is best late afternoon until sunset. The trail reenters thick woods, then shortly reemerges in patchy meadows with views of Fire Mt. above. Pass an inconspicuous trail junction (a hard right leads to more meadows, views, and a possible route to the 6,591-foot summit for the more seasoned hiker), but stay straight to pass what's left of an old log shelter and a small stream, two miles from Fire Creek (campsites nearby). Just beyond are beautiful rocky meadows with good views and lots of big boulders for sunning if the bugs are tolerable.

One can continue across the meadow and follow the trail a short distance toward a wooded crest (5,500 feet) where another opening affords a good view of Glacier Peak's icy summit. Views reach around Black Mt. above Lake Byrne to White Chuck Mt. and beyond. This is a good turn-around point. Or, walk a few paces down the other side for a good look at Meadow Mt. The trail descends about 200 feet to cross a large subalpine basin, then climbs gradually to the 6,000-foot ridge top in about two miles. From there it's another six miles to the west end of the Meadow Mt. Trail, followed by the infamous five mile walk on an old logging road to the present west trailhead (*see Hike #54 for directions*).

56. White Chuck River & Lake Byrne

Distance: 11.0 - 16.0 miles roundtrip   Time: Allow 6 - 12 hours

Elevation gain: 1,000 - 3,700 feet   Season: May - November

The White Chuck Trail is a popular access to the Pacific Crest Trail, and the principal climbers' access to Glacier Peak, as well as the busy route to Kennedy Hot Springs—which are nice but murky, often crowded, and not exactly hot. Nevertheless, the easy hike through old-growth forest close to the White Chuck River is worth a jaunt by itself. For a strenuous trudge to great views of The Volcano, go for Lost Creek Ridge and Lake Byrne, but go later in the season when the winter snowpack has had a chance to melt (usually by mid-July). A hike up Kennedy Ridge is an option, but the distance and elevation to the high meadows and views of Glacier Peak preclude this as a day hike. High camps are feasible on the ridge and at Lake Byrne, with good sites near the springs as well. Anticipate a snooping bear around the springs and hang your food.

To reach White Chuck Trail and the hot springs, take Mountain Loop Highway from Darrington to MP 6.3 and turn left on the White Chuck Rd. (USFS Rd. #23). Drive this 10.4 miles to the trailhead near its end (2,300 feet). There's a good view of the volcano from the last half-mile of road. The trail is gentle and in excellent shape to start and gains only 1,000 feet in five miles. Enter the Glacier Peak Wilderness in 0.7 mile, passing several cascading streams, and staying mostly within view of the river. Pass the Meadow Mt./Fire Mt. Trail junction at 1.5 miles, then climb occasional switchbacks to bypass slide areas. The Kennedy Ridge Trail junction is at 5 miles. In

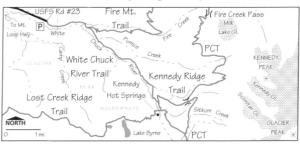

another 0.2 miles, the trail crosses Kennedy Creek on a footlog where a left leads to the Pacific Crest Trail at Sitkum Creek, but go straight. Pass a ranger cabin, and cross the river on a footbridge. The five-foot wide, five-foot deep hot springs are to the left (3,300 feet). The setting is great but primitive and heavily used, for obvious reasons — one of the busiest spots in the Glacier Peak Wilderness. Mid-week, early and late season, may be the best times to avoid the crowds. Help keep it clean by not washing or soaping up in the iron-rich (not sulphur) spring. The flow is good with temperatures in the low-90s, though there's no guarantee it's 100% free of pesky pathogens.

For the longer hike to Lake Byrne and Lost Creek Ridge, turn right after the big footbridge, go left past campsites (privy nearby), and left up very steep but good trail in woods. After a mile and two dozen switchbacks, the trail eases off, crosses an open basin, then climbs to the lake with views of Glacier Peak. The gorgeous lake is just beyond a cascade, two miles and 2,300 feet above the hot springs. Views are outstanding. Look for climbers' tracks on the Sitkum Glacier toward the center of Glacier Peak. Paths wander left and right to more views and meadows. Restoration work is underway (these high meadows are fragile). The area can remain snowbound into August with steep and potentially dangerous slopes. To continue up Lost Creek Ridge, head right over a hump then up through heather and huckleberry to a viewy crest north of the lake. A trail continues up the crest a half-mile to a rocky basin, and over a

meadowy rise toward Camp Lake (below). Mt. Baker's white cone is above the horizon to the northwest, Sloan Peak juts to the southwest, and White Chuck Mt. rises to the northwest. An intermittent path continues west along the ridge for seven scenic miles to Round Lake (*see Hike #58*). Take care not to lose the trail on the return.

Lake Byrne

57. Stujack Pass & Mount Pugh

Distance: 7.0 - 9.5 miles roundtrip   Time: Allow 6 - 10 hours
Elevation gain: 3,800 - 5,300 feet   Season: July - October

If you're an experienced Class 3 rock scrambler up for an easy but
exposed climb to the 7,201-foot summit, Mt. Pugh can be one of
the more enjoyable hikes you'll find in the North Cascades. The trail
to the site of an old fire lookout follows the crest of a sheer and
narrow ridge in one section, and was literally blasted out of the
cliffs in another. However, if that kind of thing is not your pod of
peas, or there's still a lot of snow up high, the more moderate hike
to Stujack Pass is a worthy destination as well. The peak is conspicuous from SR 530 and the Mountain Loop Highway near Darrington and was known as *DaKlagwats* to natives, then was named
for an area settler. The original fire lookout was built in 1919 but
was destroyed many years ago. Old cable marks the site.

From Mountain Loop Highway out of Darrington (good view of
Mt. Pugh dead-ahead near MP 5.5), turn left near MP 10 onto USFS
Road #2095 and drive about 1.5 mile to the trailhead just around a
sharp bend (1900 feet). Note this road is closed from mid-October
through May to protect wildlife. The way climbs moderately through
woods the first mile (some big trees), then steepens with switchbacks
another half-mile to the sudden appearance of little Lake Metan
(3,200 feet); stay left. A long three miles from the car meadows ap-

pear, and at 3.5 miles
Stujack Pass, a deep
notch in Pugh's
northwest ridge, is
reached (5,700 feet).
The views are excel-
lent: Three Fingers
and Whitehorse Mt.
to the west, White
Chuck Mt. and the
Mt. Baker volcano to
the north-northwest,

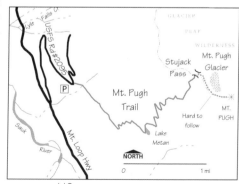

Sloan Peak to the south-southeast, and Mt. Rainier beyond and to the right.

Above the pass, the way is less defined, unmaintained, and may be snow-bound well into July. Steep snow—not to be taken lightly—requires an ice axe (and the skills to use it), and scrambling on steep rock suggests only the most experienced hikers even consider it. Wait for August for a better shot at a snow-free summit ascent. The scariest part may be a short steep section above a tiny glacier and just beyond the knife-edge ridge with a natural "sidewalk" that seems perfectly placed. Remember, too, that coming down is always more difficult than going up. The summit, a long mile beyond the pass, is broad and rounded and littered with the remains of the old fire look-out. Glacier Peak is a real loomer to the east. The sheer, 2,000-foot east wall of Mt. Pugh drops into the Pugh Creek basin. Round Lake is three miles to the southeast, and Mt. Forgotten is across the Sauk River to the southwest. Carry extra water for the longer climb to the summit.

Near the summit of Mt. Pugh

58. Round Lake & Lost Creek Ridge

Distance: 9.5 - 14.0 miles roundtrip   Time: Allow 7 - 12 hours

Elevation gain: 3,600 - 4,400 feet   Season: July - October

Near the west end of Lost Creek Ridge is a jewel of an alpine lake sunk in a bowl beneath a craggy skyline, appropriately named Round Lake. The trail leading to it links with the Lost Creek Ridge Trail and Lake Byrne, five crow-miles to the east (*see Hike #56*). Good overnight possibilities are feasible along the scenic ridge route, although water could be skimpy. To find the trail, drive the Mountain Loop Highway from Darrington to MP 13.2 and turn left on USFS Rd. #49 which climbs into the North Fork Sauk River valley (*see Walk #41 for a short side-trip to North Fork Falls*). The trailhead (1,900 feet) is on the left 3.1 miles from the junction. At a clearing a half-mile past the trailhead, Lost Creek Ridge, Bingley Gap, and steep-walled Spring Mountain are visible from the road.

The first 0.7 mile is an easy forest walk, sometimes wet, quickly becoming steep and switchbacked as the route heads upslope on better trail through more open forest (some giant trees) above a cas-

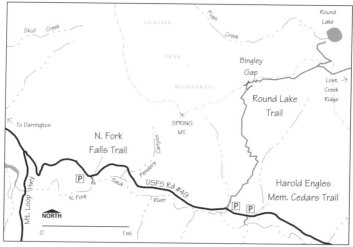

cading North Fork tributary. Look south for glimpses of Sloan Peak's summit spire across the river valley. A stiff three miles and 2,500 feet up reach Bingley Gap and the Glacier Peak Wilderness boundary that runs the ridge southwest to Spring Mountain. Mt. Pugh is visible through the trees to the northwest.

Finally, the incline moderates as the trail ascends Lost Creek Ridge to broad meadows (blueberries late summer), excellent views of Sloan Peak, and a junction (stay left) and saddle 4.5 miles from the start (5,500 feet). From higher ground east or west of the saddle, the views are exceptional, including Mt. Baker, Glacier Peak, and Mt. Rainier. To reach the lake, settled in a west-facing cirque nearly 500 feet below, take the 0.7-mile trail that drops steeply from the saddle. Or skip the lake and wander eastward along Lost Creek Ridge as far as time allows. Just around the next spur ridge (0.3 mile) is a great view of Glacier Peak. Beyond, the trail can be hard to follow, and is non-existent in some places, so best to memorize the terrain.

Round Lake

59. North Fork Sauk River

Distance: 1.0 - 18.6 miles roundtrip   Time: Allow 1 - 12 hours
Elevation gain: 100 - 4,400 feet   Season: May - November

If a terrific old-growth forest hike on mostly level trail far from
civilization sounds appealing, check out the trail up the North
Fork Sauk River valley, southeast of Darrington. Two miles in you
might even see a mountain goat grazing the cliffs high above the
trail. If that seems too easy, there's an abrupt 3,000-foot climb out of
the valley about five miles upriver for great views and a strenuous
workout. Longer multi-day back-country trips into the heart of the
Glacier Peak Wilderness and along Pilot Ridge could also start here.

From Darrington, follow the Mountain Loop Highway to the
North Fork Sauk River Rd. (USFS Rd. #49) at MP 13.2. Turn left and
drive 6.6 miles to a junction; stay left again to reach the trailhead
(2,100 feet) just ahead (or stay right to drive through a lovely stand
of old-growth forest). Almost from the start, giant Douglas fir and
western red cedar trees up to nine feet in diameter line the first mile
or so of trail, with some of the biggest ones near the wilderness
boundary a half-mile in—a possible turn-around point for an easy
stroll. Other lowland tree species like western hemlock, bigleaf
maple, and red alder seem to have bumped into the lower limit of
Pacific silver fir, producing an exceptionally diverse forest. Red
huckleberry, vine maple, several ferns, and the dreaded (but easily

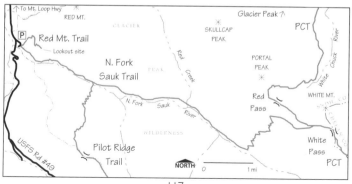

avoided) devil's club add to the mix.

Often close to the river, the wide path wanders along, a little up and down, past more big trees, passing several openings and an avalanche-hammered slope and creek crossing at 1.3 miles. Just across the creek look back over your right shoulder for a great view of the 7,835-foot summit of Sloan Peak and the Sloan Glacier to the west. A junction is reached in two miles (2,400 feet) where the trail to Pilot Ridge heads off to the right across the river (the old footlog over the river is gone but another one just downstream made a reasonable crossing in 1997 — check with the Forest Service to be sure — then expect a steep, 3.5-mile, 3,000-foot climb to excellent ridge top views). Just past the junction pan the cliffs above for mountain goats. There's a high, three-tiered waterfall here, although it peters out later in summer.

After a longish five miles and a gain of only 900 feet, the Mackinaw Shelter is reached. Just beyond, the trail begins an abrupt climb of 3,000 feet in nearly three miles to join the Pacific Crest Trail (PCT)

near White Pass (6,000 feet). Views improve rapidly about two miles up. Only the strongest hikers may have the legs for this one. If that's you, go right a half-mile to sprawling views from the pass, or take a left and walk an easy mile or more to the grand spectacle of Glacier Peak. Then comes the long knee-pounding descent...

Giant Douglas fir tree

60. Red Mountain Lookout

Distance: 1.8 miles roundtrip
Elevation gain: 700 feet

Time: Allow 1 - 2 hours
Season: May - October

The hike to the old Red Mt. lookout site above the North Fork Sauk River is short and steep, but plenty scenic. Early summer or fall are good times to visit — even November is good if the snow hasn't started to pile up in the middle elevations. Maybe combine the walk with a two-mile stroll up the North Fork Sauk River (*Hike #59, same trailhead*), or with North Fork Falls (*Walk #41*), and the Harold Engles Memorial Cedars trail (*Walk #42*). The trailhead is south of Darrington off the North Fork Sauk River Rd. From MP 13.2 on Mountain Loop Highway, turn east onto USFS Rd. #49 and drive 6.6 miles to the Sloan Creek trailhead on the left (2,100 feet).

Walk a short distance up the North Fork Sauk River Trail and turn left on the Red Mountain Lookout Trail. The narrow path among giant trees quickly finds steeper terrain, then switchbacks up the lower west slope of Red Mountain. At about 0.5 mile Sloan Peak comes into view at a small clearing. At 0.9 mile, the trail forks near a collapsing shed. The lookout site is a few paces to the right (2,800 feet). There is a great view of Sloan Peak and the Sloan Glacier to the southwest across the North Fork valley. Bedal Peak's summit rocks jag to the right. To the south, the Monte Cristo peaks tower above the Cadet Creek valley and Pride Basin six miles away.

It's feasible for expert hikers to continue three miles up Red Mt. on steep, intermittent trail all the way to tiny Ruby Lake and meadows 2,500 feet above. From the lookout site, the old trail heads up and right to a switchback then a short, steep, exposed rock scramble with an okay view. Confident route-finding skills are mandatory, especially for the descent (a few old blazes). Carry extra water for the ascent.

Sloan Peak and Glacier

61. Bedal Basin

Distance: 6.0 miles roundtrip   Time: Allow 4 - 6 hours
Elevation gain: 2,300 feet   Season: July - October

This is a more difficult hike on a rough, unmaintained trail into the upper basin of Bedal Creek, a modest tributary of the South Fork Sauk River. The trail is remote and doesn't normally see a lot of use, although it was once the principal climbing route to Sloan Peak, one of the more striking summits in the region. Harry Bedal built a small trapper's cabin in the meadows here, most of which has been reclaimed by the winds and whims of nature. When the snow recedes, some limited wandering is feasible above tree line, but routefinding skills are needed both to keep it safe and to find the way back home. Best to save this trek for better weather. And even then, only the more experienced pathfinder should attempt it.

From Darrington follow the Mountain Loop Highway to Bedal Campground and the bridge across the North Fork Sauk River. Continue another 0.7 mile (MP14.4) and turn east onto USFS Rd. #4096. Drive this road three miles to the trailhead (2,800 feet; *map, p. 122*). The old road is blocked beyond this point. Expect steep and rough sections on the drive in, as well as good views about two miles up of, right to left, Mt. Pugh (due north), White Chuck, Forgotten, Stillaguamish, Vesper, Sperry (to the southwest), and Morning Star Peaks. The trail climbs moderately from the start and steepens higher up. Expect mud, rocks, windfall, and brush in places.

The first 1.5 mile is in pleasant old-growth forest, with some open areas, before crossing Bedal Creek on logs and rocks. In another

half-mile or so, the trail becomes a dry creek bed for a short distance, then runs close to Bedal Creek again. Cross, or not, depending on conditions. Remember this section for the return. There can be some old avalanche

Sloan Peak

Monte Cristo Peaks from the ridge above Bedal Basin

snow and debris to negotiate here as well. Heading up the creek, the immense rock wall of Sloan Peak looms ahead. Cascading tumults add to the scene in mid-summer. As you reach what starts to feel like the head of the creek, step up and right onto boulders and a good view of Bedal Basin (about 5,000 feet). Several route variations are feasible. Either drop down to Bedal's cabin below, or continue up a wooded ridge to more openings with views of Mt. Baker, Three Fingers, Whitehorse, Bedal (north), Sloan, and the Monte Cristo Peaks (south), as well as the Sauk River valley below. Keep an eye trained for mountain goats as well. Retrace your steps for the return (dry creek bed will be on the left). There were a number of trees across this trail in 1997.

62. Elliot Creek & Goat Lake

Distance: 9.0 miles roundtrip   Time: Allow 5 - 7 hours

Elevation gain: 1,300 feet   Season: June - October

The five-mile hike up Elliot Creek to Goat Lake can sometimes be done as late as November and is often snow-free by June, making it a good early-summer hike when many other mountain trails are still buried. The downside is it's popular all summer and into the fall. Pick a weekday or an imperfect weekend to better avoid the crowds. It seems hard to fathom, but in the 1890s an eight-mile puncheon wagon road from Monte Cristo to the lake was constructed via Elliot Creek (old puncheon is still visible near Mt. Loop Highway). A number of cabins, a hotel, and other buildings existed near the lake's outlet, most of which have been destroyed by fire.

About 3.5 miles north of Barlow Pass on the Mountain Loop Highway, turn east on USFS Rd. #4080 (MP 16.8) and drive 1.2 miles

to the trailhead (limited parking; 1,900 feet). The hike is straight-forward, initially passing through young alder and hemlock on easy grades. The major portion of the current trail follows an old logging road instead of the original wagon road and soggy path next to the creek. The tread is in good shape with nice views along the way. Huge cedar trees stand near the Henry M. Jackson Wilderness boundary about four miles from the start. The old trail merged with the current path about a half-mile below this point. The last half-mile to Goat Lake steepens to switchbacks where McIntosh Falls makes a headlong tumble to the right.

At the lake (3,200 feet) one can wander the lakeshore toward a waterfall (gets brushy) while watching for jumpers (trout), or gaze up-basin toward snowy Ida Pass and Cadet Peak for signs of the determined prospectors who roamed these craggy mountains in search of the mother lode. An old road/trail along the northeast shore linked the mining "town" near the lake outlet with the basin above the lake, and more trails led to Ida Pass and the Foggy Mine near the base of Cadet Peak, 1,500 feet above the lake. The extensive mining bustle that occurred here a century ago is really hard to fathom.

*Goat Lake and
Cadet Peak*

63. Barlow Point

Distance: 2.2 miles roundtrip
Elevation gain: 900 feet

Time: Allow 2 - 3 hours
Season: June - November

At the headwaters of the Sauk and Stillaguamish Rivers near
Barlow Pass, a low ridge with a rocky top affords good views
of the upper basins of both watersheds. Depending on snow conditions, the Barlow Point Trail can open by mid-spring and makes a
nice early season jaunt when higher trails are snowbound. Although
it's just one long mile to the top, expect a steep workout with plenty
of switchbacks. Barlow Point is also a good place for a summer sunrise (or set). There is no water on this trail. From Granite Falls head
east on Mountain Loop Highway thirty miles to MP 30.5 and park
up the hill on the left just before the pass (2,400 feet; *map, p. 126*).

The trail leaves the north side of the parking area and bounces
up and down through woods, over a rocky hump, then downward
beneath several large rock outcrops. Just past a clearing the trail
splits. Left drops 50 yards to the old Monte Cristo Railroad grade.
Stay right for Barlow Point. At another junction close by (0.3 mile
from the start), a left follows the hardly used Old Government Trail
leading back down the valley, meeting the highway near the Sunrise Mine Rd. Instead, go right and climb to the ridge crest in 0.3
mile more. Continue up to more switchbacks with an occasional
glimpse of Sheep Mountain to the southeast. Finally, the top arrives
about 1.1 mile from the start (3,300 feet). Trees prevent a full panorama, but views are excellent nonetheless. To the west Big Four
and Hall Peak are dramatic above the South Fork Stilly. Twin Peaks

and Mt. Dickerman are to
the north and northwest, the
South Fork Sauk valley extends northeast toward Mt.
Pugh, and Sheep Mt. stands
close by to the southeast.
Drop-offs along the crest
deserve some respect.

Sheep Mt. from Barlow Point

64. Monte Cristo & Glacier Basin

Distance: 8.5 - 14.0 miles roundtrip
Elevation gain: 400 - 2,300 feet

Time: Allow 4 - 10 hours
Season: June - October

The popular hike to the old mining townsite of Monte Cristo east of Granite Falls follows an old road along the South Fork Sauk River and is an easy four-mile stroll, except for two potentially tricky river crossings on collapsed bridges. The longer hike past Glacier Falls and up into Glacier Basin, two miles beyond the townsite, is real work with a hard, steep section near the end that may not be total fun for everyone. The historic townsite was developed in the 1890s after a promising discovery of rich gold ore high on the ridge southwest of Glacier Basin. Millions of dollars were invested in mines, trams, a railroad, and infrastructure for a small city of 2,000

people in this wild and remote setting, yet the effort never broke even and was largely abandoned in 1907. The townsite is a fine destination by itself, but for the bigger scenic payoff you'll have to trudge up to Glacier Falls or Glacier Basin (may still be under snow in June).

From Granite Falls head east on the Mountain Loop Highway about 30 miles to Barlow Pass (2,400 feet) and park near the end of the pavement. Walk the obvious gated road leading to Monte Cristo. Cars are banned, but bikes are okay. After

Glacier Basin

the first mile reach the old river bridge that has seemingly been collapsing, slow-motion-like, since a big flood in 1980. It's been patched and repatched and was barely passable to foot traffic in 1997. Watch your step crossing, and continue upriver on a pleasant woodsy road. Bypass a washout, then finally reach another newly collapsed bridge at the edge of the townsite, just over four miles from Barlow Pass. This bridge also could be trouble due to severe damage from heavy snow and flooding in 1996-97. There are private cabins and a lot of recreation interest in the area, as well as the U.S. Forest Service and the non-profit Monte Cristo Preservation Association to help look after the town. Hopefully, repairs will be made soon. Check with Verlot Public Service Center to be sure.

Cross the creek-sized river on the collapsed bridge if passable. (Note that the old trail continued up-valley from the campground road and crossed Glacier Creek on a bridge higher up. This bridge

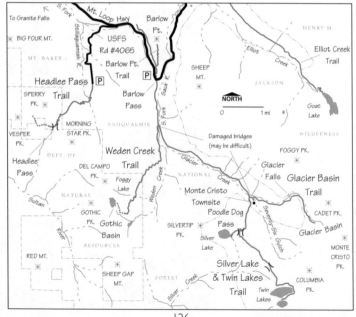

was destroyed by a major spring avalanche a few years ago and now requires a ford.) Pass the Silver Lake Trail junction (*see Hike #65*) and wander into "town" where several historic cabins, a railroad turntable, and the site of an old lodge surround a grassy clearing (2,800 feet). The lodge operated until it burned in 1983. Cross Seventy-Six Creek on a good footbridge (left) and follow Dumas St. past Peabody's Garage and Kyes Memorial (a WWII Navy commander who, as a boy, planted this tree in front of the Royal Hotel). At a four-way junction go straight (right passes the sites of a schoolhouse, assay office, hotel, and blacksmith shop on the way to Sunday Falls which is beyond another collapsed bridge and a bit hard to reach; a left at the junction goes to the site of the large Boston-American Concentrator that prepared the mined ore for shipment to a smelter in Everett). In its heyday Monte Cristo supported at least five hotels, three saloons, a newspaper, and the railroad. Most miners, amazingly, lived on the higher slopes close to the mines.

The main trail merges with the old Mine-to-Market Road and continues to the brink of an eroding slope above the creek with good views of surrounding peaks, Glacier Falls, and other waterfalls up-valley—the lacy and thundering ones are most impressive early season. Either turn around here or head for the basin 1.5 miles beyond. The trail climbs straight up the mountainside just right of the falls and enters the Henry M. Jackson Wilderness. Pass a rock outcrop next to crashing water then keep climbing the steep bedrock path (tougher coming back down) until the trail finally eases off at Mystery Ridge and the entrance to the basin (4,500 feet). The creek meanders peacefully through fragile meadows. Look for the old mine "road," cables, clutter, and waterlines upslope in talus that lead toward the main part of the basin, before rejoining a path near the creek. Keep wandering all the way up Ray's Knoll to admire Monte Cristo Peak rising from the head of the valley. Cadet Peak is to the northeast, and the huge maze of rock walls and towers known as Wilmans Peaks and Spires is to the south and west. The highest mine in the area—the 3,000-foot long Comet Mine—was 1,000 feet up this ridge, although it too has collapsed.

65. Poodle Dog Pass, Silver & Twin Lakes

Distance: 12.5 - 18.0 miles roundtrip   Time: Allow 7 - 12 hours
Elevation gain: 1,600 - 3,400 feet   Season: July - October

The steep trail to Poodle Dog Pass begins at the old mining town of Monte Cristo east of Granite Falls and climbs two miles to the subalpine meadows around Silver Lake (*see Hike #64 for directions to the townsite; map, p. 126*). For backpackers and marathon dayhikers, a continuation to Twin Lakes adds another 5.5 miles roundtrip and 2,000 feet of climbing (in and out), although you can trim more than a mile and cut a third of the elevation gain by zipping over for the view and not dropping down to these latter lakes. Silver Lake, on the other hand, is an easy walk from the pass.

Cross the uppermost reach of the South Fork Sauk River just as you enter Monte Cristo (bridge may be out; a crossing is probably doable, but check with Verlot Public Service Center to be sure), and find the trail junction close by (2,800 feet). The rough, steep, rocky, rooty trail quickly sets aim for Poodle Dog Pass 1.8 miles ahead. Ignore spur trails and stay on the most traveled track. Scrubby forest is quickly replaced by more mature trees with lots of openings and good views of Foggy and Cadet Peaks and Addison Ridge. At the end of an old section of mine road, enter the Henry M. Jackson Wilderness and continue steep climbing to Poodle Dog Pass (4,400 feet). The name is one given by early prospectors to the furry marmots commonly seen here and throughout the western slopes of the North Cascades. (Incidentally, the trail to Poodle Dog Pass is slated for reconstruction in the late 1990s.) Silver Lake is an easy quarter-mile walk to the west. The pretty lake is enclosed in the meadowed arms of Silvertip Peak rising 1,800 feet above the shore. Supposedly, the gold rush of Monte Cristo began near this peak in 1889 when Peabody and Pearsall spotted iron-rich deposits on Wilmans Spires two miles to the east. From the lake an old trail once descended Silver Creek to more old mining claims, Mineral City, and the road to Index and U.S. Hwy. 2.

If the snow is mostly gone and a longer hike beckons, head up from the pass on a generally good trail through woods and meadow,

Columbia Peak from the trail to Twin Lakes

climbing to the crest in less than half a mile with more good views that get better as you go. The trail traverses open slopes then descends to bypass a large rock face before climbing a short distance to woodsy Wilmans Pass. Follow the trail to the next rocky hump on the ridge for an excellent panorama, 1.5 mile from Poodle Dog Pass. Seventy-Six Gulch, spectacular Wilmans Spires, and Columbia Peak (the close one) and its waterfalls dominate the view. Sheep Gap Mt. and the Crested Buttes scratch the sky to the west. Ahead, lingering snow fields may prevent safe passage without an ice axe until mid-July or later. Expect minor rock scrambling as the route runs the ridge another half-mile then ducks right around the high point to reach a fantasmical view of Twin Lakes set in Columbia Peak's huge western cirque (5,400 feet). Lovely mountain hemlock trees frame the view. An interesting isthmus separates the two lakes. It's less than a mile but almost 700 feet down to the lakes from here, which is a tad more than most sane hikers would be apt to try in a dayhike from Barlow Pass.

66. Weden Creek & Gothic Basin

Distance: 11.0 - 13.0 miles roundtrip   Time: Allow 7 - 10 hours
Elevation gain: 2,600 - 3,300 feet   Season: Mid-July - October

With all the great trails and spectacular mountains clustered around the headwaters of the South Fork Sauk and South Fork Stillaguamish Rivers, one might think there would be at least one easy route to the alpine zone. If there is, the old miners' trail to Gothic Basin isn't it. Stronger hikers can make a reasonable day of it, but anticipate a longish climb on steep trail to the little lakes, tarns, meadows, and rocky terrain that beautify the basin. The lower half of the trail is in National Forest, but the upper half traverses land managed by the Washington Department of Natural Resources (DNR) as the Morning Star Natural Resources Conservation Area. In fact, 6,610-foot Del Campo Peak at the head of the basin, and one of the region's most striking and dominant summits, is within this NRCA—representing the highest point of state land in Snohomish County.

The trail is reached from Barlow Pass and the old road to Monte Cristo (*map, p. 126*). Park near the pass, about thirty miles east of Granite Falls on the Mountain Loop Highway. Walk the gated road about a mile to the collapsed bridge over the South Fork Sauk. The Weden Creek Trail is on the right just before the bridge. The first mile of trail is easy, but possibly crummy and mud-slathered early summer (the slather was slated for repair with reconstruction of the lower section in 1998). The trail crosses an unnamed creek and heads steeply up a ridge west of Weden Creek, then traverses, skipping over several plunging streams with waterfalls and mountain views— and possible snow bridges, avalanche danger, and high runoff early season. Gain 2,500 feet in three miles to rocky meadows and the first little lakes and tarns (5,000 feet). The twin summits of Sheep Gap Mt. rise to the south.

Either hang out at the tarns, wander the ice-carved rocks, or head northward over a rise about 0.3 mile to fishless Foggy Lake (also known as Crater Lake), an icy jewel beneath Del Campo Peak. The lake often holds ice into September, sometimes all year. From near

Three Fingers and Whitehorse Mt. from Gothic Peak

the outlet it's possible to hike/scramble up the rocky slopes of Gothic Peak for a great view from the ridge crest (for climbers the summit is a short class 3 scramble from here). Tin Cup Lake is the little puddle east of Foggy. A few old inconspicuous mine shafts and adits and other traces of the area's mining history are visible south of the tarns and along the trail. O. N. Weedin, from whence the name comes, apparently got in a land fight with three settlers on the upper Sauk River, and killed them.

67. Headlee Pass

Distance: 4.8 - 6.0 miles roundtrip   Time: Allow 4 - 7 hours
Elevation gain: 2,300 - 2,600 feet   Season: July - October

If steep and scenic suits your wilderness hankerings, an ascent of the old miners' trail to Headlee Pass and beyond may be a perfect candidate. Views are great from the start and only get better with elevation. And the elevation comes quick. After an easier first half-mile, expect a 2,500-foot climb in less than two miles more to the pass. But steep is good in this instance, or this would be a much more popular place. (Experienced climbers can also look forward to a Class 2 or 3 scramble up Vesper or Sperry Peaks; ice axe strongly recommended.) This trail is not a good choice for beginners.

The scenic trailhead is west of Barlow Pass at the end of the Sunrise Mine Rd. (USFS Rd. #4065). Leave the Mountain Loop Highway at MP 28.6 and drive Rd. #4065 2.2 miles to the parking area (2,400 feet; *map, p. 126*). To the south the layered slabs of Del Campo Peak rise up the valley beyond Morning Star Peak. Sperry Peak is the giant pyramid to the southwest. Follow the trail a short distance up a small creek and cross on a bridge. Cross another on rocks, then a bigger stream—the veritable South Fork Stillaguamish River—in a half-mile, which can be tricky or dangerous if the water's high (in August 1997, the footlog was lying lengthwise in the middle of the creek). Turn back if uncertain. Just before the "river" watch for a spur to the left leading to the collapsed Manley miner's cabin.

The path quickly enters open avalanche slopes and climbs several switchbacks before rounding a ridge to enter rocky Wirtz Basin between Sperry and Morning Star Peaks. There are forty switchbacks in the upper basin, many of them short and steep over loose rock. Just before the craggy wooded pass, named for prospector F. M. Headlee (4,700 feet), there is a glimpse of Glacier Peak to the northeast. Note that hard snow may persist in the chute below the pass into mid-summer, suggesting the need for an ice axe (and the skills to use it) even in July. Forget it if it's questionable. Take care not to dislodge rocks onto other hikers.

Beyond the pass, the route briefly traverses a wooded slope to steep, loose scree and talus. There are a couple of tricky spots, although the path is generally good here. Head westward to a little cascade (Vesper Creek) then northwest into a pretty snowy basin with a little icy lake between Sperry Peak (northeast) and Vesper Peak (southwest), less than a half-mile from the pass. From the cascade, a steep climbers' path ascends a meadowed ridge to Vesper's snowfields and bigger views. (Experienced climbers with an ice axe should be able to find their way up either peak without difficulty. There are sheer drop-offs at both summits. Avalanches can be a concern early season.) To see the Sunrise Mines, look across the valley from the east edge of the scree slope near Headlee Pass.

Steep swithbacks below Headlee Pass

68. Mount Dickerman

Distance: 8.6 miles roundtrip   Time: Allow 6 - 9 hours
Elevation gain: 3,700 feet   Season: July - October

Few trails lead to the summit of a mountain in the North Cascades of Snohomish County. However, the Mt. Dickerman Trail is, happily, one of them. And that suggests two things: one, great panoramic views, and two, a long haul up. With regard to the first, the views are indeed splendiferous, from Glacier Peak, Mt. Baker, Mt. Rainier, and the Olympics in the distance, to Stillaguamish Peak and Mt. Forgotten, neighbors to the north, Sloan and Bedal Peaks (right of Glacier Peak) to the east, the Monte Cristo peaks to the southeast, Del Campo and Morning Star Peaks to the south, Sperry and Vesper Peaks, Big Four, and Hall Peak to the southwest across the South Fork Stillaguamish River valley, and Three Fingers and Whitehorse to the northwest. Way down Dickerman's northwest

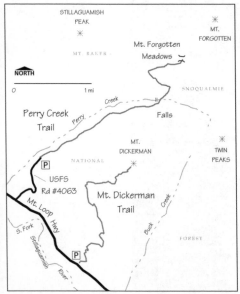

face—3,000 feet below—Perry Creek tumbles through its lush valley. With regard to the up part, there's definitely a lot of it. The trailhead, at 2,000 feet, is not 100 feet above the river, which puts the 5,723-foot summit 3,700 feet higher. Go early to beat the heat—and maybe the crowds. This is, needless to say, a popular place.

The trailhead and parking area are east of Granite Falls on the north side of the

Mountain Loop Highway just beyond MP 27. The trail immediately heads up through an attractive old forest of Douglas fir and western red cedar. The smaller trees attest to a big forest fire here early this century. Dozens of switchbacks and a couple miles later the route begins traversing northward past big cliffs and a tarn not so steeply, with views increasing exponentially with elevation, especially to the southwest. From the tarn at 4,500 feet, the trail wanders to ridge crest views, and bends east to climb through rock garden meadows of heather, huckleberry, and wildflowers. Good trail and maybe some lingering snow lead to the final summit hump and the 360-view. Volunteers made some significant trail improvements here in 1997. Note that water can be hard to come by later in summer.

Big Four Mt. from Mt. Dickerman Trail

69. Perry Cr. Falls/Mt. Forgotten Meadows

Distance: 3.8 - 8.0 miles roundtrip   Time: Allow 3 - 8 hours
Elevation gain: 1,100 - 2,900 feet   Season: June - October

By late spring the trail up Perry Creek may be snow-free and passable to Perry Creek Falls, as a half-year of winter relents and the low to mid-elevations of the Cascades begin to open up. The route to the meadows, however, will likely be under snow until July. Although a May or June hike to the falls has some appeal, serious avalanche danger can persist during these (and prior) months, particularly below the huge gullies coming off Mt. Dickerman. Otherwise, the trail can be rough, brushy in spots, but is generally easy to follow. Unique plant communities make the area particularly sensitive to disturbance. To ensure its protection and to further ongoing scientific study in the valley, the Forest Service established a Research Natural Area at Perry Creek in 1997.

The trailhead (2,100 feet) and a skinny parking area are a mile up the Perry Creek Rd. (USFS Rd. #4063) which heads north from the Mountain Loop Highway at MP 26.3 east of Granite Falls. Stay left at a fork in 0.6 mile (*map, p. 134*). Big Four Mt. is visible downvalley. The trail drops slightly at first, then quickly enters open slopes and abundant fern gardens with great views of the northwest face of Mt. Dickerman (*see Hike #68*). The peak rises abruptly out of the valley across the South Fork of the Stillaguamish River. High waterfalls tumble down big rock walls, especially in spring and early summer. Stillaguamish Peak rises above the north side of the valley. Look for a variety of ferns, wild ginger, trillium, meadow rue, fringe cup, and miner's lettuce among the wild bouquets of the lower valley.

Perry Creek Falls (3,200 feet) is reached at just under two miles from the start, a good place to relax or turn back early in the season (privy and campsites nearby). Or, continue up more steeply through old-growth forest and switchbacks another 1.7 miles until the first high meadow is finally encountered just below the crest of a ridge (5,000 feet). The views of snowy peaks and rocky summits are excellent — and so are the blueberries which should be pickable by mid-

Montane residents, more often hanging out in the woods

summer. The ridge is the official end of the hikers trail, although a climber's path continues up the nicely meadowed south and southeast flanks of Mt. Forgotten close by, with views of Glacier Peak between Sloan Peak (right) and Mt. Pugh (left). Steep snow and rock make the final ascent of the 6,005-foot peak something better reserved for experienced mountaineers (a non-technical ascent is feasible). From the end of the hiking trail, another wandering track heads west toward Stillaguamish Peak a mile and a half away.

Tiger lilies

70. Big Four Ice Caves

Distance: 0.5 - 2.5 miles roundtrip   Time: Allow 1 - 2 hours
Elevation gain: 0 - 200 feet   Season: May - December

One of the more spectacular views of jagged peaks in the North Cascades is at the new viewpoint and trailhead for the Big Four Ice Caves. High snowfields, awesome cliffs, and waterfalls produce a dramatic scene entirely visible from the trailhead, and even more amazing near the ice cave viewpoint a mile away. The caves are melting tunnels beneath snow and ice that accumulate when winter snows avalanche down a major gully and pile up at the base of the mountain. Portions of walls and ceilings, literally tons of ice, collapse routinely from spring through fall, thus the wise warnings not to enter. Avalanches are a serious matter in winter and spring, keeping the upper part of the trail closed until things settle down a bit, usually by May or June.

From Mountain Loop Highway east of Granite Falls, turn right into the big new parking lot at MP 26 (1,700 feet; *map, p. 140*). Either take the boardwalk trail (left of the restrooms) through woods toward the South Fork Stilly bridge (0.3 mile), or follow the connector

trail above wetlands to the old parking lot, a sunny picnic area, great views of the mountain, and the site of the former Big Four Inn which burned in 1949 (next to a 9-hole golf course—it's gone too, of course). Here, a paved path and boardwalk also goes to the river bridge (0.3 mile), passing a junction with the first boardwalk just before the Stilly. Both routes are barrier-free and together they form a pleasant nature loop suitable for almost everyone.

From the bridge it's another 0.7 mile and a 200-foot elevation gain to

Big Four Mt. from the trailhead

the ice caves viewpoint in a clearing near the base of the cliffs. Some years the caves may be buried in snow into July. The ice was called "Rucker's Glacier" at one time and may be the lowest perennial ice in the Cascades. Be aware at all times of falling snow, ice, and rock from above. The unusual circumstances that have created this unique place have also produced unique and sensitive plant communities. Don't (need we say?) pick or trample the flowers.

71. Coal Lake & Pass Lake

Distance: 0.5 - 1.5 miles roundtrip   Time: Allow 1 - 2 hours
Elevation gain: 0 - 300 feet   Season: June - October

When all you need is a quick dip in a cool mountain lake a stone's throw from the car, Coal Lake is a pretty reasonable choice, but expect to bump elbows with fellow lake-lovers on nice summer weekends. Weekdays or off-season will give you more room to thrash. If the lake is busy look for peace and serenity at Pass Lake, shallow, inviting, still a short walk, and accessed from the same parking lot. From Mountain Loop Highway east of Granite Falls turn north onto the Coal Lake Rd. (USFS Rd. #4060) just before the new entrance to Big Four Ice Caves (MP 26). Drive this road 4.5 miles to the parking area on the left (3,400 feet; *map, p. 140*). Several short paths across the road lead to Coal Lake and the narrow valley that contains it. The area is heavily used. For a bit of privacy try the talus on the north shore or paddle, row, or swim up-lake as desired.

Walk up the road 0.1 mile to find the Pass Lake Trail on the right. After 0.3 mile of moderate climbing in woods, skirt right of a pretty meadow, then rise briefly to the lakeshore beyond. The unmaintained trail continues and descends to North Fork Falls Creek (brushy).

Pass Lake

72. Independence Lake & North Lake

Distance: 1.5 - 8.0 miles roundtrip   Time: Allow 2 - 8 hours
Elevation gain: 300 - 2,300 feet   Season: July - October

The hike to Independence Lake is an easy one, and at 0.7 mile each way it's unsurprisingly popular too, despite some ups and downs on the way. North Lake, on the other hand, is a grind, requiring a steep climb of 1,200 feet beyond Independence Lake followed by a drop of nearly 800 feet to the seldom visited lakeshore. Views are excellent and the hike is worthwhile even without descending all the way to North Lake. A lake-sized tarn (not shown on some maps) and many small pools add some pizzazz to the trek. If you're lucky, you might see an osprey take a fish from one of the larger lakes. Listen for its high-pitched chittering. Volunteers made some nice improvements to the lower trail in 1996-97.

The trailhead is at the end of Coal Lake Rd. (3,600 feet), 0.3 mile beyond the Coal Lake parking lot (*see Hike #71 for directions*). The path climbs out of the old 1961 clearcut past monkey flowers, pearly everlasting, grass of Parnassus, foamflower, fireweed, and cow parsnip. The way soon enters old-growth forest, then descends on a moderate grade over the next quarter-mile, before regaining the elevation lost, plus 100 feet or so. A big rock wall east of the lake comes into view just before the lake does. The trail crosses the outlet stream and passes above the west shore, then descends to a lovely meadow at the north end about a mile from the trailhead (good campsites in woods, privy nearby). Here the trail heads right to steep switchbacks through trees and flowery avalanche slopes, climbing 1,200 feet in the next 1.2 miles. After a brief descent to a small clearing the path climbs to a crest with a view. Walk left a few yards for a look, but to continue go right 0.1 mile to an inconspicuous junction just past a little tarn. The North Lake trail heads left up a small rockslide (yellow paint marks the spot), or go straight another 0.1 mile to pass between two lovely tarns, the larger of which is highly swimmable by mid-summer. There are good views of Whitehorse Mt., Three Fingers, and Devil's Thumb nearby.

Heading up from the rockslide junction, enter woods again and cross a saddle (4,900 feet) in another 0.1 mile, with views of North Lake and Glacier Peak not far beyond. White Chuck Mt. and Mt. Pugh (just left of Glacier Peak) are also prominent. The trail to this modest-sized lake descends almost 800 feet in a long, circuitous mile in meadows, rock slabs, and trees. The route goes well left, then right, passing numerous tarns, pools, and good campsites on the descent. One could hike down 0.2 mile for a better view of the lake and stop there, avoiding the long climb back to the ridge.

Independence Lake

73. Deer Creek Pass & Kelcema Lake

Distance: 1.0 - 2.2 miles roundtrip   Time: Allow 1 - 2 hours
Elevation gain: 0 - 300 feet   Season: June - November

A short walk to a pretty mountain lake, this one too sees a lot of use since it's so easy to get to. The trail seems like a good candidate for reconstruction to a barrier-free standard so that the less mobile among us might be able to enjoy the experience. That would probably increase use somewhat, but the payoff for kids, seniors and others may be worth the cost. For now, we can settle for a mostly good trail with some rough spots and a little mud. From MP 23.4 on the Mountain Loop Highway, east of Granite Falls, turn north on the Deer Creek Rd. Beyond, the highway is often closed and under snow in winter; the large parking area accommodates skiers and snowmobilers (the latter are banned from Deer Creek Rd. in winter to protect wildlife). To reach Kelcema Lake, drive the Deer Creek Rd. 4.2 miles to the trailhead and parking area on the left. Walk the easy trail less than a half-mile to a big campsite that's obviously too close to the lakeshore. Wander left to a log jam and a nice view, then go right along the shore to a giant boulder with a scrabble path up the backside. This perch makes a good destination, with deep water for a swim close by. Expect lots of company on sunny weekends.

From the same trailhead, wander up the road fifty feet to the Deer Creek Pass trail on the left. This old unmaintained trail climbs through minor brush to slightly better trail in the woods above. Reach the wooded pass in about 0.6 mile. Contour around to a west-facing avalanche slope and a good view of Three Fingers, Big Bear, and

Liberty Mts. Poke around the trees some to find a view of Whitehorse Mt. right of Three Fingers. The trail continues down and northward a short mile to the Clear Creek logging road, though not quite worth the trouble.

Kelcema Lake

142

74. Bald Mountain & Cutthroat Lakes

Distance: 7.0 - 15.0 miles roundtrip   Time: Allow 4 - 10 hours

Elevation gain: 1,100 - 3,000 feet   Season: June - October

Impressive views from the summit ridge of Bald Mt. and the enchanted meadows around Cutthroat Lakes are main attractions of this moderate hike into the state-owned highlands between the South Fork Stilly and Spada Lake. Part of the Mt. Pilchuck Natural Resources Conservation Area, the mountain is a rugged six-mile ridge that divides the Stilly from the Sultan River. Just east of the mountain's middle, a craggy granite summit rises to 4,851 feet near Cutthroat Lakes. Three trailheads allow access from the east, west, and north, creating several options for moderate to strenuous dayhikes or overnight treks. The east trailhead (3,000 feet) is above Williamson Creek at the head of Spada Lake (*see Park #55 for directions*). This trail begins on an old road and climbs 1,500 feet in 3.5 miles to meadows and a junction near the summit (see below). However, to visit the lakes—and a veritable galaxy of tarns and pools

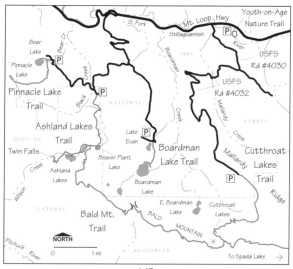

that surround them—head for the new '"Walt Bailey Trail" at Mallardy Ridge. Then either hike up and back for a seven to ten-mile roundtrip, or spot a car at the Ashland Lakes Trailhead (*see Hike #76*) for a classy, one-way, 15-mile trek.

To reach the trailhead, head east from Granite Falls on the Mountain Loop Highway to MP 18.1 and turn right on USFS Rd. #4030, just west of the South Fork Stilly bridge. Follow this one-lane paved road 1.3 miles and turn right on USFS Rd. #4032 (pavement ends here). The trailhead is 5.7 miles ahead at the end of the road, but since there is very little room to park or turn-around, it's easier to stop at a shoulder parking area 0.1 mile from the road end (3,200 feet). There's more parking and a good view of Mt. Pilchuck about 0.8 mile back down the road. The trail climbs the bank and soon enters old-growth forest, then a few small meadows. Pass a much larger meadow at the foot of Bald Mt. before crossing a narrow, pretty brook at 1.6 miles. Although the trail tread is sometimes good and sometimes not due to slippery roots and occasional mud holes, the quality of the work that's been done to improve this trail is excellent. Much progress has been made to upgrade the worst parts and it will surely get better over time. Kudos to CCC-veteran Walt Bailey and other volunteers for all the good work that's been done.

Some minor ups and downs lead to an open basin and meadowy talus with a waterfall close by. The trail reenters forest at two miles, climbs to another broad flat, then switchbacks up more talus and woods to big subalpine meadows and the first tarn at three miles. There are views here of Big Four Mt. and Sperry Peak. Reach a much larger tarn just ahead then several more beyond, each one seemingly prettier than the last. Pass above lower Cutthroat Lake, then cross the cascading outlet of the upper lake at 3.4 miles (4,200 feet). Spur trails leads to a number of excellent campsites. Either relax near the lake, take a dip, and head back from here, or wander the meadows around the upper lake. Note some local landmarks—like this lake's small rock island and peninsula, each with a single tree, and the summit crag of Bald Mt. to the south—to lessen the odds of ending up somewhere down Boardman Creek, discouraged and/or lost. The main trail runs along the south shore of the lake and climbs in trees and meadow, with views of Three Fingers and

Whitehorse Mt. to the north, to a hidden junction with the official Bald Mt. Trail at 4.0 miles. If you miss the junction, you'll cross the ridge in another 0.1 mile and begin descending to the Spada Lake trailhead. When you find the junction, take this less-used path down slightly then across gentle rocky meadows 0.2 mile to the ridge crest south of the summit crag. There's an amazing view here of Spada Lake, Mt. Rainier, and dozens of other peaks on the horizon.

For the longer trek to Ashland Lakes, keep walking. The next 0.5 mile of trail swings west around the summit and climbs to an even better view from a ridge leading directly up to the top. Everett, the Sound, and the Olympics are all visible. Experienced rock scramblers can follow a faint boot track and possible cairns up and right to an easy class 2-3 route to the summit (may be a loose block on top). The seldom-hiked trail winds along the rocky-wooded crest of Bald Mt. for the next six miles with a few major ups and downs, and views of the lakes and tarns that characterize the region, and mountains beyond. The path finally descends 1,000 feet in two miles to the Ashland Lakes Trail, two miles from that trailhead (2,500 feet).

Tarn near Cutthroat Lakes

75. Boardman Lake & Lake Evan

Distance: 0.5 - 2.0 miles roundtrip   Time: Allow 1 - 3 hours
Elevation gain: 0 - 300 feet   Season: June - October

Lake Evan, while just a hundred easy yards from the parking lot, hardly counts as a hike, but the setting is pleasant and surely worth a visit. Via the same trail, the hike to Boardman Lake is still an easy trek for most of us, and is far more interesting. Not only is the lake more dramatic, but the forest walk getting there winds through beautiful old-growth Douglas fir, red cedar, western hemlock, and silver fir, all perfectly placed among huckleberries (usually pickable by August). Note that some years the area may be accessible in May. The hike can also be combined with Ashland or Bear and Pinnacle Lakes nearby (*see Hikes #76 & #77*).

From Mountain Loop Highway east of Granite Falls, turn right at MP 15.8 onto USFS Rd. #4020, signed for Ashland Lakes. Stay left at a fork in 2.7 miles and drive another 2.2 miles (some views) to the obvious trailhead just beyond a sharp bend (2,800 feet; *map, p. 143*).

The trail rounds the marshy shore of Lake Evan, climbs slightly through big trees, then eases off before climbing again to a low ridge north of Boardman Lake 0.7 mile from the start (3,000 feet). Descend to a little gravel beach and log jam at the lake's outlet which happens to be Boardman Creek. If the water isn't too high it should be easy to cross here, climb steps, and follow paths to nearby campsites or to a good resting perch along the rocky shore. The steep wall to the south rises to Bald Mountain (*see Hike #74*).

Lake Boardman

76. Ashland Lakes & Twin Falls

Distance: 5.8 - 10.4 miles roundtrip Time: Allow 2 - 6 hours
Elevation gain: 400 - 1,000 feet Season: May - October

I believe it was a dayhike with the Pilchuck Audubon Society in the late 1970s that introduced me to Ashland Lakes. The trail, including much boardwalk, was a relatively new facility built by the DNR and we were eager to see what was there. The lakes were quiet, mysterious, and thoroughly inviting, despite a morning of drizzle and mist permeating our raingear. In late 1997 the hike was still just as enjoyable, and true to form. The clouds and mist hung just as stubbornly as before from a dripping tarp sky. Then just as we were leaving, the clouds parted, confirming that a sunny day at Ashland Lakes is not, after all, impossible.

To reach the trailhead from Mountain Loop highway east of Granite Falls turn south onto USFS Rd. #4020 at MP 15.8. Stay right at a fork in 2.7 miles (USFS Rd. #4021), then left 1.4 miles beyond. The trail and parking area (2,400 feet) are 0.2 mile up this steep, bumpy road (*map, p. 143*). The trail follows an old logging road through second-growth forest and crosses Black Creek in the first half-mile. Stay left at a road junction (and former trailhead) and soon enter old-growth forest. The trail deviates from dirt to mud to single and double-plank boardwalk to log rounds to rock steps to whatever it takes to get a hiker through the woods on generally wet ground. Reconstruction is ongoing to fix up the bad spots, although most of the trail is quite walkable. Plan on a 400-foot elevation gain to the first lake, then easy grades to the next two.

At a junction about 1.8 mile from the start, head left 0.1 mile to Beaver Plant Lake (2,800 feet) and an entertaining half-mile board-walk that loops around the lake. Hop across the inlet and outlet streams on the far side. For some uncertain reason this is a fun lake to walk around. Scenic too. From the last junction, stay right 0.2 mile to reach a junction with the Bald Mt. Trail on the left. (This trail climbs about 1,000 feet in two miles to the top of a six-mile long ridge known as Bald Mt. More trail runs the length of the ridge and provides a link with the Walt Bailey Trail and Mallardy Ridge to the east; *see Hike #74 for details.*) For the lakes, keep right to reach another fork in 0.1 mile. The left fork leads around the south side of Upper Ashland Lake. The right fork is in better condition and runs along the north shore. The two rejoin at the west end of the lake in less than a half-mile. This is a good turn-around point for the shorter 5.8-mile hike. Or, continue on the main trail about 0.3 mile to one more junction. Left drops a short distance to Lower Ashland Lake and more boardwalk that runs along the west shore (an old abandoned trail, rough and overgrown, continues all the way around). Right at the junction drops about 1.6 miles to Twin Falls, a spectacular waterfall conveniently interrupted by a pool known as Twin Falls Lake (2,300 feet). The trail makes a steep descent of about 400 feet to the falls, elevation that must be regained on the way out.

Boardwalk trail, Beaver Plant Lake

77. Bear Lake & Pinnacle Lake

Distance: 0.6 - 4.2 miles roundtrip   Time: Allow 1 - 4 hours
Elevation gain: 100 - 1,200 feet   Season: May - October

The easy walk to Bear Lake is a good choice in spring when the higher trails are still snowbound, and in the fall when nature pencils in some color along the lakeshore. Like anywhere else in the Cascades, early to mid-summer can be buggy around the lakes. And if a 0.6-mile roundtrip adventure to Bear isn't quite the workout you had in mind, continue on to Pinnacle Lake, not quite two miles farther, but almost 1,100 feet higher. This lake usually needs more time to melt out in the spring than Bear Lake, but the latter's lower elevation means the trail to it can be snow-free in some years by April. The hike to these lakes can also be combined with an easy trek to Ashland Lakes or Evan and Boardman Lakes close by (*see Hikes #76 & #75*).

To find the lakes from Granite Falls, leave the Mountain Loop Highway at MP 15.8 and head south on USFS Rd. #4020. Stay right

Placid Bear Lake

at a fork in 2.7 miles (USFS Rd. #4021), and right again in 1.4 miles (Ashland Lakes Trailhead is to the left). Reach the trailhead near the road end 1.6 miles beyond (*maps, p. 143 & 152*). The trail climbs moderately then eases off as it winds through an attractive stand of old-growth hemlock and big cedars with gnarly tops. The trail to Bear Lake is well maintained. Reach a junction in about 0.2 mile and stay right to find the lake about 0.1 mile beyond. A rough fisher's path leads along the shore, but mud and brush make a circumnavigation unappealing. Horsetails and meadow patches rim the lake in soft layers of green.

A left at the junction leads to Pinnacle Lake, about 1.8 miles ahead. The tread worsens as the trail climbs to a ridge crest, passing a very large western hemlock tree before gaining a view of Bear Lake through the woods (on the right). As the grade lessens, water and mud make the going slightly cumbersome in places, but worth the effort. Patchy meadows appear and a large tarn with two rock islands is passed on the left where scattered boot tracks can confuse the route. The main trail heads down a draw to Pinnacle Lake only two hundred yards past the tarn. The lake is narrow and settled in a steep basin below the eastern ramparts of Mt. Pilchuck. Big boulders make good sundecks near the lake's outlet, and a cool cascade drops to another small tarn below.

Pinnacle Lake

78. Lake Twenty-Two

Distance: 5.5 miles roundtrip

Time: Allow 3 - 5 hours

Elevation gain: 1,400 feet

Season: May - November

A good early season hike in the North Cascades, the modest climb to Lake Twenty-Two is not unpopular. Big trees, lovely waterfalls, and nice views from the cliffy carved basin that holds the lake are the treats. The trail ends at the 2,400-foot level where winter snows usually vanish long before the higher alpine country has seriously begun to release its heavy snowpack. Probably best to go early in the year, even April if it's mild, when the falls are up and the crowds are down. In July, watch for marbled murrelets, a small-

ish seabird (a federally-listed threatened species) that nests in old-growth forests. The birds are sometimes visible from the lower trail.

From Granite Falls take Mountain Loop Highway to MP 13; the trailhead is to the right. The trail is an easy stroll the first half-mile, then begins to climb steadily, but moderately. Soon pass the first low falls on a footbridge. Big western red cedar trees are scattered up and down the hillside. Another falls, somewhat hid-

Puncheon, Lake 22 Trail

den from view, is passed but sheer cliffs make it difficult to get a good look at (an invitation to trouble for those who can't stand not seeing every square inch of every waterfall). More impressive waterfalls are passed higher up, about half-way to the lake. Savor an earful of water music, then continue the climb to Lake Twenty-Two, 2.7 miles from the start.

The steep cirque surrounding the lake is a half-mile deep, and just a mile east of the summit of Mount Pilchuck. The lake (it's deep too), the trail, and 790 acres of land that contain them comprise the Lake Twenty-Two Research Natural Area, established in 1947. A mere postage stamp in size by today's National Wilderness standards, it's a pretty big deal that an area like this was set aside a half-century ago just to keep it wild. By designating such areas, foresters could evaluate the effects of logging on a forest ecosystem. Imagine what the watershed might be like had we kept the experiment to 790 acres of logging, and left the rest wild. What a concept.

To help keep this natural area natural, camping and fires are not allowed.

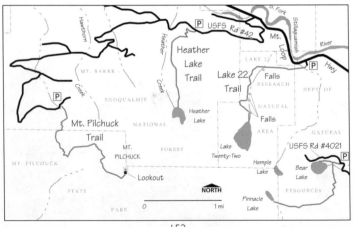

79. Heather Lake

Distance: 4.0 - 4.8 miles roundtrip Time: Allow 2 - 4 hours
Elevation gain: 1,000 feet Season: May - November

The hike to Heather Lake is only moderate, but the scenic payoff at trail's end is heavy-duty. The lake lies at the base of a deep cirque carved from the north face of Mt. Pilchuck by a glacier that only "recently" disappeared. The setting is remarkably comparable to that of Lake 22 (*see Hike #78*) and its deep cirque immediately east of Heather Lake. On a quiet day, big trees, high cliffs, snowfields, and streaming waterfalls are reflected in the cool still water. From the Mountain Loop Highway east of Granite Falls take the Mt. Pilchuck turnoff (USFS Rd. #42) at MP 12 and drive 1.4 miles to the trailhead (1,400 feet; *map, p. 152*).

The first half-mile is part of a recent reconstruction that bypasses the former start up an old logging road. Large cedar stumps suggest a magnificent stand of trees here not so long ago. The trail climbs moderately and rejoins the road briefly before the tread narrows and enters old-growth forest in about a mile (stay right at an apparent junction). Hike through overgrown talus on good trail, followed by a small cascade and rockier trail above. The final quarter-mile descends slightly through big trees, with Heather Creek close by, lamming noisily down the mountain. Cross footbridges to reach the lakeshore (2,400 feet), at two miles. In spring and early summer a dozen waterfalls tumble down the cliffs in a scene from a Chinese

painting. The USFS plans to construct a loop trail around the lake in 1998 (0.8 mile). Until that happens, one can wander the lakeshore with boulder-hopping and minor bushwhacking. A few campsites exist near the lake where snow sometimes lingers into early summer.

Heather Lake

80. Mount Pilchuck

Distance: 6.0 miles roundtrip
Elevation gain: 2,200 feet

Time: Allow 4 - 7 hours
Season: July - October

Of the hundreds of peaks in the North Cascades that are climbed each year, Mt. Pilchuck is one of the most popular, especially on decent summer weekends. A good trail and a short easy rock scramble (optional) near the top make the ascent feasible for almost anyone in average or better shape. The old fire lookout up top, one of only a few that remain in the state, was restored in the late 1980s by the Everett Mountaineers in cooperation with Washington State Parks. Oddly enough, Mt. Pilchuck is not on federal land like most peaks in the Northwest, but is part of Mt. Pilchuck State Park which supported a small downhill ski area from 1957 to 1980. A small picnicking and tent camping area exists just above the trailhead.

To bag the summit of this prominent peak (highly conspicuous from the west county area), wait for the weather to clear and the snowpack to recede then drive east from Granite Falls on the Mountain Loop Highway. The peak is quite visible near Robe, and with a sharp eye you can see the lookout on the summit. Turn right on the Mt. Pilchuck Road (USFS Rd. #42) at MP 12. Follow this road seven miles to the wide parking area and viewpoint at 3,100 feet (*map, p. 152*); the last two miles are paved. The trail was under reconstruction in 1997, including relocation of about half the distance, plus a real trail to the summit bypassing the optional rock scramble. The work should be completed by late summer, 1998. Until it's finished, expect some rough, slippery, mucky, and/or clumsy sections. There is much rock after the first mile on good new trail. Old-growth forest gives way to a twenty year-old clearcut and views open up the second mile. The route becomes a mix of trail through granite rock gardens. Until the new trail is completed, easy scrambling leads past painted wolf prints marking the old way to the top (cute, but cairns are fine, thank you). Above timberline, lingering snow patches may require an ice-axe (and the skills to use it). A slip on firm snow can send even the most winsome biped careening into rocks or over cliffs, and the steeper snowfields can be an avalanche hazard early in the season. If you aren't sure don't chance it. And by all means, don't lose the trail. Finally, giant boulders and a short ladder take you to the summit lookout (5,324 feet). A fine interpretive exhibit gives a brief history of the place, while the views in all directions offer a raptor's insight into the North Cascades' magnificence.

Mt. Pilchuck summit lookout

81. Saddle Lake & Goat Flat

Distance: 5.0 - 14.0 miles roundtrip   Time: Allow 3 - 10 hours
Elevation gain: 700 - 3,800 feet   Season: July - October

The hike to Goat Flat, in the heart of the Boulder River Wilderness, is one of the region's more popular treks, and understandably so. The view across meadows and glacier to the three towering summits of Three Fingers Mt. is a true North Cascadian alpine scene. This locally famous mountain is widely visible from the western county and beyond, and along highways near Granite Falls and Darrington. Amazingly, a fire lookout was constructed on the higher south summit in the early 1930s. Before it was ever climbed, the top fifteen feet of the summit was blasted away by Harry Bedal and Harold Engles (*see Walk #42*) to accommodate the little building which has since been restored and maintained by the Everett Mountaineers. Unfortunately for some, an ascent to the lookout requires basic mountaineering skills, like sure proficiency with an ice axe. Still, there's plenty to look at from the meadows below — including many other people looking. Go mid-week to see less of them. Along the way, Saddle Lake and huckleberries are added incentives.

From Mountain Loop Highway east of Granite Falls, turn north at MP 7.1 on Green Mt. Rd. (USFS Rd. #41). Stay left at a fork in two miles (pavement ends) and continue 16 long miles to the signed

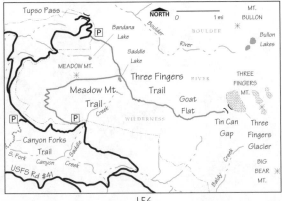

trailhead (3,100 feet) above Tupso Pass. From here it's an initially steep, then easier, but rocky, wet, and rooty, 2.5-mile climb to Saddle Lake (3,800 feet), with a peak at Three Fingers along the way. Just before passing the lake, an old unmaintained trail leads over Meadow Mt. about five miles west and south to a former Goat Flat trailhead (on USFS Rd. #41 near Saddle Creek, 11 miles from Mt. Loop Highway). No camping is allowed within 200 feet of the lake, and no fires beyond this point. Stay on the main trail as it climbs a ridge to meadows, tarns, huckleberries, and better views of Three Fingers. The big view from Goat Flat (5,000 feet) is at 4.8 miles. Big Bear and Liberty Mts. are to the southeast, the Boulder River descends to the northwest, and Mt. Baker cuts the sky forty miles north. The meadows are colorful summer and fall. Forty goats were spotted here in the summer of 1931. The path continues another 1.5 miles along the south side of Tin Can Ridge to a small saddle overlooking the glacier (5,700 feet). From this point, lingering steep snow requires an ice axe (and the skills to use it). For experienced climbers, the route generally continues along the ridge, sometimes on its north side, to easier terrain, followed by steep rock scrambling and a series of ladders going straight up to the lookout, precariously perched on the 6,854-foot south summit (1-2 hours from the saddle). There's a sheer drop of 2,000 feet out the east window. It's easy to dawdle at Goat Flat and beyond, so allow time to scoot back before dark.

82. Greider Lakes

Distance: 4.2 - 6.4 miles roundtrip Time: Allow 3 - 6 hours
Elevation gain: 1,300 - 2,100 feet Season: June - October

Of the few maintained trails in the Sultan River Basin, Greider Lakes is a good choice. While steep and a little rough in places (partially rebuilt in 1996), the two lakes it leads to offer fine scenic payoffs for the effort. A cliffy viewpoint high above Big Greider Lake adds an adventurous side trip — not recommended for younger kids or acrophobic others. The elevation of both lakes is just under 3,000 feet which suggests an earlier season than many other Cascade hikes; however, a large avalanche slope between the two lakes makes the going unadvisable when there's still much snow above.

Find the trailhead near the east end of Spada Lake northeast of Sultan (road is open only from late April to late October). From U.S. Hwy. 2, turn north on the Sultan Basin Rd. near MP 23, just east of the town of Sultan (big sign). Follow this about 13.5 miles to a fork in the road just past a registration pull-out where recreation users are invited to fill out a form. Note that the lake basin is closed at night, and no camping is allowed, except at backcountry sites near the lakes. Stay right at the fork and continue another seven miles to the obvious trailhead on the right (1,600 feet). The trail leads past a

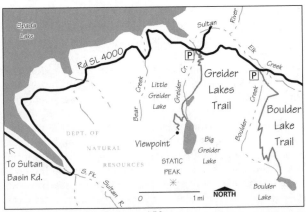

Little Greider Lake

rustic woodsy picnic area and a junction with short loop trail around a pond (comes out 100 yards up the road from the trailhead). A giant hemlock tree on the right makes a whale of a nurse-log exhibit — it most likely sprouted from a big rotten log centuries ago. Stay right and wander up increasingly steeper trail past a waterfall, some big trees, and a mostly obscured view of Spada Lake below.

After about three dozen switchbacks, the path tops a shoulder and levels out. Little Greider Lake is just beyond, two miles from the start (2,900 feet). The trail wanders past several campsites and crosses the outlet (Greider Creek) on a footbridge above a cool cascade. A good turn-around point for an easier trek. The path rounds the lake and crosses the broad avalanche slope before reentering woods near Big Greider Lake. Head left at a junction for the short descent to the lake (more campsites), a half-mile past Little Greider. Or, stay right for a steep 600-foot climb over 0.7 mile to the aforementioned precipitous viewpoint (3,600 feet). The unmaintained path can be tricky to follow in talus and brush; don't lose it. When you reach the larger talus in trees at the base of a big rock wall the trail skirts left below boulders and quickly emerges at the brink of a sheer drop-off overlooking Big Greider. Holy cow.

83. Bridal Veil Falls & Lake Serene

Distance: 4.2 - 8.0 miles roundtrip   Time: Allow 3 - 6 hours
Elevation gain: 1,000 - 1,900 feet   Season: May - October

The popular climb past Bridal Veil Falls to Lake Serene south of Index might have been the worst 'trail' listed in this guide. In fact, it's been known as more of a climbing route than a trail, requiring routefinding skills and scrambling on steep terrain. Despite the miserable way up through brush, logs, mud, rock, and roots, several beauteous waterfalls and a pretty lake in a rugged setting made it worth the grunt. The good news, however, is that a totally new trail was under construction in 1997-98 that will not only make the hike more humane, but dramatically reduce the damage to thin soils and vegetation occurring along the old route. The Forest Service expects the new trail, over a mile longer than before, to be open by summer or fall of 1998. Hikes will begin from a lower trailhead, not from a steep spur farther up the mountain—a good change.

To reach the trailhead, turn south off U.S. Hwy. 2 at MP 35.2 onto Mt. Index Rd., just before the bridge over the South Fork Skykomish River. Stay right in a quarter-mile and find the big parking area on the left just ahead (600 feet). Once the new trail is completed, the way should be obvious. The route will follow an old gated logging road, staying right at a fork, then continuing another mile, partly by way of an easement across private timber land, past a blocked road on the left (a former access). The new trail

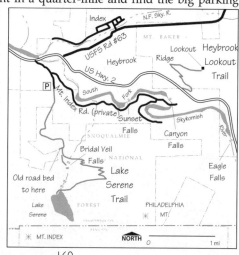

begins on the left shortly beyond this point. As for the old trail, it's thoroughly confusing and most likely closed so don't even bother. It ain't worth it.

The new trail will cross Bridal Veil Creek near the base of the falls less than two miles from the start. A 0.4 mile spur trail (planned for construction later in 1998) will climb to a higher viewpoint between the falls. From the creek, the main trail traverses steep, rocky slopes to the east and begins a long series of switchbacks and steps, climbing about 1,000 feet over the next mile, then bears westerly for the lake (2,500 feet), 3.6 miles from the trailhead. The lake can hold ice even in July, but the trail is generally snow-free by May. The massive rock walls and pinnacles of Mt. Index rise to the south and west. The lakeshore is fragile and somewhat abused, and res-

toration work is underway; no camping or fires allowed. The hike offers great views of waterfalls, nearby peaks, and the South Fork Skykomish River valley below, including Sunset Falls to the northeast. Heybrook Ridge and a decoration of high voltage transmission lines (*see Hike #46*) divide the South Fork from the North. Even without a good trail, Lake Serene has been a very popular place. To avoid the crowds, try going on a weekday or a not-so-sunny weekend.

Bridal Veil Falls

84. Barclay Lake

Distance: 4.0 - 7.6 miles roundtrip   Time: Allow 2 - 6 hours
Elevation gain: 300 - 1,700 feet   Season: May - October

One of the highest rock faces in the Cascade Range, the north wall of Mt. Baring rises an abrupt 3,000 feet above the south shore of Barclay Lake east of Index. The view, needless to say, is impressive, but so are the crowds on a sunny summer weekend when forty cars or more can jam the trailhead. Go super-early, or pick a weekday in cooler weather to avoid the throngs. Then expect a pleasant two-mile hike through mature forest to a placid mountain lake. A few western hemlock giants line the trail. In a setting like this it's easy to forget that much of the watershed has been hammered by clearcut logging.

From U.S. Hwy. 2 a few miles east of Index (MP 41.1) turn north onto USFS Road #6024 and drive just over four miles to the trailhead at the road end (2,200 feet). Mt. Baring is the big peak straight ahead; across the valley are Gunn and Merchant Peaks. The trail is gentle and in generally good shape all the way to the lake, and even a little enchanted with all the puncheon to walk between mossy rocks and slopes. At about 1.4 miles the way crosses Barclay Creek on a footlog

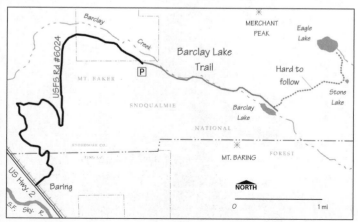

and reaches the west end of the lake at just under two miles (2,500 feet). The trail continues along the north shore another 0.3 mile, passing several campsites and wide open views of Mt. Baring. The face was climbed in 1960, but it took a tragedy to pull it off (several years earlier a climber fell while descending after an unsuccessful attempt). Later in summer, the water level drops to expose narrow beaches rimming the lake.

From near the east end of Barclay Lake, a rough unmaintained trail heads left and steeply up the mountainside to two other lakes 1,400 feet above. The rough path can be difficult to follow in places; after climbing through woods followed by a brushy talus slope, watch for a fork where the path seems to go up a gully, but stay right to find the trail in woods nearby. Tiny Stone Lake is just ahead, and Eagle Lake, set in a broad subalpine-like basin (extensive wetlands known as Paradise Meadow), is not far beyond, less than two miles from Barclay Lake. Mountain views are really no better here than at Barclay, but the lakes add a scenic extension for those looking to burn off a few more grams of breakfast.

Mt. Baring over Barclay Lake

85. Lake Elizabeth

Distance: 0.7 mile loop
Elevation gain: None

Time: Allow 1 hour
Season: May - November

The easy loop trail around Lake Elizabeth is not officially in Snohomish County, but is accessed from U.S. Hwy. 2 and a logging road a few miles east of Index. The little lake is somewhat isolated at the headwaters of Money Creek, in a narrow valley shared by headwaters of the Tolt River to the west. Oddly, the designated Tolt Watershed boundary splits the lake in two (according to the Mt. Si Green Trails™ map). The trail is generally suitable for kids and seniors, although it can be muddy in spots early or late season. It winds 0.7 mile through open forest and lush meadows bordering the lake. The drive in can be rough.

From U.S. Hwy. 2 at MP 45.9 turn south at the sign for Money Creek Campground, just before a tunnel. Continue past the campground, cross the railroad tracks, then go right onto USFS Rd. #6410 a mile from the highway. Immediately take another right on Rd.

#6420 (signed for Lake Elizabeth) and drive this about seven miles to the lake and trailhead on the right (2,900 feet). On the drive in there is a nice view of the high meadows and snowfields of Goat Basin just inside the Alpine Lakes Wilderness Area. A slide area about two miles short of the lake can be trouble early in the year if maintenance crews haven't made the rounds here yet. Expect rough road from here to the lake (possibly four-wheel-drive).

Lake Elizabeth

86. Blanca Lake

Distance: 8.0 - 11.0 miles roundtrip
Elevation gain: 3,300 - 4,000 feet

Time: Allow 6 - 10 hours
Season: July - October

Blanca Lake, the largest high-elevation lake in Snohomish County, and one of the North Cascades' most spectacular (and surreal), lies in a deep glacier-carved basin on the southern edge of the Monte Cristo Range. The chalky-green water contains the suspended dust of granite that is continually being carved away by the Columbia Glacier not far above the lake. The glacier is unique as well. Flanked by Columbia Peak on the west, Monte Cristo Peak to the northeast, and Kyes Peak to the east, it is nearly a mile long and a half-mile wide, which makes it exceptionally large for a south-facing glacier at this elevation and latitude. The hike to the lake, though strenuous, offers magnanimous views of big trees, water, rock, and ice.

To reach the trailhead, leave U.S. Hwy. 2 at the sign for Index (MP 35.7) and head north on the North Fork Rd. (USFS Rd. #63). Drive 15 miles to a fork; stay left on Rd. #63, then in two more miles stay left again to find the trailhead just up the hill (1,900 feet). The first half-mile follows good trail through an old clearcut, then steepens before entering old-growth forest with many large Douglas fir and western hemlock trees six feet or more in diameter. After three dozen switchbacks and a three-mile trudge, the trail enters the Henry M. Jackson Wilderness at the crest of a ridge. Glacier Peak is visible to the northeast. A slight descent leads past tiny Virgin Lake cupped in a saddle near 4,600 feet.

Blanca Lake is less than a mile farther but it's nearly 600 feet downhill on rougher trail. Nevertheless, this colorfully intriguing gem is well worth the descent and the steep climb

165

on the return. When the water isn't too high, one can cross a log jam at the lake outlet (Troublesome Creek) and follow a rough path along the west (left) shore of the lake. More adventurous hikers can scramble up the basin to a closer view of the Columbia Glacier and the peaks that cradle it. Travel on the glacier, of course, requires climbing gear and mountaineering skills. Waterfalls tumble into the basin. Note that routefinding can be tricky early season when the upper portions of the trail are under snow.

Blanca Lake

87. N. Fork Skykomish & W. Cady Ridge

Distance: 0.5 - 17.0 miles roundtrip   Time: Allow 1 - 12 hours
Elevation gain: 0 - 3,600 feet   Season: May - November

The trailhead near the end of the North Fork Skykomish Rd. north-east of Index offers a choice between three different trails, from easy to strenuous—from a short stroll in old-growth forest on a gentle trail, to a steep climb to alpine meadows above, and the option of a strenuous 17-mile loop. A 1.5-mile road walk (possibly four-wheel driveable) leads up to the former North Fork trailhead (3,000 feet) and several miles of mostly easy trail beyond. A moderate four-mile hike to Curry Gap and beyond leads along the Quartz Creek Trail and to Bald Eagle Mt. Or, an easy 0.3 mile walk to the river on the West Cady Ridge Trail, followed by three miles of steep trail, leads to four miles of great ridge walking and the long loop via Pass Creek. The latter offers the best views for the effort. All three are good old-growth forest hikes.

From U.S. Hwy. 2 at Index (MP 35.7) turn north up the North

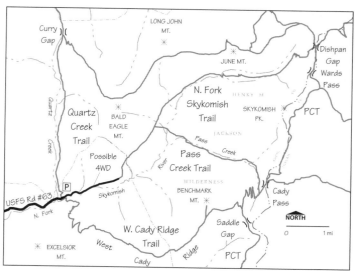

Fork Rd. (USFS Rd. #63), pass the bridge into town, and continue another 14 miles to a fork; stay left. The trailhead is 4.5 miles ahead (2,500 feet). Quartz Creek Trail heads left (north), quickly entering the Henry M. Jackson Wilderness Area, and climbs a moderate mile to a broad meadowy flat just above a noisy Quartz cascade. Turn around here for the easier walk, or continue as far as Curry Gap three miles ahead (3,900 feet). The Monte Cristo Peaks, close by to the west, are largely obscured by forest. An old trail drops from the gap (pass) to Cadet Creek, but the better option is to head right up Bald Eagle Mt. for views near the ridge crest a steep mile beyond.

Across the road from Quartz is the West Cady Ridge Trail, leading a flat quarter-mile to a stout footbridge over a scenic narrows in the North Fork. Beyond, the trail steepens and doesn't relent for over three miles, after forest gives way to wildflower meadows and vistas north and south. In 3.5 miles more, a good panorama is had from the 5,816-foot summit of Benchmark Mt. (stay left at a junction) also inside the Wilderness Area. From the junction, strong hikers could descend steep trail 1.5 miles to the east to the Pacific Crest Trail; turn left, then left again in 1.6 miles on the Pass Creek Trail,

and left again in about four miles on the North Fork Trail, 1.5 miles upstream of the road end. This strenuous loop is about 17 miles long, two-thirds of it in woods. West Cady is a popular horse trail, but has been well maintained after a rebuild in 1995.

As for the North Fork, it too quickly enters the Wilderness, and climbs to the PCT at Dishpan Gap (5,600 feet) in about 7.5 miles—but save the longer trek for an overnighter. Many fine loops are feasible.

North Fork Sky near the trailhead

88. Evergreen Mountain Lookout

Distance: 3.0 - 15.0 miles roundtrip　　Time: Allow 2 - 9 hours
Elevation gain: 1,300 - 3,000 feet　　Season: July - October

The trail to the newly refurbished Evergreen Mountain Lookout north of Skykomish is only 1.5 miles long but it's a steep 1,300-foot gain which makes it something more than a cakewalk for many of us. But that may be the easy part. The old road getting there is probably closed, adding six miles of additional walking both directions (and a 1,700-foot elevation gain). At the time of publication, the issue was in debate as competing interests argued over the monetary and environmental costs of keeping the road open or closed. A forest fire (1967), storm damage, logging, repair and maintenance costs, as well as potential overuse are among the testy issues being discussed. If the road reopens—or you don't mind the added miles—the view is certainly worth the trek. Check with the Skykomish Ranger Station for the latest scoop.

From U.S. Hwy. 2 just east of Skykomish (MP 49.3), turn north on the Beckler River Rd. (USFS Rd. #65) and drive this about eight miles to a junction at Jack Pass. Turn right on USFS Rd. #6550, then left in 1.1 miles on Rd. #6554 which, in late 1997, was closed at Evergreen Creek (2,600 feet). Walk (or drive) another six miles across burned and logged slopes and up a few switchbacks to the trailhead (4,300 feet). The hike is straight-forward, but steep, up through a clearcut, then woods, before reaching a saddle and viewy meadows. Continue up the ridge to the

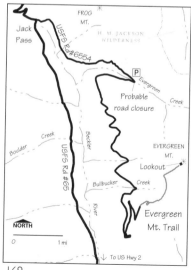

summit lookout at 5,587 feet. The view is excellent: the Monte Cristo peaks to the north, Glacier Peak to the north-northeast, the Cascade Crest to the east, Alpine Lakes Wilderness and Mt. Stuart to the south and southeast, Mt. Rainier and Beckler River to the south-southwest, and Mt. Baring, Townsend Mt., and Merchant and Gunn Peaks to the west-southwest. Go mid-week in late July and early August for less people and more flowers, including lush drifts of lupine, paintbrush, tiger lilies, asters, and valerian. Kudos to the volunteers who've helped to restore the lookout.

Sunset from Evergreen Mt.

89. Lakes Valhalla, Janus & the PCT

Distance: 5.5 - 8.0 miles roundtrip   Time: Allow 3 - 6 hours

Elevation gain: 800 - 1,300 feet   Season: July - October

The longest trail in the state, the Pacific Crest Trail (PCT), is also one of the hardest to get to locally. It does not cross a single road in Snohomish County, as it winds around Glacier Peak and along the Cascade Crest. In most areas, an overnight backpack is required to reach it. A number of spur trails, often eight miles or more in length, lead to the PCT from the east and west. To the north, the trail doesn't touch a road until High Bridge on the Stehekin River, twenty miles outside the county. However, the PCT does cross U.S. Hwy. 2 at Stevens Pass, and although the pass is a couple miles south of the county line, the gravel road up Smith Brook just east of the pass offers the easiest approach to Snohomish County's portion of the PCT. Here, a spur trail not quite a mile long, leads to the east county line at Union Gap, and the official crest of the North Cascades. While the Smith Brook trailhead might not be the ideal place to begin a multi-day backpack, it makes a great start for a dayhike.

Head east on U.S. Hwy. 2 to Stevens Pass, about 65 miles from Everett. Continue down the highway to a hidden left turn at MP 68.7, just beyond the point where the highway divides. Cross the westbound lanes *cautiously* to USFS Rd. #6700, then drive this road 3.4 miles to the trail on the left; shoulder parking only (4,200 feet). The trail climbs gently across open slopes (can be brushy in summer) then steepens in forest on the sub-one-mile trek to Union Gap and the PCT (4,700 feet). Right goes to Lake Janus; left to Lake Valhalla. It's a bit under 2.5 miles and a 700-foot descent (plus a slight gain) in woods and meadow on less than perfect trail to pretty Lake Janus. Either continue north on the PCT another two to five miles for good views from the crest, or for an easier option with impressive views, stay left at the gap for Lake Valhalla.

The trail to Valhalla is surprisingly flat much of the way, with occasional views of Nason Ridge (east), Smith Brook valley, and Lichtenberg Mt. (south). After 1.5 miles the trail rises gradually to a saddle (5,000 feet) and an excellent lake vista just beyond. The lake is an easy descent in 0.3 mile from the saddle. Just before the saddle, a narrow path leads northwest less than a half-mile up a meadowy ridge with abundant mountain ash and even better views, including Mt. Stuart (south-southeast) and the jagged summits of the Alpine Lakes Wilderness. It's feasible to continue to the summit of Mt. McCausland or to the ridge on the right for a good view of Glacier Peak to the north. From Lake Valhalla, one could also continue on the PCT for about five miles back to Stevens Pass, if a ride can be arranged. From the lake, the trail climbs over a low ridge then descends about 1,000 feet in the next two miles before a long easy stretch overlooking Stevens Creek and U.S. Hwy. 2.

Lake Valhalla

90. Cady Ridge & Dishpan Gap

Distance: 9.0 - 16.0 miles roundtrip   Time: Allow 7 - 12 hours

Elevation gain: 2,400 - 3,300 feet   Season: July - October

Some of the best high mountain scenery in the county is found along the Cascade crest, the natural divide that keeps western Washington west and eastern east. The Pacific Crest Trail (PCT) more or less follows this divide through the state, with the exception of a wide swing west around Glacier Peak. The area is beautifully remote—not a single road crosses the crest anywhere in Snohomish County (Stevens Pass is over the line in King County). As a result, hikes in the area are long, far from the urban masses, and generally better suited as overnighters. Nevertheless, several dayhikes are possible, including a 6.5-mile run up Cady Ridge from the Wenatchee River (*see also Hike #89*). There are also two options for longer loops via Cady Pass and the Little Wenatchee River. Note that water is skimpy later in summer.

Head east on U.S. Hwy. 2 over Stevens Pass to the Lake

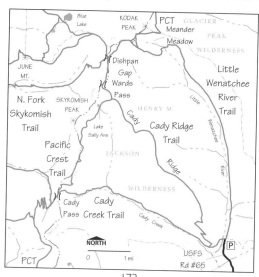

Wenatchee turnoff at MP 84.5. Go north on SR 207 past the state park at 4.5 miles, and cross the White River bridge 6.5 miles beyond (becomes USFS Rd. #65). Sockeye salmon spawn here late summer and fall. Near the bridge, watch for Glacier Peak twenty miles up-valley—maybe the best view of the mountain anywhere from a paved road. It's about fifteen miles from here to the trailhead and the end of the road at Little Wenatchee Ford Campground (3,000 feet). Figuring one latte and a pit stop, this is a three-hour drive from Everett (several campgrounds on the way).

The trail is well marked, descends slightly to cross the bouldery river, and reaches a junction in a half-mile. The easier hike to the crest at Cady Pass is via Cady Creek, but it's nearly all in woods— and so is the pass, five miles up. The better plan is to head right up Cady Ridge. The trail wastes no time gaining elevation (and views) as it winds up through pine, fir, and hemlock forest. Trees thin out as you approach the ridge crest and subalpine fir appears. Clearings with huckleberry, lupine, and mountain ash lure you on to bigger meadows, and at four miles, a great view of Glacier Peak, the hidden volcano, distinct and impressive, now just 11 miles to the

Cady Ridge

north. This is a good turn-around point for a 9-mile day. If a more grueling hike is in order, continue two more miles in meadows to the PCT (5,300 feet), then choose one of two 16-mile loops for the return.

Left leads a half-mile to Lake Sally Ann, becharming, clear, and cold, with more tarns above. The trail skirts below Skykomish Peak and touches the Cascade Crest (and the east county line) before descending to Cady Pass (4,300 feet) 3.5 miles from Sally Ann. There are views west to the Monte Cristo Peaks, and northwest to Sloan Peak on this stretch. From the pass it's an easy five miles down Cady Creek to the junction near the trailhead. The second loop option heads right at the Cady Ridge/PCT junction and climbs 400 feet to Wards Pass (and the county line) in 0.6 mile. Another 0.9 mile of up and down leads to a convergence of four trails at Dishpan Gap (5,600 feet). The North Fork Skykomish River valley falls away to the left, and June and Johnson Mountains beckon to the northwest. Stay right on the PCT about 0.8 mile, fork right, then right again at Meander Meadow in 0.3 mile. Amble down a mile-plus, then descend steeply to the Little Wenatchee River and the starting point, seven miles from the PCT.

Alternative transportation on the Cady Ridge Trail

Other Walks & Hikes

Needless to say, not every trail in Snohomish County is listed in this guide. Space limitations, access problems, private property issues, safety concerns, changing conditions, and other factors make it difficult for anyone to produce a truly comprehensive work. Nevertheless, we've tried to be reasonably complete with this first edition of *Hiking Snohomish County*. (We welcome your suggestions and corrections for future editions, as noted on page ii.)

Of the trails that aren't listed, many are "unofficial" paths, particularly in the lowland and foothills areas, and were likely excluded because they cross private land. Rural areas are notorious for private property frustrations that range from legitimately concerned but accommodating, to pissed off and ridiculous. On state and private timber land, access is generally a little easier and old road grades offer potential access to wide areas and a range of destinations. A little detective work will surely reward more ambitious hikers with some dazzling possibilities. But do get permission where necessary.

Historically, urban areas have been slow to develop their own trail systems, although things are picking up in that regard for some communities. Nevertheless, a strong argument can be made that there is a real deficiency of good hiking trails in most (but not all) populated areas of the county. At the same time, new trail systems are developing, in both urban and rural areas thanks to the good work of trails enthusiasts, volunteers, agency staff, and other concerned citizens.

On National Forest lands, where trail development (and trail eradication) has been underway for more than a century, the situation is actually much better. Like many other areas in western Washington, Snohomish County enjoys a good number of trails and trail miles on federal lands in the North Cascades, despite the loss of many miles over the past several decades from logging and road-building. In recent years, however, the number and miles of trails seem to have stabilized, more or less, and many of them are listed in this guide. Others are not but they are still worth exploring (a few are briefly mentioned below). Consult with the U.S. Forest Service for the latest information on these and other trails in the National

Forest. And while you're at it, write your Congressional representative and demand better funding for trails. The Forest Service is willing to make needed improvements, but Congress has had a habit of gutting the trails budget.

As for other walks and hikes that wouldn't fit in this edition (for whatever reason) here are a few more to ponder:

COASTAL AREAS

Stillaguamish River Delta

Some dikes and levees along the lower Stillaguamish River and delta near Stanwood have obvious appeal for walking, but most are on private land without public access or with limited fishing and hunting access. It would be great to see more areas opened up for hiking, especially when the public contributes a major share of the financing needed for dike construction and maintenance. Opening up the dike from Big Ditch Slough back to Stanwood has been discussed as one of several attractive possibilities. The planned new riverfront park in Stanwood has potential to improve access as well.

Tulalip Reservation & Other Tribal Lands

Of the several native tribes living in Snohomish County, only the Tulalip Tribe controls access to a large area of land and water. The Tulalip Reservation extends from I-5 west to Possession Sound and from the Snohomish River delta north to McKees Beach near Kayak Point. Non-natives should respect the tribe's sovereignty over these lands and seek out permission for access where necessary. Areas that are perhaps of most interest to hikers are the saltwater beaches near Priest Point, Mission Beach, Tulalip Bay (*see Walk #3*), and north along Port Susan where wild beaches rest at the base of steep bluffs 300 to 400 feet high.

Mission Beach

Mission Beach occupies a unique landform, a high, narrow, eroding, glacially-deposited peninsular bluff that defines the southwesterly shore of Tulalip Bay, west of Marysville. While public access is somewhat complicated by this thing called private property, it's feasible to walk a good chunk of the shoreline when the tide is more out than in. On the southwest side a piling sculpture of sorts frames the view. Hat Island is anchored straight away in the middle of Possession Sound, Port Gardner and the Everett waterfront are visible to the left, and the Mukilteo Ferry cuts across the water between. Lots of homes line the better beaches, with wilder shores between.

Snohomish River Delta

In addition to existing public trails around Spencer Island and along the river at Langus Park (*see Walk #28*), there are many more miles of unofficial trails, roads, and walkable dikes along the lower sloughs and main channel of the Snohomish River. Some are reasonably accessible; others display super-sized no trespassing signs. Secure permission where necessary.

Richmond Beach

See Richmond Beach Park (*Park #41*) for directions to this walkable beach just south of the county line. A mile or more of easy beach wandering (depending on tides), and another half-mile of upland paths await itchy feet. Theoretically, one can motate northward all the way to Edmonds during a low tide. However, sundry physical, aesthetic, procedural, industrial, and railroad obstacles make that not a terribly appealing endeavor at the moment.

Urban Areas

Parks, Promenades, Etc.

Most urban parks of any size have at least minimal facilities for walking. If something less than a half-mile of path is all that exists at any particular park, it's probably been excluded from this guide. That's not say that these little paths aren't worth walking. Urban waterfront areas, too, often include some kind of walkway or promenade between buildings and the water where a little nature experience might be combined with some window shopping or a winter tea break. Marinas are explorable also, although you might need an in with someone (or a boat) to get past the security gates. Other possibilities are sure to exist in and around every town, and the more dedicated outgoer will find them.

Historic & Cultural Sites

Formal and informal sites of cultural or historic interest abound in Snohomish County, some with short walking paths, sidewalks, or parks nearby. Check maps, libraries, roadside markers, and the like, or find the original downtown core and residential districts of almost any community in the county for insights into our regional past. Everett, Edmonds, Stanwood, East Stanwood, Arlington, Snohomish (*see Walk #11*), Monroe, and Index are especially interesting, but so are several others. Easy strolling, say, from a little park to a bakery or museum and back, makes a good outing on all but the blusteriest days of the year. In fact, every small town in the county has something unique to offer, from antiques and used books to funky espresso stands and squeaky floor cafes. With or without a path, they're all worth a visit. In Everett a hillside residential area of narrow winding streets, older homes, and nice views affords interesting wandering too. Maybe start at Rucker Hill Park near the west end of 33rd St. Check with the Edmonds park department for brochures describing walks there focused on local art and history.

Pigeon Creeks

In south Everett's Howarth Park, a minor trail system accesses Pigeon Creek #2, and short paths meander along Pigeon Creek #1 at lower Forest Park, an unofficial trail network that may eventually become part of a larger system linking the parks and waterfront.

Boeing / Paine Field

This might have been listed as a veritable hike, considering Boeing's official walking tour of the world's largest building — birthplace of the 747 — takes over an hour and covers a third of a mile. Instead, call the tour folks (800-464-1476) and schedule a visit to this monster airplane palace on one of our scarce rainy days.

Mill Creek

Lots of urban paths meander through the planned community of Mill Creek, and while some are public, many are limited to residents and guests. Still some exploring is feasible. Find a good map, then try Library Park off the Bothell-Everett Highway, or Heron Park on Village Green Dr. for two possible starts.

Burke-Gilman & Sammamish River Trails

Just across the line in King County, two major urban trails can be easily accessed from south Snohomish County. They are, of course, the famed Burke-Gilman Trail that links north Lake Washington with downtown Seattle, and the equally popular Sammamish River Trail which passes through Bothell on its winding way to Redmond. The river trail is generally open to a variety of user groups from walkers and bikers to wheelchairs and roller blades, plus horses in some areas. Access this elaborate, paved, and busy trail system from parks on Lake Washington, or, from Bothell, turn south off Main St. on 102nd Ave. NE and cross the bridge to Sammamish River Park on the right. Blyth Park (*Park #48, also on the King County side of Bothell*) is a long block south and a couple more west on W. Riverside Dr. This park offers a pleasant 0.7-mile interpretive walking trail.

Other Urban Trails

Over time, new trails can be expected in urban and outlying areas as the population expands and the demand for new facilities increases. Coastal ravines from Everett to Edmonds (Big Gulch, Japanese Gulch, etc.) are prime locations for new trails. So unless overzealous budget-cutting politicians consistently get their way, this should mean new trail opportunities for everyone. Contact local park offices or Snohomish County Parks and Recreation on occasion to see what's in the works and how you might help safeguard the trails budget, or make new projects happen.

Lowlands & Foothills

River Dikes & Levees

Snohomish County and the City of Everett, among others, have worked to establish trails along dikes and levees and more can be expected as the concerns of diking districts and landowners are addressed. Considering the level of public investment in building and maintaining such facilities, it's only reasonable that public access to dikes and levees be accommodated wherever possible. Many areas along the Snohomish and Stillaguamish Rivers are especially attractive and physically accessible already. Get permission if required.

Stimson Hill

The hills northeast of Arlington include much publicly-managed land (DNR), largely dedicated to timber production, and sorely lacking in trail or vehicle access for the general public. Locked gates are the norm unless there's logging underway, which is not the time to be putting around these places anyway. Stimson Hill used to be a regional favorite because of the great views opened up by clearcutting—which is not to say views are more important than trees. However, the gate on the main access road had six locks on it at last count. The trees, fortunately, are coming back and the views have moved to other clearcuts. Diehard forest walkers might try parking near (not in front of) gated roads off Cedarvale Rd., among others, and wandering old grades with a map and compass. Check with DNR for a map and for walkable (bikeable?) roads where the buzzsaws are dormant.

Frailey & Wheeler Mountains

Old roads and trails exist within large areas of public and private timberland in the hills between Arlington and Darrington, particularly on Frailey Mt. and Wheeler Mt. Clearcuts have opened up some nice views in many areas, but newer cuts and ongoing reforestation mean the big panoramas have a way of moving around over time. Old logging grades still make for interesting expeditions to good views, a few big trees, water access, cascades, and various geologic nuances. Much of Frailey Mt., straddling the Snohomish-Skagit County line, is managed by DNR, while the U. S. Navy (Jim Creek Naval Radio Station) controls a principal access to Wheeler Mt. Changing road conditions and gate closures complicate exploration.

Perhaps the best place to reach Frailey Mt. is from the Lake Cavanaugh Rd. east of Arlington. Head east on SR 530 to MP 32.7 and turn left just before the river bridge, quickly crossing the Darrington Branch railroad grade (and future trail). About 3.5 miles up on good road, a gated spur road on the left leaves a right-hand switchback. Park here and wander up the road leading to Frailey's long ridge and 2,666-foot summit about three miles west. Good views can be had of Lake Cavanaugh, Mt. Higgins, and Whitehorse Mt.

As for Wheeler, you probably need to know someone connected

to the Naval Station to get access as a guest. If so, turn south from SR 530 at MP 25.6 onto Jim Creek Rd. and drive to the Navy guardshack seven miles ahead. The trailhead is just inside on the left. Old logging roads and trails, popular with equestrians, wind around the hillsides to little lakes, views, and the 3,604-foot summit. If you don't have a connection and do have a fishing pole, you can access a mile of trail at Twin Lakes several miles south of the gate, but only during fishing season. There are extensive wetlands and little lakes here as well, all draining into Cub Creek's narrow canyon. (It may be feasible to access Wheeler Mt. from the south via USFS Rd. #41, #4150, and long spur roads of uncertain status.)

Hubbard Lake & South Fork Stillaguamish River

With the support of concerned citizens, Snohomish County recently acquired nearly 1,000 acres of land around Hubbard Lake and along the South Fork Stilly east of Granite Falls. The potential for park and trail development, as well as open space and habitat protection is excellent. The land, called Robe Canyon Historical Park, includes the Old Robe Trail (*see Hike #44*) and an extensive gorge along the river. By the turn of the century, major new trail opportunities appear likely in this area. Eventually, a new bridge over the river will allow a complete link between existing and future trail systems. The worrisome part of it all is a gigantic gravel pit and rock quarry that's been proposed immediately north of the park—considered by many to be one of the more important environmental battles in the county.

Spada Lake & Sultan Basin

The Spada Lake reservoir northeast of Sultan has a number of developed picnic sites and viewpoints with short walking paths, much of which is barrier-free (*see Park #54 for details*). Several North Cascades hikes can be accessed from the area as well (*see Boulder Lake below and Hikes #74 & #82*).

Boulder Lake

The trail to Boulder Lake, perched in a cirque above Spada Lake, begins a little more than a mile beyond the trailhead for Greider Lakes (*see Hike #82 for directions*). Expect a comparable climb over four steepish miles, some on old road bed.

Haystack Lookout

South of Sultan, gated DNR roads lead to a lake and former lookout site with a view on Haystack Mt. Find a good map, then take a bike to Rd. #22000 off the Ben Howard Rd. south of the Skykomish River and west of 311th Ave. SE. Follow the main road to Airplane Lake (deteriorates after five or six miles) and the lookout site beyond. The Sultan Mt. summit is close by. Watch out for log trucks.

North Cascades

Niederprum Trail

The main climber's route up Whitehorse Mt. near Darrington, this trail is very steep and in generally bad shape. It's a long haul to meadow views, with potentially dangerous snow slopes beyond (maybe best to let the more experienced peak baggers ponder the rest). To find the trailhead, turn south off SR 530 on Mine Rd. and drive about 2.5 miles (road becomes USFS Rd. #2030); angle left between houses where pavement ends. Trail's on the right.

Huckleberry Mountain

A long trudge (4,500-foot gain) on good trail to alpine meadows overlooking Buck Creek, the Suiattle River, and a sky full of summits, Glacier Peak included. As the name suggests, expect some sweet edibles in season. Go east on Suiattle River Rd. (#26) to MP 14.4 and a parking area on the left next to the trail. Water gets scarce up high later in the summer. Limited views on the way up.

Downey Creek

This old trail through deep forest leaves the Suiattle River Road near the bridge over the creek and gradually climbs into some of the most remote and precipitous wildland in the North Cascades. The lower stretch was recently improved by volunteers, but brush and a creek crossing five miles in are problematic. Above this point, the route's appealing to mountaineers with at least four days to burn, but otherwise not recommended.

Sulphur Creek

The curious thing about this little hike is the 'hot springs,' which might better be described as "tepid puddles," elusive, strong-smelling from sulphurous gas, and otherwise uninviting. Unlike the iron-rich mineral water bubbling through Kennedy Hot Springs, the source and nature of this spring is, perhaps, more intimately linked with the Glacier Peak volcano, an easy crow-fly to the southeast. However, the trail up the creek passes through nice old-growth so let that be the main attraction. Many down trees in 1997. Find the trailhead west of the creek directly across from the Sulphur Creek Campground near the end of the Suiattle River Rd. (MP 22.5).

Circle Peak

If the road's passable, the old and almost forgotten trail up to a lookout site on Circle Peak, east of White Chuck Mt., is still a good trek. From Suiattle River Rd. (#26) take Rds. #25 and #27 to #2703 and look for the trail at or near the road end. Woods and meadow lead to summit rocks in 2.5 miles. Strong routefinding skills are a plus.

Crystal Lake

Crystal and Meadow Lakes, near the west end of the Meadow Mt. Trail, are reachable as a long dayhike (*see Hike #54 for details*), but a 3.5 to 5.0 mile road walk (each way) makes the area more appealing as an overnighter. If Crystal Lake is the objective, walk the road about 1.7 miles to the fork before Crystal Creek. Left goes to the old Crystal Lake Trailhead in about 1.5 miles. The scenic lake is about 1.7 steep, muddy miles away (an old fire line), just beyond a waterfall. Or stay right at the road junction for the longer approach via Meadow Lake. Near the road end (at five miles) head up the Meadow Mt. Trail for less than two miles to a junction. Right goes on to Meadow and Fire Mountains. Left leads down several hundred feet in less than a mile to Meadow Lake. A fisherperson's trail continues over a ridge a long mile to Crystal Lake. A complete loop of about 14 miles is feasible, but expect some brush and crummy trail.

Peek-A-Boo Lake

Southeast of Darrington, the old trail to Peek-A-Boo Lake climbs a wooded ridge to a fragile meadow in two miles, then drops to the forested lake in another half-mile. From Mountain Loop Highway at the confluence of the White Chuck and Sauk Rivers (MP 6), turn west on USFS Rd. #2080, stay right at a fork (sign), then right again on Rd. #2083 in 1.7 miles, and left on Rd. #2086 in another 1.7 miles. The trail's 1.3 miles beyond at a right-hand switchback. Mt. Pugh and White Chuck Mt. are visible on the drive up.

Cougar Creek

An old and beauteous trail now used mostly by climbers headed up Sloan Peak begins on the right a few miles up the North Fork Sauk River Rd. The problem, however, is The River. It must be crossed to get to the main trail leading to meadows north of Sloan. Fording anytime but at low water is either impossible or possibly deadly (it takes so little current to jam a body under a log or stump in the river...). Maybe let the more experienced mountain brutes bag this one. (*See Hike #61 for a more inviting alternative just over the ridge.*)

Old Government Trail

An easy, seldom used, 1.6-mile trail from Barlow Point Trail (*see Hike #63*) running down-valley to near the Sunrise Mine Rd. east of Granite Falls. This is a remnant of a much older trail that paralleled the old Monte Cristo Railroad grade, and predates construction of the Mountain Loop Highway.

Marten Creek

Marten Creek is a steep and not terribly interesting hike up an old grade off the Mountain Loop Highway near MP 20.4 east of Granite Falls. The first mile is very steep and was built in the 1940s to access the Marten Creek Mines. The route passes the site of a Douglas fir "heredity experiment" begun in 1916. Seedlings from all over the Northwest were planted here to compare growth characteristics in the decades-long quest for the perfect timber tree. Signs explain the project and results. The trail eases off in Marten Creek's upper broad valley, then crosses the creek, before disappearing in brush less than three miles from the road. The old trail continued another two miles and climbed 500 feet to Granite Pass on the way to Darrington.

Canyon Lake

A three-mile road walk leads to a short path to a fishable lake on the southwest edge of the Boulder River Wilderness. Take Green Mt. Rd. (USFS Rd. #41) from Mountain Loop Highway at MP 7.1, then stay right on Rd. #4110 in two miles, and right on Rd. #4111 in two miles more. The road is probably closed at 2.7 miles, leaving about three miles to the lake. Trail's on the left.

Lake Isabel

Isabel: a big mysterious lake in a remote area that, surprisingly, lacks a good trail. To search it out, more experienced trekkers could leave U.S. Hwy. 2 at Gold Bar heading for Wallace Falls State Park, then go right at the intersection with May Creek Rd. In another mile look for a rough old logging road on the left just past a gravel pit. Park and walk (or bike) this roadbed past powerlines (maybe four-wheel-driveable) a long mile to May Creek; scamper across on rocks if the water isn't too high. Beyond, a veritable maze of ORV trails makes any route description difficult. A little trial and error may be needed to find the correct path to an old railroad logging grade that gently climbs to the east. It's easy to become a missing person here, so memorize your progress and don't disorient. A steep section higher up leads to a flat grade, and an upper creek crossing on stringer logs left over from a former bridge, then more steep and rocky road-bed. Follow this well past the first bend, pass a "view trail" on the right, and look for the old trail to the lake heading uphill to the left (three-plus miles to here). Climb briefly then follow easy but rough trail northward past big cedars. Near the base of a big beautiful waterfall, follow very steep and poor trail (some old puncheon) almost straight up to the lake, coming out near a stream with a gauge (another mile to here). Campsites nearby. One can wander west, some on path, some not, to a second, westerly outlet. Expect slippery logs and rocks to clamber over. Warning: this is not a hike for the more casual adventurer.

Curry Gap & Bald Eagle Mt.

Bald Eagle Mt., overlooking the North Fork Skykomish River, is doable in a day, but limited views make the trek somewhat less appealing than nearby alternatives like Blanca Lake and West Cady Ridge (*see Hikes #86 and #87*). From the Quartz Creek Trailhead figure four miles to Curry Gap and three more to Bald Eagle. The route is of some interest as an overnighter and can be continued as a two or three-day loop via June Mt., Blue Lake, and the North Fork Trail.

Iron Goat Trail

In King County, west of Stevens Pass, twelve miles of abandoned railroad grade with tunnels and switchbacks have been undergoing reconstruction for trail purposes for several years, the bulk of it done by volunteers (still ongoing). Over half the distance was open in 1997; the first (lower) mile is barrier-free. To find it (late spring through fall), turn north off US Hwy 2 at MP 55 onto the Old Cascade Hwy, then left in 2.3 miles on USFS Rd. #6710; the trailhead is 1.4 miles farther. The railroad history is amazing (*see Walk #48*).

Pacific Crest Trail

If you happen to find your calendar open for four or five months late spring through summer, consider a little 2,500-mile-plus jaunt from Mexico to Canada via the Pacific Crest Trail (PCT). Or, if you only have a week or two to spare, take a serious look at doing the chunk of it that runs along the east boundary of Snohomish County which also happens to be the Cascade Crest. The trek from Steven's Pass north to Cloudy Pass and the Suiattle River, or on to Rainy Pass or Canada's Manning Park makes an extraordinary outing that, for obvious reasons attracts a lot of bipedal pack luggers (and a few super-light, high-tech scamperers) each year. If you're in shape and you happen to catch mostly good weather along the way, it can be a trip of a lifetime. If not, well, there's always next year. Several of the dayhikes listed in this guide can be used to access the PCT or at least follow it for a short distance (*see Hikes #51, #56, #59, #87, #89 and #90*). If a longer hike is the plan, refer to one of many guidebooks available that discuss the trail in detail. Because of high elevations and lingering snowpacks, August is typically the best month for an extended hike on the local segment of the PCT.

Buck Creek Pass

Really an overnight backpack, the 20-mile roundtrip to the pass and back is more than most people will attempt in a day. The pass is on the east county line at the Cascade Crest where easy summit scrambles offer great panoramas. Views of Glacier Peak and neighboring summits are exceptional. The trailhead is at the end of the Chiwawa River Rd. (USFS Rd. #62) in Chelan County.

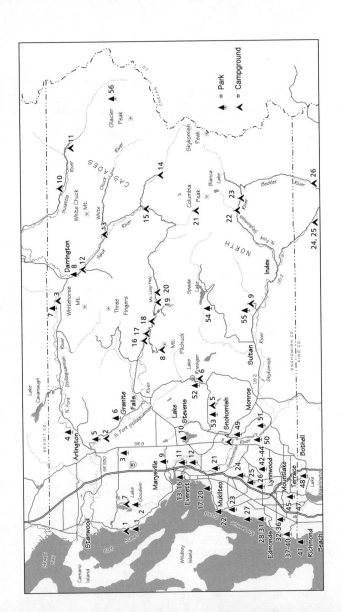

Parks

Almost every community in Snohomish County has at least one park of some kind, and though some may be on the meager end of the excitability spectrum, many others are surely worth a visit. Some of the nicer ones are listed below. The availability of walking paths is noted. If good parks and trails are lacking in your community, call the mayor to see what you can do to help rectify things.

In 1997 the county started charging fees to park or launch a boat at Kayak Point, Wyatt, and Flowing Lake Parks. Day use was $3 and an annual pass could be purchased for $40. Check with the county park department for details. Some state parks charge similar—or slightly higher—day use fees as well. Hopefully, such fees will remain nominal so that those who can least afford it are not excluded from the joy and enrichment that comes from our parks and trails. Keeping these facilities free for kids, seniors, and the disabled also seems like a good idea, as well as giving a break to cyclists and walk-ins who don't generate car-related impacts and expense on the park system.

Parks listings are loosely organized from north to south (locations are noted on the facing page). A few non-park sites, like the Sultan Basin Recreation Area, are included because of obvious recreation value.

1. Kayak Point Park

Adjacent to some of the prettiest marine shoreline in the county, Kayak Point County Park northwest of Marysville is a good starting point for some excellent beach wandering (*see Walk #2 for directions*). The 428-acre park was acquired from ARCO in 1972 after the company shifted its refinery plans north to Cherry Point in Whatcom County. The park offers camping, picnicking, a barrier-free fishing pier, scenic paths, fine sunsets, and great views of Port Susan, Camano Island, and the Olympic Mountains. Expect to share the place with many other folks late spring through early fall. You might even catch a glimpse of a whale, though don't go expecting that on your first visit. Bring binoculars to better the odds. A public golf course adjoins the park to the east.

2. Wenberg State Park

Wenberg is a heavily visited, semi-urban state park on just 46 acres on the east side of Lake Goodwin. The 550-acre lake is scenic if you can see it between all the people and boats. For some quiet, visit on a crummy day or in the off-season (November through March). From the Smokey Point exit on I-5 north of Marysville, head west on SR 531, turning right at a stop sign, then left at the park sign almost five miles from I-5. Park entrance is on the right in another 1.5 miles. Good picnicking (with grills), beach sunning, swimming, motor and non-motor boating, and camping. A few short paths wind along the shore and through Doug-fir and red-cedar forest.

3. Gissberg Twin Lakes Park

Next to I-5 north of Marysville is this green but predictably noisy county park built around two artificial lakes that formed after the state excavated a zillion truckloads of fill to construct I-5. Besides fishing, swimming, and picnic potential, an easy, pleasant walk in the grass circles both lakes (*see Walk #25*). Find them west of the freeway, 0.7 mile south of SR 531 (Smokey Point exit).

4. Twin Rivers Park

A 44-acre county park at the confluence of the North and South Forks of the Stillaguamish River with ballfields and several paths in woods by the river (*see Walk #23*). The park is on the left near the river as you head north out of Arlington on the new SR 530 bridge. The City manages another much smaller park with a play area, Haller Park, off the south end of the SR 9 bridge over the Stilly.

5. River Meadows Park

East of Arlington this excellent riverfront park on about 200 acres was once a dairy, and a native Stillaguamish settlement before that. The county park fronts the South Fork Stilly for a mile and contains mixed forest, lovely fields (grass and wildflower meadows), the site of a historic homestead, picnic areas, tent camping, and six miles of easy walking paths (*see Walk #24*). From SR 530, a half-mile north of the new South Fork bridge at Arlington, turn right on the Jordan Rd. Stay right in a mile and continue another three miles to the park entrance on the right. Closes at dusk.

6. Jordan Bridge

To reach this mini-park and suspension footbridge over the South Fork Stillaguamish River, take SR 530 a half-mile north of the new South Fork bridge in Arlington and turn right on Jordan Rd. Stay right at a junction in one mile and drive another six miles to the footbridge and parking area on the right. A 0.6-acre parcel on the Stilly was donated to the county in 1974 to preserve this famous landmark, since rebuilt. Stairs lead to a little beach below the bridge.

7. Squire Creek Park

This 28-acre, nicely wooded county park is primarily of interest to campers. Good fishing access to Squire Creek. The park is off SR 530 about 4 miles west of Darrington.

8. Backman Park

This small fishing access on the Sauk River is about 2.6 miles south of Darrington on the Mt. Loop Hwy. Turn left on Clear Creek Rd. just before the Backman Creek bridge. Park is 0.4 mile ahead on the right. No facilities.

9. Jennings Nature Park

A large city park with it all: rolling lawns, play and picnic areas, duck pond, extensive wetlands, a creek, woods, walking paths, ballfield, a demonstration garden, a big cannon, an historic barn, several parking lots, and more. Considering the serious crowd factor on a nice weekend, one gets the impression Marysville may be short of parks. At other times, it's a pleasant place to wander, hold hands, watch birds, read books. (*See Walk #10 for directions.*)

10. Lake Stevens Area

Perhaps the nicest park on Lake Stevens is Lundeen County Park at the north end of the lake. Though small, it offers a nice view of the water plus a swimming beach, barrier-free fishing dock, play and picnic areas, a basketball court, and minor wetland interpretation. From SR 9, head east on Lundeen Parkway (signed to City Center) only 0.8 mile; park is on the right. Other parks on the north end of the lake include the City Swimming Beach west of the city center, and North Cove Park next to the police station downtown. Wyatt

County Park and its popular swimming beach are on the lower west shore of the lake off S. Davies Rd.

11. Langus Park

The 96-acre Langus Park, acquired from DNR, was named for an avid park supporter. The park and a 2.3-mile nature trail along the river were dedicated in 1991 (*see Walk #28*). Future trail extensions are possible. Also considered is a rather ambitious footbridge to be hung underneath the I-5 Snohomish River overpass to link Langus Park to the rest of the river trail system. The land was originally inhabited by native people.

12. Spencer Island & Steamboat Slough

Spencer Island, part of the Snohomish River delta in north Everett, is a haven for both wildlife and recreation. Snohomish County owns the southern portion, while the Washington Department of Fish and Wildlife owns the lion's share on the north end. The island attracts hunters and photographers, and both come here often, both looking for a good shot. Despite the apparent conflict, the area has become a birdwatcher's paradise in winter and spring. A fairly extensive trail system also exists (*see Walk #28 for details*).

13. Legion Memorial Park

Land donated to the city by the American Legion in 1932 led to the development of this multi-faceted park with walking paths, play areas, tennis courts, ballfields, golf course, a small arboretum, horticultural center, garden compost demonstration site, meeting hall, and good views of Everett's industrial waterfront and beyond. See Walk #12 for a good waterfront loop that can begin at this park.

14. North & South View Parks

These two pocket parks on the north Everett waterfront are on a narrow strip of land between the water and Marine View Dr. and just southwest of the Maulsby Swamp. A good paved path links them together (*see Walk #12*).

15. Marine Park

On the Everett waterfront, Marine Park offers water access to Jetty Island, Port Gardner, Possession Sound, and the Snohomish River.

Short walking paths, small floats, fishing pier, lawns, sea sculpture, and viewing areas warrant at least a brief visit. Expect a lot of traffic at the major multi-laned boat launch (a couple of slots are reserved for non-motorized craft). The city runs a summer foot ferry to Jetty Island from here, and a private ferry links with Hat Island (no public facilities). The park is at the west end of 10th St. off Marine View Dr. (*see also Walk #12*).

16. Jetty Island Park

On the Everett waterfront, Jetty Island is a 210-acre, two mile-long landform created by modern homo sapiens from harbor dredge spoils dug from Port Gardner waterways. Yet the island offers a surprising respite from city life a stone's throw away, and includes a two-plus-mile beach, an interpretive nature trail, barking sea lions on occasion (fall and winter), and sometimes even warm saltwater for swimming. A foot ferry shuttles island goers to and from the Jetty in summer (*see Walk #4 for details*).

17. Forest Park

It seems amazing to think it now, but Forest Park once supported a zoo with exotic animals from around the world, including elephants, bears, and kangaroos. Now only a petting zoo of familiar domesticated farm animals exists, a transition that seems entirely appropriate given humanity's increasing concern for the welfare of our planet's endangered wildlife. The park's current 111 acres includes play areas, short forested walking paths, lawn areas, a public swimming pool, tennis courts, horseshoes, a ballfield, picnicking, the historic Floral Hall (a lovely old log building on the National Historic Register), plus a separate 60-acre chunk of park land on Pigeon Creek #1 with more trails, views, and 3,000 feet of saltwater shoreline. Jackson Elementary School kids have worked for years to reestablish a healthy salmon run in the creek. An interpretive trail along the entire length of Pigeon Creek has been proposed. From Evergreen Way, follow 41st St. west (becomes Mukilteo Blvd.) a few blocks to find the park just around the bend on the left. Or continue past the second entrance to a sharp right on Pigeon Creek Rd. to reach the lower 60 acres.

18. Howarth Park

This big little park off Mukilteo Blvd. has tennis courts, playground, nice woods, bluff trails, views, and picnicking. A high footbridge leads across railroad tracks to a viewing platform and a fine gravel and sandy beach below (*see Walk #5*). The bridge can be reached from the main park area above or from the Pigeon Creek #2 parking area below. Howarth Park is about 1.5 mile southwest of Forest Park. The eastern park entrance off Olympic Blvd. was still closed in late 1997 due to a major slide early in the year. Repairs could take awhile. Use the west entrance near Seahurst Ave. and Mukilteo Blvd.

19. Harborview Park

For an excellent, unobstructed view of Possession Sound, the Everett waterfront, Mt. Baker, the Olympics, and Whidbey, Camano, and Hat Islands, try this little view park between Everett and Mukilteo, a half-mile west of Howarth Park. There's real interest in acquiring a trail down the bluff to Darlington Beach to access 4,600 feet of public shoreline near the mouth of Merrill Creek. Stay tuned.

20. Walter E. Hall & Kasch Memorial Parks

These two adjacent south Everett parks are not of much interest to walkers but they do offer limited play and picnic areas in addition to all the busy ballfields and golf course that occupy most of the parks' 200 acres. There's some interesting history here: Hall was built over a landfill, and Kasch used to be a Bomarc missile site. Reach the former from W. Casino Rd. west of Evergreen Way, and the latter from Airport Rd. to the west.

21. Rotary Riverfront Park

This 11-acre park in the Lowell area of south Everett is a recent addition on the lower Snohomish River near the former home and lumber mill of E.D. Smith, founder of Lowell in 1861. The park includes a river boat launch and trailhead parking for the Lowell Riverfront Trail (*see Walk #29*). There are also nice views of the river, the Mt. Baker volcano, and other peaks of the North Cascades.

22. Mukilteo State Park

Next to the Mukilteo ferry terminal, this inconspicuous 18-acre state park has 1500 feet of walkable public shore (*see Walk #6*), interpretive exhibits, a fishing pier, picnicking, and ferry-watching, once you get past a gigantic parking lot used by island commuters. This is also Point Elliot, one of western Washington's most important historic sites. It was here that 2,000-plus members of native tribes in the region gathered in 1855 to witness the signing of the Elliot Point Treaty by 82 Indian leaders. This lone act essentially gave all of Northwest Washington to non-native settlers in exchange for peace, a few small reservations for some of the tribes, and a promise for equal access to traditional fishing and hunting grounds. Many non-natives have groaned about the latter ever since. A skimpy sign near the restrooms commemorates this immense historic event. A historic lighthouse, the U.S. Coast Guard Lightstation Mukilteo, built in 1905, stands to the north (open for tours on spring and summer weekends). The lighthouse was restored in 1987.

23. 92nd Street Park

On the east side of the Mukilteo Speedway and south of 92nd St. SW is an attractive park with large rolling lawns, forest, and two small wetlands, as well as play and picnic areas and nearly a half-mile of trails in trees and sun.

24. Thornton A. Sullivan Park

This is the popular 110-acre Everett city park on Silver Lake in south Everett (on Silver Lake Rd. off 19th Ave. SE). The park includes a swimming beach, small boat rentals, picnic and play areas, and a nature path across Silver Lake Rd. (*see Walk #13*). Look for a wild sea monster in the trees north of the beach behind Camp Patterson. The park gets really busy in summer.

25. McCollum Park

What used to be a county landfill is now 77-acre McCollum Park, one of the western county's more attractive regional parks. There are play and picnic areas, a swimming pool, ballfields, and walking trails in the woods (*see Walk #14*), as well as a BMX racetrack and WSU Cooperative Extension facility next door. The Adopt-A-Stream folks have developed an educational facility here as well. The park is south of 128th St. several blocks east of I-5.

26. Martha Lake Park

The county park on Martha Lake is small (6 acres) and a little noisy — not from users but from traffic on 164th St. SE. In fact, the park is hardly used at times other parks are crowded, despite several hundred feet of attractive natural shoreline. The park entrance has a slightly run-down feel to it, but the lakeshore is worth a look nonetheless. Early morning visits spring through fall may be best when traffic isn't so obnoxious. Turn north off 164th St. onto East Shore Dr. and find the park just ahead on the left.

27. Picnic Point Park

This 54-acre county park has 1200 feet of walkable public shore, most of it sandy beach, although the beach connects with a much more extensive and walkable beach running northward to Mukilteo and south to Edmonds and beyond (*see Walks #6 and #7*). The park was donated to the county for park purposes and has been developed with paths, viewing areas, a pedestrian overpass across the railroad tracks, picnic area, and portable restrooms. The park is at the west end of Picnic Point Rd. between Edmonds and Mukilteo, and can be reached via Highway 99 and Shelby Rd. which becomes Picnic Point Rd. The park opens early and closes at dusk.

28. Meadowdale Beach Park

Just north of Edmonds is this 105-acre park with one major trail to the beach (*see Hike #8*), lots of nice woods, and 800 feet of public beach. The highlight of the park and natural area is, in fact, the mile-long trail to the beach. A small play area and Lunds Gulch Creek are the other main attractions. The park is off 156th St. SW about a mile west of 52nd Ave. W.

29. Meadowdale Playfield

An urban park and sports complex in Lynnwood, Meadowdale Playfield has ballfields, picnic and play areas, a duck pond, rock sculpture, and a mile of mostly paved paths (*see Walk #16*).

30. Southwest County Park

Another large (115 acres) and largely undeveloped county park in the Edmonds area, this site includes a lot of nice forest and a fairly good, albeit limited trail system, but no other facilities (*see Walk #17 for details*). Park on Olympic View Dr. near 180th St.

31. H. O. Hutt Park

This small (7 acre) natural area in Edmonds contains an attractive grove of Douglas fir trees, but no facilities. A short walking path leads past two giant firs. The trailhead is on 187th St. SW, just east of 94th Ave. W. Parking is problematic.

32. Sierra Park

The interesting thing about this small Edmonds park off 80th Ave. W and 190th St. SW is the short Path for the Blind (*see Walk #19*). There are also a small arboretum, picnic area, play area, basketball court, and ballfield here.

33. Lynndale Park

Lynndale Park off Olympic View Dr. is a surprising spot on 37 acres near a confluence of power lines. Despite the obvious electrical downside, there are significant amenities here, including pleasant 'campy' picnic sites in the woods, picnic shelters, play areas, an amphitheater, tennis courts, ballfield, basketball courts, and a fine little trail system, some of which is paved and barrier-free (*see Walk #18*). Access the park from Olympic View Dr., near 73rd Ave. W.

34. Daleway Park

This long and skinny park in Lynnwood has play and picnic areas, a kids' spray pool (in summer), basketball courts, horseshoe pits, some woods, and a 0.2 mile trail running the length of the park. Access it from 64th Ave. W, a few blocks north of 196th St. SW.

35. Scriber Lake Park & Wilcox Park

One of Lynnwood's few natural gems, Scriber Lake is a veritable paradise among the steel and concrete of southwest Snohomish County's immoderately crowded landscape. A lovely path circles the lake (*see Walk #20*), and a diversity of birds and small mammals have scratched out a living here. The paths, wetlands, a marshy lake, woods, benches, and blinds for birdwatching are the principal amenities. Wilcox Park to the north across 196th St. SW is developed with the more urban-traditional play and picnic areas among nice trees. The parks are not linked but can be mutually accessed via the crosswalk at the Scriber Lake Rd. traffic light. Reach Scriber Lake by car from 198th St.; Wilcox park from 196th St. and Walnut Way.

36. Swamp Creek Park

A 90-acre undeveloped county park site in the Lynnwood area with a planned 1.1-mile trail, in conjunction with a storm water facility. Watch for improvements soon.

37. Edmonds City Park

From the outside, the city park at Edmonds doesn't look particularly inviting, but on the inside it's nicely landscaped, well maintained, and loaded with family funster amenities. Picnic and play areas, a wading pool, a gazebo, barrier-free walking paths, a ballfield, nice trees, and lots of rich lawn should keep the kids adequately entertained. Park on 3rd Ave. north of Pine St. near downtown Edmonds. Open dawn to dusk.

38. Brackett's Landing

This beachfront city park is adjacent to the Edmonds ferry terminal and is a popular spot to watch shipping traffic and the ferry come and go. Interpretive facilities, benches, nice walkways, a good chunk of public beach, a small jetty, and views of Mt. Baker to the north as well as Whidbey Island, Kitsap Peninsula, and the Olympics. Scuba divers frequent the area and an underwater park has been established around an artificial reef. Outside cold showers are also available. The park spans both sides of the ferry terminal and makes a good starting point for a beach walk to the north (*see Walk #7*). Or, wander south to Olympic Beach and the long fishing pier where a great poster shows you how to properly fillet a fish. Then head east up Main St. to the historic downtown area near 5th Ave.

39. Marina Beach Park

Another small but nice city park in Edmonds exists south of the ferry terminal at the end of Admiral Way. Lots of grass, play area, picnic tables, barbeque grills, nice beach, walking paths, pet area, and historic features. The site was originally named Point Edmund by the Wilkes expedition in the mid-1800s. The park is not well connected to the rest of Edmonds' pedestrian-friendly waterfront.

40. Maplewood, Yost Memorial & Pine Ridge Parks

Three nicely wooded parks in Edmonds offer southwest county residents a choice of destinations for walking and picnicking in a natural setting close to home (*see Walk #21*). The smallest, Maplewood, is a newer facility with short paths, play area, and semi-private picnic spots among trees and lawn. Find the elusive entrance at the end of 89th Pl., north of 200th St. SW. The larger of the three, Yost Memorial Park, covers 48 acres and offers play and picnic areas as well, plus an outdoor public swimming pool, tennis courts, and a limited trail system in a wooded ravine. From downtown Edmonds take Walnut St. up the hill (east) several blocks to the park entrance. Pine Ridge Park, at 24 acres, is less developed and serves more as a natural area protecting Goodhope Pond and surrounding wetlands. Several short paths lead to views of water and wildlife. Access this area from 83rd Ave. W., two blocks south of 200th St. SW.

41. Richmond Beach Park

Richmond Beach Park, less than a mile south of the Snohomish-King County line, offers excellent picnicking (several shelters), a number of short walking paths, a scenic play area, a fine sandy beach, and a great view of the Olympic Mountains. Beach wandering, by way of the footbridge across the railroad tracks, is best when tides are below five feet or so — and preferably on the way down, not up. Much of the park, formerly a sand and gravel pit, is ADA-accessible, although a very steep ramp leading to the beach itself may preclude wheelchair access to some otherwise nice amenities. From Richmond Beach Rd. west of SR 99, turn south onto 21st Ave. NW and drive a couple of blocks to the well-marked park entrance.

42. Silver Creek Park & May's Pond

Though small and close to power lines, Silver Creek Park south of Mill Creek has some nice amenities, including a half-mile walking trail with bridges and boardwalk among woods, wetlands, and a small pond. Enhancements to the creek have been made to help recover salmon habitat. There are limited picnicking and play areas in the park, located off 20th Ave. SE south of 180th St. SE and east of SR 527. May's Pond is close by, north of 180th St. and behind a swimming pool. There are a few short paths and a play area here as well.

43. Rhody Ridge Botanical Garden

This site southwest of Mill Creek is not a conventional park for picnicking or kids' play, but was graciously donated to the county for the benefit of people who want to experience (and maybe learn from) a well-kept, privately established arboretum. Access is by appointment only with the resident caretakers. Call the county park department for information.

44. North Creek Park

This fine nature park south of Mill Creek was developed by the county off 183rd St. SE a half-mile west of SR 527. The park has good picnic facilities, a viewpoint, and an extensive boardwalk trail system through wetlands (*see Walk #30*). Expect good birding and wildlife viewing in winter and spring. Park opens early, closes at dusk.

45. Evergreen Playfield

South of 220th St. SW on 56th Ave. W. in Mountlake Terrace, this facility is mostly made of ballfields. A good paved trail winds around the edges under conifers.

46. Terrace Creek Park

Also in Mountlake Terrace is this woodsy, 52-acre park and natural area with play and picnic areas, pool, a unique 'golf course' for disc throwers (tee off and sail it to a basket hundreds of feet away), plus a wide, easy trail running the length of the park (*see Walk #22*). Access the park and trail off 48th Ave. W., near 233rd St. SW.

47. Brier Park

Find this modest-sized city park with lots of lawn, ballfields, play and picnic areas, and walking paths on the north side of 228th St. SE near Poplar Way.

48. Blyth Park

Across the county line in King County is Bothell's Blyth Park on 37 acres with forest, lawns, play and picnic facilities, and a 0.7-mile interpretive walking trail close to the Sammamish River. The Sammamish River Trail is nearby. From downtown Bothell turn south off Main Street onto 102nd Ave. NE, cross the river and turn right on W. Riverside Dr. to reach Blyth Park.

49. Pilchuck Park

For a simple picnic break on the Pilchuck River in Snohomish, Pilchuck Park off 2nd St. and Cypress Ave. is a maybe. The park includes several tennis courts and ballfields and a paved (and uninteresting) pedestrian path around them, plus a big soccer field complex to the south.

50. Bob Heirman Wildlife Park at Thomas Eddy

A beautiful 344-acre natural area fronting the Snohomish River south of Snohomish with a good trail to river banks and bars. Also a small lake and wetlands, plus picnic facilities. Hiking only (*see Walk #31*); no dogs allowed. Access is off the Connelly Rd. east of SR 9.

51. Lord Hill Regional Park

In 1879, Mitchell Lord homesteaded on this anomalously high hill near the confluence of the Snohomish and Skykomish Rivers west of Monroe. By the 1930s the whole dern thing had been logged off and the DNR started pulling the second-growth fifty years later. Quite fortunately, Snohomish County Parks managed to rescue about 1,300 acres of the hill, including some maturing forest, substantial river frontage, several ponds, and the not quite towering Devil's Butte for a major regional park. An extensive trail system, much of it open to horses and bikes, has been developed (*see Hike #32 for details and directions*). No camping or fires allowed. The park opens early and closes at dusk.

52. Lake Roesiger Park

A small county park on 38 acres, with a swimming beach, dock, picnic tables, lawn, a short trail in the woods (that really should be extended toward the lake and made into an attractive loop), and limited camping. Park closes at dusk. The park is off Lake Roesiger Rd. about a mile north of the junction with West Shore Rd.

53. Flowing Lake Park

Located on the north shore of Flowing Lake east of Snohomish, this 33-acre rural wooded park includes a swimming beach, fishing dock, boat launch, play areas, good picnic sites, walking paths, and an attractive campground. From U.S. Hwy. 2 near Snohomish, exit to

88th St. SE, cross the highway and continue 0.8 mile to 131st Ave. SE. Turn left, then in 1.3 mile turn right onto Three Lakes Rd. Drive another 2.5 miles to 171st Ave. SE and go left 1.2 miles, then right on 48th St. SE (park signs). The county park entrance is 0.5 mile ahead.

54. Sultan Basin Recreation Area (Spada Lake)

Northeast of Sultan in the Cascade foothills is Spada Lake, a large reservoir that serves as a major component of the Everett water supply system. In fact, this water supply serves two thirds of the county population. To protect water quality, public use of the lake and watershed is strictly regulated. From late April to late October the public can access a number of improved sites and facilities during daylight hours only. Camping is not allowed, except at backcountry sites near Boulder and Greider Lakes (*see Hike #82*). Boating is okay, but not internal combustion motors, nor inflatables like tubes and rafts. Fishing with bait and swimming are also prohibited.

From U.S. Hwy. 2 just east of Sultan head north on the Sultan Basin Rd. 13.5 miles to an information/registration area at Olney Pass. The road forks just ahead. A right reaches the South Fork site (picnicking, boat launch) in 3.1 miles; the South Shore site (boat launch) in 5.0 miles; the Nighthawk site (excellent picnic area, a half-mile of walking paths, boat launch) in 5.5 miles; and the Bear Creek Overlook in 6.0 miles with an excellent view of the lake from the east. The Greider Lake Trailhead is a mile farther. From the junction near Olney Pass, head left to reach the Culmback Dam Viewpoint in 1.8 miles; go right at a tee in another 1.2 miles, then drive 1.2 miles more to the last site, North Shore, on the right. Here are more paved paths (most barrier-free), picnic sites, and another great view of the lake, this time from the north. The road eventually drops back to the lake at Williamson Creek then after two miles bends west and south to climb the east end of Bald Mt. (*See Hike #74*).

55. Wallace Falls State Park

A very popular (i.e. crowded) place in summer, this fine state park offers limited tent camping and picnicking, but is best known for the spectacular falls on the Wallace River (*see Hike #45*). The famous falls are conspicuous from U.S. Hwy. 2 near Gold Bar. Follow the signs to the park from U.S. Hwy. 2 near MP 28. Best to avoid the place on nice weekends June through September. The park charges a day-use fee and closes at dusk.

56. USFS Wilderness Areas

Considering there are more than 630,000 acres of federal land in Snohomish County — nearly all of it National Forest, including one of the most dramatic mountain landscapes in the lower-forty-eight states — there sure ought to be a slug of designated wilderness here. Right? Fortunately, there is. That doesn't mean that all the fragile places worth protecting have been saved, but great strides have been made over the past several decades to ensure future generations have more than a slim chance to experience what we can today.

Three wilderness areas have been established in the region, including the Glacier Peak Wilderness, one of the first such areas set aside anywhere in the nation. Over 570,000 acres are protected in an area covering parts of Snohomish, Skagit, and Chelan Counties. The area is entirely dominated by the state's fourth-highest volcano, *DaKobed*, or Glacier Peak, rising to just short of two vertical miles above sea level. Two other Wilderness Areas were designated by Congress in 1984: The Boulder River and Henry M. Jackson. The latter covers around 103,000 acres, mostly in Snohomish County. It includes, most significantly, the peaks and glaciers of the Monte Cristo area. The Boulder River Wilderness includes 49,000 acres and has Whitehorse and Three Fingers Mountains at its heart.

All three contain extensive trail systems, especially Glacier Peak with over 450 miles worth. Henry M. Jackson has about 50 miles, and Boulder River holds a whopping 25 miles (that's good if you really appreciate small-'w' wilderness). A number of trails in this book access these areas (*see also What to Know Before You Go, p. 13-22*). Even with these kinds of trail miles, all three wilderness areas contain plenty of places that are so wild and rugged and trail-less that no one ever visits. Check with your local climber, hunter, or fisher friend for hints on where to go to avoid humanity altogether. But beware, this is no playground for the inexperienced. Hazards are many, and more than a handful haven't come out alive. Consider a comprehensive mountaineering course if this sort of thing sounds appealing. It just might change (if not save) your life.

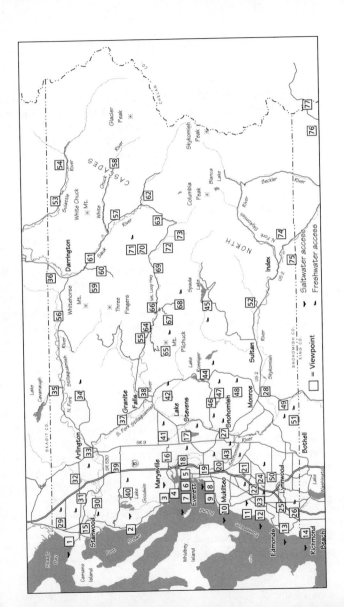

Viewpoints & Water Access

Officially, few designated viewpoints exist in Snohomish County. Yet there are still hundreds of places where there is a unique or scenic vista of something natural worth looking at: a bay, a lake or river, a waterfall or cascade, a canyon or gorge, a mountain, a glacier, a tree or a forest, an area frequented by wildlife, an uncommon ecosystem, a pretty place to snap a picture. Such places are not always located at a convenient roadside pullout, or a park, or on the brink of a steep precipice, although a few are and that makes them handy. So, while the author was making the rounds in Snohomish County checking out the trails, some of the more interesting vistas were noted. Approximate locations are noted on the facing page.

Also, there happen to be dozens of public fishing access areas on lakes and rivers that are managed by the Washington Department of Fish and Wildlife (WDFW), but which few people are even aware of. Many of these were also noted. For fishers and non-fishers alike, access areas on lakes—waters that belong to us all, by the way—make great spots to launch a canoe or kayak. Even the smallest lakes can brighten an otherwise dull day when the mountains are snowed in and woods walks just aren't on the menu. Nearly all have at least a portable privy. However, use of these sites *requires* a fishing and/or conservation license ($10 for the latter; good for 12 months). Obtain one through WDFW or your local sporting goods store.

Selected viewpoints and water access areas around the county are listed below. A '**W**' indicates water access suitable for launching a hand-carried boat. Assume that a conservation license is required for all WDFW sites. Incidentally, this is not a boater's guide. **It is the reader's responsibility to learn and practice boater safety, which includes, among other things, wearing an approved life jacket** (duh...). Cold water, wind, and changing weather are particular dangers. Currents in rivers, and both tides and currents in the Sound present additional hazards. If you're new to canoes, kayaks, or rowboats learn the ropes from someone who knows. Boldness is useless when your boat, or worse, You, are suddenly sinking to the bottom. Here's almost eighty sites to check out.

The Coast

1. Big Ditch Slough (W)

See Walk #1 for directions to this pleasant viewpoint and walk north of Stanwood along Skagit Bay and within the Skagit Wildlife Recreation Area. Views of the bay, Camano, Whidbey, Fir, and Fidalgo Islands, plus Mt. Baker, and the Twin Sisters Range. A variety of birds and other wildlife inhabit this coastal floodplain, a major habitat area that is ecologically linked not just to the bay, but to the extensive estuary and delta of the Skagit River. Nice sunsets, but closed after dark. (WDFW site.)

2. Kayak Point (W)

A good fishing and viewing pier at Kayak Point County Park, plus an excellent beach are great for a lengthy morning wander or a sentimental sunset stroll. Views are west toward Port Susan and Camano Island. Bring binoculars for birdlife and marine mammals. You could even see a whale. (*See Walk #2 for directions.*)

3. Tulalip Bay (W)

On the Tulalip Reservation west of Marysville, one can access the water and enjoy a view of the bay at Tulalip Bay Marina, as well learn some history of the place by way of an interpretive walk near the water (*see Walk #3*). From I-5 take Marine Dr. to 64th St., go left, then right on Totem Beach Rd. to the marina entrance on the left.

4. Mission Beach

Across the spit from Tulalip Bay is a good view of Possession Sound and Hat Island from Mission Beach Rd. From Marine Dr. take 64th St. to a tee, turn left. Look to the left at a sharp bend just past the cemetery, 0.4 mile from the tee.

5. Legion Memorial & Grand Avenue Parks

To reach modest-sized Legion Memorial Park, follow Grand Ave. north from downtown, passing the late Sen. Scoop Jackson's Everett home and Grand Ave. Park at 17th St. (*see Walk #12*) to enjoy a nice view of the Navy Homeport and marina. A footbridge to the waterfront has been considered here. Continue north and find Legion Memorial Park at 2nd St. Westward off Alverson Blvd. are great views of Port Gardner, Possession Sound, the Snohomish River delta, Hat, Whidbey, and Camano Islands, the Olympic Mountains, and Mt. Baker. A large wetland below, Maulsby Swamp, offers a glimpse of what some of the natural coastline may have once looked liked.

6. North & South View Parks

Two parks with a paved path connecting them and the north Everett waterfront on Port Gardner (*see Walk #12*).

7. Marine Park (W)

Water access to Jetty Island is a highlight at Everett's Marine Park, but short walking paths, a small fishing pier, and viewing areas are worth a visit. Whidbey and Hat Islands are to the west, Point Elliot and Mukilteo to the southwest. The park is off Marine View Dr. at the west end of 10th St.

8. Howarth Park & Pigeon Creek

Howarth Park offers several good viewpoints, one from the park road above the bluff overlooking Port Gardner and the Everett waterfront. Scamper down and across the grass to reach a path along the bluff and a link to the pedestrian overpass over the railroad tracks. From this bridge there is a great view up and down the coast (a good spot for binoculars or a spotting scope). The same bridge can be accessed from the Pigeon Creek parking lot below (off Olympic Blvd.; may be closed). Mukilteo and the Whidbey Island ferry are visible across Possession Sound to the southwest, Port Gardner, the Everett waterfront, Navy Homeport, and the Mt. Baker volcano (on the horizon) to the northeast, and Whidbey and Camano Islands to the northwest. (*See Walk #5 for a good beach trek here.*)

9. Harborview Park

A great viewpoint between Everett and Mukilteo, with a wide panorama of islands, Possession Sound, the Everett waterfront and Mt. Baker (*see Park #19; photo next page*).

10. Mukilteo State Park (W)

Adjacent to the ferry terminal, Mukilteeo State Park offers access to some good walkable beach (*see Walk #6*), as well as views across Possession Sound to Whidbey Island and beyond. It might also be a

Everett from Harborview Park

good place to watch the ferry come and go while you develop ideas for the perfect Northwest mystery novel. Be sure to read the interpretive signs, this place has some important history (*see Park #22*). Also, look for a small public float next to the ferry dock.

11. Picnic Point

The county park at Picnic Point offers good access to the waterfront between Edmonds and Mukilteo and is a convenient starting point for beach walks (*see Walk #7*). A footbridge over the railroad tracks accommodates partial views of the coastline, but walk down to the beach to better enjoy this attractive shore. Whidbey Island is to the northwest, and the Kitsap Peninsula sprawls west to southwest.

12. Meadowdale Beach

See Meadowdale Beach Park (*and Walk #8*) for access to the beach by way of a long path through the park. About a half-mile south of the park one can also access the beach from a tiny parking area off 162nd St. SW. Lack of parking means it's probably hopeless to try on nice weekends (be friendly and don't block the neighbors).

13. Edmonds Area Viewpoints

Several good viewpoints have been developed in the Edmonds area, including the Stamm Overlook north of town on Olympic View Dr. across from High St., with two benches, flowers, a tiny parking area, great view of sunsets and the Olympics, and two trees (a fir and a cedar) that seem to have eloped. Another overlook closer to the water but with a similar view is a few blocks south on Ocean Ave. From Olympic View Dr. turn west onto Cherry St., then right on Sound View, left on Water St., and left on Ocean (parking at south end). Note that trains move through the area fast and frequently. A few blocks south is one more developed viewpoint along Sunset Ave. reached via Edmonds St. Edmonds historic district is a delight also. Walk up Edmonds St. to 5th Ave. and take a right. (*See also Park #38.*)

14. Richmond Beach

Although it's just across the border in King County, Richmond Beach's beach is definitely worth a visit for any southern Snohomish Countian. On a cool clear winter morning the view of the Olympics is exceptional. If the tide is more out than in, there's good beach to walk as well. (*See Park #41 for directions.*)

Urban Areas

15. Rotary Riverfront Park

(Stanwood) A new riverfront park is in the works in Stanwood on the south side of SR 532 just east of Twin City Foods. Viewing potential is good and, hopefully, the park will lead to improved hiker access to river dikes. Over the long-term, connections to the dikes along Port Susan, West Pass, and Skagit Bay, as well as Stanwood's historic district, would be particularly attractive.

16. Jennings Nature Park

This Marysville park has good views of the Allen Creek wetlands. Worth carrying binoculars and a bird book in spring (*see Walk #10*).

17. Lake Stevens (W)

Although Snohomish County lacks any "really large" lakes like the ones found in surrounding counties, there is one "fairly sizeable"

North Cove Park, Lake Stevens

one, Lake Stevens, which most locals are familiar with. In the past when the lake was a little more remote from urban civilization, the area developed as a resort community, and for many, a weekend or summer hideaway. Now, of course, there is nowhere to hide. Most waterfront property that could be developed has been, and as growth and development in the region continue to explode more or less out of control, Lake Stevens is rapidly being absorbed into the greater megalopolis. All is not yet lost, however. To get a good look at what's left, try Lundeen Park on the north shore, or North Cove Park next to the city center (*see Park #10 for directions*).

18. Langus Riverfront Park (W)
Across the Snohomish River from north Everett, this park includes an extensive path and good views of the river (*see Walk #28*).

19. Viola Oursler Viewpoint, Riverside & Summit Parks
A newly developed viewpoint in north Everett looks out across Smith, Spencer, and Ebey Islands, I-5, and the Snohomish River valley to the North Cascades. On the horizon left to right, Whitehorse

Mt., Three Fingers, and Mt. Pilchuck are most prominent. Crane your neck to see Mt. Baker to the north. The Viola Oursler Viewpoint is on E. Marine View Dr. near 7th St. Trees (in summer) tend to obstruct a similar view from Riverside Park (Everett Ave. at E. Grand Ave.). The best view east, but right next to I-5, is at Summit Park (Summit Ave. and 20th St.).

20. Rotary Riverfront Park (W)

(Lowell) Try this little park on the Snohomish River southeast of Everett for a good look at the river, nearby wetlands, wildlife, and prominent peaks of the North Cascades, including Mt. Baker above the smooth moving water. The Lowell Riverfront Trail is also accessed here (*see Walk #29 for directions*).

21. Silver Lake (W)

See Thornton A. Sullivan Park (*and Walk #13*) for details and directions to Everett's largest lake. A good view from a rectangular fishing float can be found on the east shore next to 19th Ave. SE just south of 116th St. SE (limited parking). Paddling a canoe or kayak in the off-season might be worthwhile; motor boats over 10 horsepower and 8 mph are banned all year.

22. Lake Stickney (W)

A small and pretty lake with a fair bit of natural shoreline still intact is Lake Stickney in the 'burbs south of Everett. From SR 99 a mile north of Mukilteo Speedway head east on Gibson Rd. a few blocks to 17th Ave. W. Turn right and find the WDFW public fishing access just around a bend. Like most small lakes, Stickney is better as an easy paddle than as a stop on a Sunday drive.

23. Lake Serene (W)

A pretty little lake in the middle of suburbia, Lake Serene may still not be worth driving far to look at, but it does beckon an easy paddle by canoe or kayak in the off-season. Look for Canadian honkers and mallards, plus pink and white lily pads blooming in spring. The WDFW public fishing access is off Serene Way at 140th St. SW which can be reached via Highway 99 and Shelby Rd. Park across from the fire station. No internal combustion motors are allowed.

24. Martha Lake (W)

This modest-sized lake is heavily developed but worth an early morning visit when motor boats are few and noise from nearby traffic is less intrusive. Briefly stroll the south shore or launch a canoe or kayak from Martha Lake Park off East Shore Dr. just north of 164th St. SE. A WDFW public fishing access and boat ramp is adjacent to the north.

25. Scriber Lake

A nice path, floating walkway, interesting seating accommodations, and duck blinds for wildlife viewing are key features to be explored at this attractive lake and natural area in the heart of Lynnwood (*see Walk #20 for details*).

26. Lake Ballinger (W)

One of the larger lakes in the county, Lake Ballinger is probably best known for the public golf course built on its northerly shore. But there is also a public fishing access, dock, and a little swimming beach off Lakeview Dr. near 236th St. SW. Boating is allowed but internal combustion motors are not. The park is a city of Mountlake Terrace facility. May be best to avoid the area in nice summer weather, unless it's crowds you crave.

27. Blackman Lake (W)

When in Snohomish, take a look at Blackman Lake either at Ferguson Park east of Bickford Ave. just south of SR 9, or better yet, at Hill Park off Lake View Ave. north of 13th St. There's a simple woodsy urban park here with picnicking, play area, and two small fishing docks. All of it, unfortunately, is stuck behind an unsightly chainlink fence. Perhaps there's an explanation. . .

28. Al Borlin Park (Buck Island)

On the east side of Monroe between the Skykomish River and Woods Creek is Buck Island and Al Borlin Park. The park is within a wooded floodplain so facilities are limited to picnic areas, river access, and a great little trail system that links with Lewis Street Park on higher ground to the west (*see Walk #33 for details and directions*). The park opens early and closes at dusk.

29. Lake Ketchum (W)

Northeast of Stanwood is this small public access point managed by WDFW. The little lake is rather developed so don't go looking for anything spectacular here. Residents are working with state and county officials to improve water quality, reduce algae and unwanted vegetation, and restore ecological, scenic, and recreational values to the lake. From I-5 exit 215, find 300th St. NW and head west three miles to 76th Ave. NW; turn right. In less than a mile, turn left on S. Lake Ketchum Rd. Park on the right in a half-mile.

30. Stillaguamish River (W)

For a look at the lower Stillaguamish River in the county's rural nordland, try I-5 exit 210 and head west on Jackson Gulch Rd. 1.4 miles to Pioneer Highway (historic Silvana is a mile to the south). Turn right and immediately left on Norman Rd. and follow this 2.5 miles to a sharp right bend in the road with shoulder parking and a guardrail next to the river. There are good views up and down with

South Fork Stilly from Mt. Loop Highway

Whitehorse Mountain, Three Fingers, Mt. Pilchuck, wooded terraces, and surrounding farms adding to the scene. Another wooded spot to gander is farther west. Continue north and west on the Norman Rd. 2.3 miles to Marine Drive and head straight across to find a WDFW fishing access area on the left just ahead. A planned new riverfront park in Stanwood may improve access as well. Closer to I-5, you can reach the gravel bar upstream of the freeway bridge by heading west from I-5 on SR 530 to 7th Ave. NE. Turn right here and follow this dead-end road under I-5 to a wide paved shoulder just beyond. It's a 0.2 mile walk on a grassy road to the bar.

The river's two major forks are also relatively easy to view. The North Fork Stilly roughly parallels SR 531 between Arlington and Darrington (*see Walks #23 and #34*). The South Fork is especially scenic along the Mountain Loop Highway east of Granite Falls. The falls, of course, is one of the better spots, but several trails and campgrounds offer views and easy access as well (*see Hikes #44 and #70*). The forks converge at Twin Rivers Park in Arlington.

31. Sunday Lake (W)

A pretty little mostly developed lake near I-5 with a small dock and float, suitable for one or two people dying to stare at ducks and cattails. Really, what life in the Northwest oughtta be. No internal combustion motors allowed, so a friendly place to launch a canoe or kayak for a twenty-minute paddle in the off-season (forget it May through September). From SR 532 1/4 mile west of I-5, turn south onto E. Sunday Lake Rd. Look for the WDFW public fishing sign on the left in 0.9 mile. Closed after dark.

32. Pilchuck Creek

About two miles west of SR 9 on the Stanwood-Bryant Rd., and just east of the bridge over Pilchuck Creek is a small parking area next to a popular summer swimming hole, with gravel bars, woods, and a nice bit of water. Take a look on the way through.

33. Lake Armstrong (W)

An attractive little lake where motorboats are banned, Lake Armstrong is enjoyable by rowboat, canoe, or kayak. Drive a mile north of Arlington on SR 9 to a narrow steep paved road angling to the right uphill, signed for the lake. Drive this around a bend, crossing the Centennial Trail and passing the 1994 Wildlife Farm of the Year (on left). In 0.6 mile turn left on E. Lake Armstrong Rd. and find the WDFW parking area on the left in 0.4 mile. The return to SR 9 can be tricky and should be avoided during commute hours.

34. Riley Lake (W)

To reach this marshy lake east of Arlington from SR 530 (MP 25.6), drive Jim Creek Rd. six miles and go left on Lake Riley Rd. It's two miles to the lake and public fishing access (stay left at a fork). Transmission lines and homes nearby diminish the appeal, although it is pleasantly quiet. Internal combustion motors are not allowed.

35. Lake Cavanaugh Road

For a good view of the North Fork Stillaguamish valley, take SR 530 east from Arlington to MP 32.7 and turn left on the Lake Cavanaugh Rd., just before the river bridge. Narrow pavement ends in two miles but good gravel continues over the east end of Frailey Mt. another four miles to Lake Cavanaugh in Skagit County. At 2.5 miles from SR 530 there is a great view of the valley from a bump next to a road cut. Look past the beer cans and shotgun shells to the Boulder River valley (feeds the Stilly), Three Fingers and Whitehorse Mt. to the southeast. Mt. Higgins is to the east. A wide spot just beyond offers more room to park and almost as good a view.

36. North Mt. Lookout & Nels Bruseth Memorial Garden

A good view of the Sauk and S. Fork Stilly valleys and surrounding mountains can be found at the old lookout site atop North Mt., near Darrington. From Mt. Loop Hwy head west and north on USFS Rd. #28; stay right in three miles on Rd. #2810 for ten more long and potentially rough miles to the 3,824-foot summit. Also, across from the ranger station, check out the Nels Bruseth Memorial Garden.

37. Jordan Bridge

An intriguing suspension footbridge over the South Fork Stillaguamish River between Arlington and Granite Falls, accessed via Jordan Rd. Nice views up and down the river. Stairs lead to a beach under the bridge. Definitely worth a look. (*See Park #6 for directions.*)

38. Granite Falls

There are only a few waterfalls in Snohomish County that you can drive to year-round, and Granite Falls, from which the nearby timber town takes its name, is a good one despite marginal facilities for the public. Expect lots of company on nice summer weekends. From downtown Granite Falls, follow the Mt. Loop Highway north about 1.8 miles out of town to a small WDFW parking area on the left just before crossing the bridge over the South Fork Stilly. Even at low flows the falls are noisy and inviting, thundering when higher run-off races by in fall and spring. The drop is not great, but the view is good. Walk the obvious wide path (road bed) about 150 yards to stairs and either continue or drop down the steps to complete a short loop of about 0.2 mile. The big concrete structure below is a fish ladder to help ocean-going salmon and steelhead make their way up-river to spawn (no fishing allowed here). The river cuts an impressive gorge with high rock cliffs on the opposite shore. The rock can be slippery close to this tumult, so best to obey the unsightly "keep-out" signs. Big cedars and Douglas fir trees line the banks above the falls. With some creativity and minimal funding, the falls could be improved to a first-class viewing area. As it is, the signs, fencing, and concrete clash with the gem nature put here.

39. Cedar Stump

For those who have never seen a really big tree, the old cedar stump at the northbound I-5 rest area near Arlington (MP 207) is worth a gander, perhaps to spur a little consideration of what an incredible forest once existed in the region. In less than a century and a half, we humans have managed to destroy 90% of the old forests of Washington, although some will argue that we've locked up too much remaining forest in parks and wilderness. Hardly. There is a giant living western red cedar tree quite visible from I-5 a half-mile north of the rest area (on private property). The tree has a tall dead top rising well above the live crown. Few motorists are aware that the base of this tree is nearly 15 feet across.

40. Seven Lakes (W)

If it's not summery out, a visit to one or more of these little lakes northwest of Marysville makes a suitable mini-adventure when there's absolutely nothing else to do, or if you just want to see more of what this county is made of. The seven-plus lakes are scattered around Lake Goodwin (*see Park #2 for directions*). Paddlers might enjoy them in almost any kind of weather. If it's too nice, though, expect lots of folks with similar ideas. There are public boat launches and WDFW fishing access areas, and/or swimming at almost all lakes in the area. A good county map will help you find them. Better ones include Goodwin (the biggest lake, has a state park, camping, etc.), Crabapple (access on the north side, attractive, small, no motor boats allowed), Ki (access from SR 531 shoulder on the north side, slow motor boats permitted), Shoecraft (access west side, water-skiing in the middle of the lake), Martha (north side access, pleasant), and Howard (west end access, no motors). Except for Goodwin, facilities are limited, though most have at least an outhouse.

41. Lake Cassidy (W)

Of interest to canoeists and kayakers is this pleasant lake three miles north of Lake Stevens. Lake Cassidy has lots of marshy shore and wetlands nearby, within a developing rural setting. County Parks owns a big wildlife reserve on the north end, adjacent to the Centennial Trail. A WDFW public fishing access is just south of where Lake Cassidy Rd. (60th St. NE) meets S. Lake Cassidy Rd., 0.6 mile east of SR 9. Park across the road.

42. Lake Bosworth (W)

A small, pleasant WDFW fishing access exists at the north end of Lake Bosworth, a modest-sized lake with lots of homes and some undeveloped shoreline. Motor-powered boats are prohibited so it's good for a paddle. From the flashing red light in Granite Falls, head south on Granite Ave. (becomes Robe Menzel Rd.) and drive about three miles to a junction with Bosworth Rd.; stay right up the hill. In 0.8 mile, just after a sharp bend, turn right on E. Lake Bosworth Dr. and find the fishing access in a mile, off the end of this road.

43. Snohomish River (W)

The County's namesake river, and one of the region's three principal river systems, is (surprise!) the Snohomish. The river collects runoff from the Skykomish and Snoqualmie Rivers which merge to form the Snohomish two miles southwest of Monroe. Good vantage points of the lower river are at several parks and public fishing access areas. The estuary at Port Gardner in North Everett is best viewed from W. Marine View Dr. (*see Walk #12*), and from SR 529. Upriver, try Langus Park (*Walk #28*), Lowell Riverfront Park (*Walk #29*), Riverview Rd., downtown Snohomish (*Walk #11*), Thomas Eddy (*Walk #31*), Lord Hill (*Hike #32*), and Shorts School Rd., three miles south of Snohomish. For a good look at the river's broad floodplain try Summit Park in North Everett at Summit Ave. and 20th St. The best place to view the Snoqualmie River, of course, is at Snoqualmie Falls in King County. A placid stretch above the confluence is visible from the WDFW public fishing access near the junction of High Bridge Rd. and Crescent Lake Rd. For good looks at the Skykomish, skip ahead to Viewpoint #74.

44. Lake Roesiger (W)

With all its little woodsy bays and points, Lake Roesiger was once one of the more attractive lakes in the county. But like so many other lovely natural waterfronts in western Washington, humans and their houses, yards, and contrivances have encroached on the water's edge on all sides, vastly replacing the natural shoreline with a chaotic collage of development. Multitudes of boats, docks, floats, and portable comforts crowd the banks. And now that "water cycles" are the rage and singing birds are passé, even the quiet is missing from the lake most of the summer. All that said, Lake Roesiger still intrigues. At the right time of day or year (water skiing is banned October through April), there remains something to see and breathe here. Try Lake Roesiger County Park off the Lake Roesiger Rd. on the southeast shore, or the WDFW boat launch and fishing access at the south end (off Middle Shore Rd.), a mile south of the park.

45. Spada Lake (W)

Spada Lake, a large reservoir in the foothills northeast of Sultan, is the main water supply for two-thirds of the Snohomish County population. The lake was created with the completion of Culmback Dam, a rock and clay structure, in 1965. The dam was raised 62 feet in 1984, doubling the size of the lake, and a hydroelectric project was constructed by Snohomish County PUD. Recreation amenities —

mitigation for the dam and power project—were completed in 1990. Public use of the area is highly restricted to day use only (late April to late October). There are excellent picnicking facilities, limited walking paths, and good viewpoints, most barrier-free (*see Park #55 for details*). For more information, try the PUD at 1-800-562-9142.

From U.S. Hwy. 2 at the east edge of Sultan, head north on the Sultan Basin Rd. about 13.5 miles to an information/registration area and a road fork. Stay right to find Bear Creek Overlook on the left in about six miles. A short steep path offers a great vantage point for photos and sunsets (*see back cover photo*). Head left from the fork to reach the Culmback Dam overlook in 1.8 miles, with a view into the Sultan River gorge below. Continue across the dam 1.2 miles to a junction and head right another 1.2 miles to the North Shore site high on a bluff overlooking the lake and dam. Del Campo Peak is prominent to the east and Static Peak (above Big Greider Lake) is to the southeast. A 0.2-mile paved path and picnic sites are available here. The roads are unpaved but well maintained. Lake Chaplain to the west is also part of the Everett water system but is not open to public use.

46. Flowing Lake (W)

Flowing Lake is a modest-sized lake northeast of Snohomish with an attractive county park on the north end (*see Park #54 for directions*). Boating, fishing, swimming, camping, and short walks are all available. The lake can also be reached from the WDFW fishing access at the south end (turn right, or south, off Three Lakes Rd., then a quick left on Spada Rd., a left on Storm Lake Rd., and left again on Wonderland Rd.).

47. Storm & Panther Lakes (W)

Two smaller lakes near Flowing Lake, Storm and Panther Lakes, are also worth a paddle. Storm Lake's WDFW site is just a block east of the southern access to Flowing Lake (above). To reach Panther Lake's public fishing access turn north off Three Lakes Rd. onto 163rd Ave. NE, then left in a mile on Panther Lake Rd. The WDFW access is just ahead on the right. Panther is a pretty lake with woods and a marshy shore, and not too developed. Internal combustion motors are not allowed at either lake.

Wagner Lake near Monroe

48. Chain Lake & Wagner Lake (W)

A very pretty little lake with a mostly natural and marshy shore is Chain Lake, hidden in a little valley a few miles north of Monroe. A WDFW public fishing access is a half-mile east of Trombley Rd. on Chain Lake Rd. Wagner Lake, not far to the southeast, is also quite attractive and holds evidence of the area's robust logging history. The WDFW access is on the east side of Wagner Rd. about 0.7 mile north of Woods Creek Rd. Internal combustion motors prohibited.

49. Crescent Lake (W)

A small, pretty lake with a mostly natural shoreline and WDFW public fishing access. From SR 203 south of Monroe head west to Crescent Lake Rd. and a parking area on the right before reaching the Snoqualmie River bridge. Mt. Rainier is visible to the south.

50. North Creek Park

A new county park south of Mill Creek with a nice view of large wetlands; has a good boardwalk trail (*see Walk #30*).

51. Echo & Lost Lakes (W)

Two small lakes near the King County line east of Bothell can be reached at WDFW public fishing access points, though like most smaller lakes, Echo and Lost are of more interest to fishers and boaters than sightseers. Echo Lake is mostly developed. To reach it turn south off SR 522 onto Echo Lake Rd. and drive 2.8 miles to the fishing access on the right. For the other, back up a mile to Lost Lake Rd. and turn east to find the lake access a short mile beyond. Lost is smaller but less developed and somewhat appealing. Farther west, a larger lake, Crystal, can be found off Crystal Lake Rd. Unfortunately, this lake is effectively locked up by private development.

52. Wallace Falls

The best view of this high — and highly impressive — waterfall is from the trail that leaves Wallace Falls State Park (*see Hike #45*), although it's also quite visible from U.S. Hwy. 2 near Gold Bar. While you're in the area, maybe check out the Wallace River Salmon Hatchery, a mile west of Gold Bar.

The North Cascades

53. Suiattle River

Many good views of this broad swift river can be had from Suiattle River Rd. (USFS Rd. #26) which leaves SR 530 seven miles north of Darrington. From its Suiattle Glacier headwaters, this designated Wild and Scenic River winds halfway around Glacier Peak, collecting meltwater from more than three-fourths of its glaciers. At various points along the river, some of the area's dominant peaks are visible, including Whitehorse and White Chuck Mt. (prominent to the south near MP 7). Look for a few tributary waterfalls high above the road, including a nice one to the north at 4.0 miles. The road accesses several trails listed in this guide and ends at 23 miles, near Sulphur Creek Campground. The Suiattle River joins the Sauk near SR 530 and the Sauk feeds the Skagit River at Rockport near SR 20.

54. Green Mountain Road

The drive to many mountain trailheads, though at times rough, is often scenic, thanks to old-growth forest (and view-penetrating clearcuts), waterfalls, cliffs, occasional vistas, wildlife, and wildflowers. Green Mt. Rd. is one possibility (*see Hike #49 for directions*).

55. Mountain Loop National Scenic Byway

This famed highway is a 50-mile long, mostly-paved road connecting Granite Falls and Darrington by way of Barlow Pass and the South Fork Stillaguamish and South Fork Sauk River valleys. Development began in the 1890s, first spurred by mining, and later logging activity in the region. Today, numerous trails, views, campgrounds, picnic areas, and historic sites can be accessed along the way; however, winter snows near Barlow Pass prevent year-round access. The road is usually open from May until November; and from Granite Falls only to Deer Creek Rd. in winter; beyond is a popular snowmobile area (Deer Creek Rd. is closed to motorized vehicles mid-December through March). Fourteen miles of road north of the pass are unpaved, well graded, but dusty in summer, with some single-lane roadway and turnouts. Check with the Darrington Ranger Station or the Verlot Public Service Center for current conditions and a good travelers' guide to the route. Note that the drive is famous and busy on summer weekends.

56. Whitehorse Mt. & Three Fingers

Even the locals will tell you that the most spectacular thing about the little logging town of Darrington is the backdrop: 6,852-foot Whitehorse Mt. The peak, visible from much of the western part of the county, rises abruptly just a mile from a town that's barely 500 feet above sea level. This remarkable glacier-carved mountain is steep and impressive from all sides, although the long steep glacier on the north makes it particularly gorgeous from the Darrington area. The mountain is visible from many roads in and out of town. Try a turnout at MP 45 on SR 530 where an open field offers a great wide-open view of both Whitehorse Mt. and Jumbo Mt. behind and to the left. If drivable, USFS Roads #28 and #2810 up North Mt. just north of the Darrington Ranger Station offer excellent views of these and other neighboring peaks. The triple summit of Three Fingers is also prominent from many areas of western Snohomish County, including I-5 north of Everett, SR 530 east of Arlington (around MP 34), and SR 92 heading into Granite Falls. From these distances, in good light and with ordinary binoculars, you should be able to make out the old fire lookout atop the south summit.

View from the White Chuck Mt. Viewpoint, south of Darrington

57. White Chuck Mt. & Mt. Pugh

Good mountain views exist at a number of turnouts along the Mountain Loop Hwy. between Darrington and Granite Falls. The White Chuck Mt. viewpoint at MP 6.9 is a good picnic stop, small and scenic with a wheelchair-accessible restroom (bullet holes courtesy of the Northwest's gun-totin'-bottle-chuckin'-sign-shootin'-back-woods-pick-up-truckers). White Chuck is the obvious big one across the Sauk River. Nice. Downriver are the layered summits of Mt. Higgins, and Jumbo Mt. to the left. Around MP 4 and 5, among other places, are good views of Mt. Pugh, also visible from SR 530 west of Darrington. The north side of White Chuck Mt. is prominent from the Suiattle River Rd. near MP 7.

58. Glacier Peak, Mt. Baker & Mt. Rainier

The highest bit of terra firma in Snohomish County (*front cover photo*) is the 10,541-foot summit of DaKobed, the "Great Parent," or as most of us know it, Glacier Peak, Washington's fourth highest — and least active — volcano. Its last significant eruption was about 12,000 years ago when a huge mudflow reached pre-Darrington. The summit is only a few feet shy of standing two vertical miles above sea level, yet it is almost entirely invisible over vast areas of the county. Mt. Baker to the north and Mt. Rainier to the south are far more conspicuous from many locations, not just because they are higher (Mt. Baker is 10,781 feet and Mt. Rainier is 14,440 feet), but because they don't sit behind crowds of high rugged peaks like Glacier does, say, when viewed from the Everett area. While Glacier Peak is closer to Everett than its two neighbors, it is buried much deeper in the Cascades than the others. Still, it can be seen up close from a number of trails in the mountains, and with a careful eye, from a distance as well (*for the former, try Hikes #50, #55, #56, and #90*). White Chuck River Rd. appears to offer the best view from a road. From Mountain Loop Highway, head east on USFS Rd. #23 about 7.5 miles to a signed viewpoint, then continue two more miles to a good view of the peak six miles away and straight above the road near the White Chuck River Trailhead. One can also catch a glimpse of Glacier Peak from SR 530 west of Darrington near MP 42 and 43. The volcano is just right of White Chuck Mt. and left of Mt. Pugh.

For the distant view, wait for mid to late summer or fall when most of the snow has melted off the lower peaks and then try to pick out the more conspicuously snowy (icy) one in the background. The mountain is visible at several points along I-5, but also try Home Acres Rd. a half-mile south of U.S. Hwy. 2, where Glacier Peak appears only a few degrees right of Mt. Pilchuck. If you're fanatic about it, you'll find all three volcanoes visible from a single point. From the east side, there's a good view from a paved road northwest of Lake Wenatchee (*see Hike #90*). It should be added that from a few select locations, Mt. St. Helens, well over a hundred miles to the south, is also visible, but barely. In a geology class at Everett Community College in 1980, we all walked out to the parking lot to watch it erupt.

59. Squire Creek Wall

This immense granite wall, 2,500 feet high, plus the east face of Three Fingers are visible from near the end of USFS Rd. #2040. (*See Hike #53 for directions.*)

60. Clear Creek & Asbestos Creek Falls

Clear Creek is one of many attractive, cascading streams crossed by the Mt. Loop Highway. When all you feel like doing is watching water go by, pack up the lawn chair and head for Clear Creek Campground near Darrington. Look for a view of the creek's little gorge close by (*see Walk #36*). Or head up Clear Creek Rd. (USFS Rd. #2060), across from the campground entrance, to check out the creek's interesting watershed. The road can be rough at times. At three miles, park on the left just before the shallow creek flowing over the roadway (Asbestos Creek). A long series of falls, partly visible, but mostly not, tumbles down the east wall of Jumbo Mt. The name may be uninviting, but the view isn't. Unfortunately, the view doesn't get any better than right from the road due to vista-blocking vegetation higher up the slope. If the stream and road are passable, drive another 2.6 miles to a junction. Right leads 0.5 mile to a view of two high rock walls and the east trailhead for Squire Creek Pass (*see Hike #53*). Left goes to a bridge over Clear Creek in 0.2 mile and more views of more walls, partly obstructed by trees. A washout blocks progress in another 0.8 mile where there's a nice mountain view of the peaks south of Three Fingers. This old road leads about three miles to the north trail to Deer Creek Pass (*see Hike #53*).

61. Sauk River

The Sauk River, a major fork of the Wild and Scenic Skagit River, begins in the heart of Snohomish County's North Cascades. The North and South Forks, plus the White Chuck and Suiattle River tributaries downstream, drain much of the Glacier Peak and Henry M. Jackson Wilderness Areas. Good views of the Sauk are found along the Old Sauk, Beaver Lake, North Fork Falls, and North Fork Sauk Trails (*see Walks #37, #38, #41, and #59*), and at many Forest Service campgrounds and pull-outs along the Mountain Loop Highway north of Barlow Pass (*see also Park #8*). The old Monte Cristo Rd. (*see Hike #64*) parallels the South Fork for three miles. The South Fork takes a steep scenic drop just below Monte Cristo Lake, 2.5 miles north of the pass, and is impressive at high water. Near MP 19 is a good view of Sheep Mt. towering above the road. Whitewater boaters congregate near the confluence of the Sauk and White Chuck

Rivers and often put in at a launch off USFS Rd. #22 about 0.2 mile off the Mountain Loop Highway (from Darrington turn left at MP 6.2). One can also check out the White Chuck River at a bridge on USFS Rd. #23, 5.5 miles east of Mountain Loop Highway.

62. North Fork Sauk Falls

An impressive waterfall anytime of the year, and a definite stop for hikers exploring the Mountain Loop Highway region. The viewpoint is at the end of a moderately steep 0.2-mile trail that switchbacks down into a canyon. There's a sheer drop-off at the trail end so younger kids may need to be roped in close. (*See Walk #41 for directions.*)

63. Monte Cristo Lake

In a broad floodplain of the South Fork Sauk River about 2.4 miles north of Barlow Pass lies Monte Cristo Lake, worth a quick visit in the spring or fall. Myrtle Lake is across the road at a bend. At a turnout near the lower end of the lake (marked by a modest cedar tree next to the road) look for a short path leading to a small sandy bank on the lake. The river begins a steep drop just below this point.

64. Verlot Public Service Center

This unusual viewpoint is included because of the giant tree section on exhibit and other interpretive exhibits, plus an opportunity to learn to identify local trees, shrubs and flowers (ask for the walking tour brochure at the Service Center). The site is east of Granite Falls next to the South Fork Stillaguamish River near MP 11 on the Mountain Loop Highway. Short walks, barrier-free restrooms, and camping are available nearby, and information on the National Forest and Wilderness Areas can be found at the center, formerly the Verlot Ranger Station. The big Douglas fir tree across the road was at least nine feet in diameter and over 700 years old before it was cut in 1969. Various events through history are marked along the rings, since we know that one new tree ring is added to a live tree each year. Amazingly, the tree was already about six feet across when Balboa sighted the Pacific Ocean in 1513. Millions of big trees have been logged in western Washington since the first mills were established in the mid-1800s. Now only a relative few remain.

65. Mt. Pilchuck

Not only does western Snohomish County afford good views of Mt. Pilchuck, one of the region's more prominent landmarks, the drive up the mountain (summer and fall) offers even more impressive views of the county. From Mountain Loop Highway (MP 12) turn south on USFS Rd. #42 and follow this seven miles to a big parking area and viewpoint near the former ski area. Then try to figure out what's what (a good topographical map helps). For the splendid panorama from the summit, try the Mt. Pilchuck Trail (*see Hike #80*).

66. Gold Basin Mill Pond & Hemple Creek Picnic Area

The upper valley of the South Fork Stillaguamish River is rich in timber and mining history, and the mill pond at Gold Basin is one of many historic sites that are easily accessible by car or on foot. Hemple Creek Picnic Area (with room for at least three dozen picnics, including some barrier-free) is nearby across the highway. From Granite Falls drive the Mt. Loop Highway to MP 13.5 and find the signed parking area on the right, across from Gold Basin Campground. A short paved interpretive walk (wheelchair accessible) leads to a few remnants of the early 1900s sawmill and nice views of the mill pond. The impoundment formed behind a small dam and was used for log storage until the mill folded in 1913. The scenic pond has been enhanced to support young coho salmon. Hemple Creek Picnic Area, next to the campground (to the west), contains a small interpretive display. The area is accessible nearly year-round.

67. Bear Lake (W)

The trail to Pinnacle Lake (*see Hike #77*) quickly reaches Bear Lake, affording a nice view of the wooded lakeshore with minimal effort.

68. Lake Evan (W)

A very short walk from the Boardman Lake Trailhead leads to this little mountain lake surrounded by old-growth forest (*see Hike #75*).

69. Dick Sperry Picnic Area & Sperry-Iverson Mine

A nice lunch spot on the South Fork Stilly east of Granite Falls at MP 21 on the Mountain Loop Highway. Upriver, the broad west face of Stillaguamish Peak is prominent. The Sperry-Iverson Mine entrance (closed) can be seen across the highway 200 yards farther east, and a short path leads up the wooded hillside to Sperry's old cabin site. Just up the highway is a turnout near the site of a three-mile aerial tram that carried gold and silver ore over Marble Pass. In another half-mile is the old mining town of Silverton.

70. Coal Lake Road Overlook

Photographers seeking an easy vantage point for a rugged mountain scene might try turning north off the Mountain Loop Highway at MP 25.9, east of Granite Falls. Drive up the Coal Lake Rd. 2.7 miles to a big turnout on the left side. The view of the South Fork Stillaguamish valley is excellent. Fall is especially nice when there is more color and the chance of a little fresh snow dusting the summits. Hall Peak and Big Four Mt. are to the south, with Sperry and Vesper Peaks behind and left. The road continues to Coal Lake and nearby trails (*see Hikes #71 & #72*).

71. Coal Lake (W)

From the Coal Lake Rd. overlook (above) continue up the road to the Coal Lake parking area (*see Hike #71*) and wander the short trail to a good view of another lovely montane lake. Watch for pikas whistling warnings in the rocks.

72. Big Four Ice Caves

For awesome views of some big peaks of the North Cascades, head for the new Big Four Ice Caves Trailhead. (*See Walk #70 for directions and a description of the easy hike to the ice caves.*) Big Four Mt., a real neck-craner, and Hall Peak's big spire dominate the skyline. If you don't care to hike a mile up to the cave viewpoint at the base of Big Four, try the level half-mile paved path and boardwalk nature loop with a visit to the Stilly River footbridge mid-way (barrier-free to bridge). Big avalanches thunder down the mountain's precipitous slopes in winter and spring, producing the snow and ice accumulation in which the caves form. They are unsafe to enter, by the way. Early season, avalanche danger is still very high so the trail may be closed past the river bridge. The peak is named for a snowpatch high above that resembles the number "4" in summer (there's also a leaning "7" above it, and sometimes a "witch on a broom" to the right, best seen from the Coal Lake Rd. junction where a keen eye might make out a sounding "sperm whale"). The area is generally inaccessible from January into April, sometimes longer, because of deep snows that close the Mountain Loop Highway.

73. Sunrise Mine Road

One of the more dramatic close-up views of some impressive North Cascades peaks and waterfalls can be found at the end of the Sunrise Mine Rd. 2.6 miles southeast of the Big Four Ice Caves. East of Granite Falls, turn south off the Mountain Loop Highway at MP 28.6. Best late spring through fall. Waterfalls run their highest in the spring and early summer. Even in cloudy weather, the views of stark, vertical rock walls may be worth a visit. From the road-end (at 2.2 miles), visible peaks include Del Campo Peak (the steeply layered summit directly up the valley), Morning Star Peak (closer to the right), and Sperry Peak (a towering pyramid to the southwest). Lewis Peak is visible just before the road-end, left of Del Campo. On the drive in, the spires of Big Four Mt. and Hall Peak are sublimely inexplicable. For a good strenuous summer hike in the area try Headlee Pass (see Hike #67).

74. Skykomish River

To check out the lower reaches of the Skykomish River (a state-designated Scenic River) try Monroe's Buck Island (see Walk #33), and these WDFW fishing access areas: on the north side of the river west of Lewis St. in Monroe; on the north side of Ben Howard Rd. two miles east of SR 203; north of U.S. Hwy. 2 on the west side of Sultan (picnicking), and on the south side of the river east of 311th Aveune SE at Sultan. A short reach of the Snoqualmie River which joins the Skykomish southwest of Monroe is also accessible. Look for a WDFW public fishing access near the junction of High Bridge Rd. and Crescent Lake Rd. west of SR 203. The latter will take you south to the famous falls in King County, still a half-hour drive from here.

One of the more famous stretches of whitewater in the state is Boulder Drop, about two miles west of Index. Pull off on the north shoulder of U.S. Hwy. 2 east of MP 34 where you can see the river near the top of the drop. Fleets of rafts and kayaks float this area in spring and summer, an exhilarating run, to be sure. For a chance at

North Fork Skykomish River

a spur of the moment, half-day ride (for a fee, of course), look for a guide early morning at the Big Eddy River Access on U.S. Hwy. 2 about 3.5 miles downriver. It's a common meeting place and take-out for commercial raft trips on the Sky.

The North and South Forks of the Skykomish converge just below Index near the U.S. Hwy. 2 bridge west of town. The North Fork parallels USFS Rd. #63 (or vice-versa) with good views viewable at the old bridge into Index a mile north of the highway; just past Howard Creek at MP 9.1—turn left on USFS Rd. #6330 and immediately cross a bridge over the North Fork; park at the other end then walk out on the bridge for good views up and down the river, plus Mt. Index and the high rock wall leading right to Mt. Persis; farther up the North Fork Rd., there are several scenic stretches of bouldery, cascading whitewater. More serious and skilled adventurers might look around the Bear Creek confluence for more river views; *see also Hike #87.*

The South Fork begins near the town of Skykomish (in King County) with the merging of the Beckler and Tye Rivers east of town.

Waterfalls make these rivers intriguing, especially the Tye at Deception Creek (*see Walk #48*), and the South Fork between Index and Baring where three significant waterfalls are visible to searching eyes. Public access improvements to all three are non-existent (this really ought not to be so). Sunset Falls is a spectacular sliding cascade that drops to a wide bend in the river 1.5 miles up the Mt. Index Rd. from U.S. Hwy. 2. Another 1.3 miles up is Canyon Falls, just below an arched bridge. Here, the river seems to be sucked into a dark hole in the Earth, reappearing as foam in a gash below. Poking around these falls is not only potentially dangerous (no facilities), access is complicated by extensive private development. The Mt. Index Rd. beyond the Lake Serene trailhead (*see Hike #83*) is intended for residents and guests only and big signs warn that your presence is unwelcome. Lacking a good connection, try Eagle Falls farther upriver, but only when you're headed east on U.S. Hwy. 2. Pull off at a turnout at MP 39 and follow a short rough path to a good view of this falls. The drop isn't great but it's quite scenic, especially in afternoon light.

75. Mt. Index & Mt. Baring

From many areas of southwest Snohomish County one can look to the Cascades and easily spot several sharp peaks and a deep gash in the skyline where Mt. Index, Baring Mt., Gunn and Merchant Peaks, and their neighbors rise like sentinels over the Skykomish River. The peaks are visible at various locations along U.S. Hwy. 2 east of Everett, with good pastoral views from the backroads between Snohomish and Monroe. Mt. Index becomes prominent east of Gold Bar and is most impressive up close near the town of (where else) Index. This peak's near vertical north face is one of the Cascades' classic mountaineering objectives. Behind the town to the west is Town Wall, a rock climber's paradise whenever the rain quits. To get closer to the peak maybe try the really steep hike to Lake Serene (*see Hike #83*). Heybrook Ridge offers a good view that should get a whole lot better in the near future (*see Hike #46*). Mt. Index and the wall of cliffs leading to Mt. Persis to the northwest produce an impressive scene from the North Fork Rd. at about MP 3.5.

Equally impressive is Mt. Baring, farther east and across the river valley from Mt. Index. From the west, Baring stands out like some kind of petrified rocket launcher, albeit far more beautiful. While there is a good view of the peak just east of MP 36 on U.S. Hwy. 2 (straight down the highway), the best view from a road is at the end of USFS Rd. #6024 where the trail to Barclay Lake begins (*see Hike #84*). Things get dramatic a bit over three miles from the highway, beginning with the impressive southwestern rampart of Merchant and Gunn Peaks on the left (clearcuts below), followed by a good view of Baring's precipitous upper wall just beyond. The north face, nearly 3,000 feet high, is one of the highest cliffs in the Cascades. At mile four near the Barclay Lake trailhead a big waterfall slices the slopes of Merchant Peak.

76. Deception Falls

Although Deception Falls is across the line into King County, it is a favorite stopping point on the drive to Stevens Pass. Several falls on the Tye River and Deception Creek are an easy stroll away, and partly barrier-free (*see Walk #48*).

77. Stevens Pass

Also just outside the county, Stevens Pass is where the railroad and U.S. Hwy. 2 breach the crest of the North Cascades. There are no towering peaks here, but the drive over the 4,000-foot pass is scenic and popular year-round. A ski area operates in the winter, and the PCT crosses the highway here as well (*see Hike #89*).

Public Campgrounds

Local, state, and especially federal land management agencies provide abundant camping opportunities in a variety of settings, usually for a fee (often $10 to $15 per site). Many sites fill up in summer. Camping by reservation is a relatively new concept, but one that has taken hold as the demand for camping increases, and budget-cutting politicians earmark fewer funds to look after the little things like public campgrounds. (Congress especially seems happy to support corporate welfare programs, then puts the squeeze on when it comes to basic environmental and recreation programs. Go figure...)

Free camping is sometimes available in the off-season. Many sites close altogether since there is not enough staff to pick up the trash, pump the toilets, or scare off mindless vandals—scourge of the wilderness—who torch outhouses and blow bullet holes through anything that clinks. Despite the problems, agency staff and campground hosts should be commended for the great work they do to keep a struggling but good system alive. Some sites have potable water and chopped firewood in season. Nevertheless, always carry jugs of drinking water, and pack out your garbage and recyclables. Douse fires completely, just like the bear says. Incidentally, burning plastic and aluminum trash in firepits is not only uncool, it's toxic.

In addition to all the campgrounds found along Mt. Loop Highway, and the Skykomish and Suiattle Rivers, the Forest Service maintains several smaller group facilities, by reservation only. Informal camping occurs along many roads and rivers but this "cheap" alternative is often too damaging to vegetation, soils, and water quality to be recommended (if legal). These might also be the places where the familiar phrase "watch your step" was originally coined.

For more information, contact the appropriate agency (or concessionaire). To make a campsite reservation at a National Forest site, try calling (800) 280-CAMP. This number was valid in 1997, but could change in the future. You can also get camping information from a local USFS office, or try the toll-free information line in Mountlake Terrace at (800) 627-0062. Reservations are not usually required October through March when most campgrounds are either closed or available first-come, first-serve only. Reservations at most state parks can be made by calling (800) 452-5687. Again, this is generally unnecessary October through March. (*See map, p. 188.*)

City & County Campgrounds

1. Kayak Point Park
The county operates a decent little campground with some barrier-free sites at Kayak Point Park above the beach south of Stanwood (*see Walk #2 and Park #1 for details and directions*).

2. River Meadows Park
Limited walk-in tent camping is available at this county park on the South Fork Stillaguamish River (*see Walk #24*).

3. Squire Creek Park & Campground
To find this attractive county facility, turn north off of SR 530 about 4 miles west of Darrington (park sign). Beautiful Douglas fir and sword fern forest on 28 acres next to Squire Creek. Many relatively private sites for tents and RVs, plus group camping with a large picnic shelter.

4. Ferguson Park Campground (Snohomish)
A small, urban campground on Blackman Lake in Snohomish is run by the city. Find it next to a busy shopping complex east of Bickford Ave. south of SR 9. Named for E. C. Ferguson, founder of the city in 1859.

5. Flowing Lake County Park
A nicely wooded park with decent campsites, some barrier-free, just above the lake (*see Park #54 for details and directions*).

6. Lake Roesiger Park
The county operates a small campground in the woods at Lake Roesiger Park, across the road from the lake (*see Park #53*).

Washington State Campgrounds

7. Wenberg State Park
On Lake Goodwin northwest of Marysville, a few dozen sites and a lot of boats on the lake (*see Park #2 for directions*).

8. Mt. Pilchuck State Park
A few nice tent sites in the trees near the Mt. Pilchuck Trailhead (*see Hike #80 for directions*).

9. Wallace Falls State Park

North of Gold Bar, there are only a few tent sites at this park famous for the three-mile hike to the falls (*see Hike #45 for details*).

National Forest Campgrounds

In addition to the sites listed below, several group campgrounds are open by reservation only, including Beaver Creek, Coal Creek, Esswine, Marten Creek, Tulalip, and Wiley Creek. All are on the Mt. Loop Highway east of Verlot. In the off-season, call the local office if you need to know which areas are open, or stop at Darrington or Verlot on the way.

10. Buck Creek Campground

An attractive, remote, modest-sized campground in big trees on a rushing creek above the Suiattle River (*see also Walk #40*).

11. Sulphur Creek Campground

About 30 sites at the confluence of Sulphur Creek and the Suiattle River, off USFS Rd. #26 at MP 22.5. Stand near the creek and your olfactory may just pick up a hint of sulphur, derived from the hot springs (i.e. warm puddles) a mile up the trail. The popular Suiattle River Trailhead (*Hike #51*) is also just up the road, so expect some traffic.

12. Clear Creek Campground

A small area in trees next to the Sauk River, close to the road and close to Darrington. Frog Lake Trail (*see Walk #36*) is across the road.

13. White Chuck Campground

South of Darrington with only a couple of primitive sites, better for picnicking. Just across the White Chuck River bridge on USFS Rd. #22, and around the corner from the White Chuck Bench Trail (*Hike #39*).

14. Sloan Creek Campground

In a nice remote location next to North Fork Sauk River and Trail (*Hike #59*) with easy access to big trees.

15. Bedal Campground

Attractive remote setting at the confluence of the North and South Forks Sauk River, 18 miles from Darrington. Some barrier-free sites. Many trails in the area, including North Fork Falls (*Walk #41*).

16. Turlo Campground

Westernmost USFS campground on Mt. Loop Highway, at Verlot, 11 miles from Granite Falls. Perched in nice woods on the South Fork Stilly.

17. Verlot Campground

A nice early and late season campground with about two dozen sites, next to the river just upstream from Turlo. An easy trail links both with the Verlot Public Service Center.

18. Gold Basin Campground

What once was a town is now a large campground with almost 100 sites (some barrier-free), and a number at the edge of the South Fork Stilly. Some walk-in tent sites in mature forest. Playfield and amphitheater, too. East of Granite Falls at MP 13.5 on the Mt. Loop Highway.

19. Boardman Creek Campground

On the river in hardwood forest, a small tent-only area at MP 16.9 on the Mt. Loop Highway.

20. Red Bridge Campground

Smallish area east of Boardman on the Mt. Loop Highway at MP 18.4. Private sites with good river access.

21. Monte Cristo Campground

A small walk-in (or bike-in) area near the old townsite, a four-mile hike from Barlow Pass along the old road; on the left before crossing the creek-sized river (*see also Hike #64*).

22. Troublesome Creek Campground

Nice sites in forest near the creek and North Fork Skykomish River northeast of Index. A good nature trail nearby with two footbridges over the creek (*see Walk #47*).

23. San Juan Campground

A smaller site two miles east of Troublesome Creek.

24. Money Creek Campground

Just south of U.S. Hwy. 2 near MP 46. Nice sites in big trees along the river, plus a good picnic area.

25. Miller River Campground

In King County, two miles south of Money Creek CG.

26. Beckler River Campground

Nice area on a small river, not quite two miles north of U.S. Hwy. 2 on USFS Rd. #65.

Agencies & Organizations

• ALL EMERGENCIES (including search & rescue) **CALL 911**

Organizations

• Adopt-A-Stream Foundation, (425) 316-8592
• Everett Mountaineers, (425) 316-0881
• Pilchuck Audubon Society, (425) 252-0926
• Washington Trails Association, (206) 625-1367
  [http://www.wta.org./wta/]

City & County Government

• Edmonds Parks & Recreation, (425) 771-0230
• Everett Parks & Recreation, (425) 257-8300, or (425) 257-8399
• Lynnwood Parks & Recreation, (425) 771-4030
• Snohomish County Parks & Recreation
  3000 Rockefeller Avenue, M/S 303, Everett, WA 98201-4046
  (425) 339-1208, or (800) 562-4367

State Government

• Washington State Parks & Recreation
  7150 Cleanwater Lane, KY-11, Olympia, WA 98505
  (360) 902-8563, or (800) 233-0321
  Campsite reservations, most state parks (800) 452-5687
• Mukilteo State Park, (425) 353-2923
• Wallace Falls State Park, (360) 793-0420
• Wenberg State Park, (360) 652-7417
• Department of Natural Resources (DNR), Northwest Region
  919 North Township, Sedro Woolley, WA 98284
  (360) 856-3500, or (800) 527-3305
  (800) 562-6010 (forest fires only)
• Washington Department of Fish & Wildlife, Regional Office
  16018 Mill Creek Blvd., Mill Creek, WA 98012, (425) 775-1311
• Skagit Habitat Management Area, (360) 445-4441
• Washington Department of Transportation
  Mountain Pass Report, (888) 766-4636

Federal Government

- Mt. Baker-Snoqualmie National Forest
  21905 64th Avenue West, Mountlake Terrace, WA 98043
  (425) 775-9702, or (800) 627-0062
  Recreation Information Center, multi-agency, (206) 470-4060
  Campsite reservations (800) 280-CAMP (number may change)
- Darrington Ranger Station
  1405 Emmens Street, Darrington, WA 98241
  (360) 436-1155, or (425) 259-7911
- Verlot Public Service Center
  33515 Mt. Loop Hwy., Granite Falls, WA 98252, (360) 691-7791
- Skykomish Ranger District
  P. O. Box 305, Skykomish, WA 98288, (360) 677-2414
- Lake Wenatchee Ranger District
  22976 SR 207, Leavenworth, WA 98826, (509) 763-3103

Other Useful Information

- Avalanche Hazard & Snow Information, (206) 526-6677
  [http://www.nwac.noaa.gov]
- National Weather Service Forecast
  (206) 464-2000, then press 9000 (Seattle Times Info Line)
  [http://www.seawfo.noaa.gov]

Law Enforcement Agencies

- All emergencies, CALL 911
- Everett Police Department, (425) 257-8400
- Snohomish County Sheriff, (425) 388-3393, main line
  (425) 388-3328, search & rescue staff
- Washington State Patrol, (360) 658-1345 (Marysville)

Index